Aborigine Trail

Aborigine Trail

Trials, Travail, and Triumph Using
Psychology with Aborigine Police

Daniel Rudofossi and Matt Moloney

<teneo> //press
AMHERST, NEW YORK

Copyright 2019 Teneo Press

All rights reserved.
Printed in the United States of America

No part of this publication may be reproduced, stored in or introduced into a retrieval system, or transmitted, in any form, or by any means (electronic, mechanical, photocopying, recording, or otherwise), without the prior permission of the publisher.

Requests for permission should be directed to
permissions@teneopress.com, or mailed to:
Teneo Press
100 Corporate Parkway, Suite 128
Amherst, New York 14226, USA.

ISBN: 978-1-93484-424-3

Table of Contents

Foreword vii

Preface xiii

Acknowledgments xvii

Introduction 1

Chapter 1: Witnessing Wisdom in Aborigine and Police Eco-Ethological Existential Niches 9

Chapter 2: In, But Not Of: An Observing Participant Amongst the First Australians 49

Chapter 3: Primer for Training and Learning as Conduits with Indigenous Officers 75

Chapter 4: Torres Straits Island Police and the Thwarted Shark Attack – An Eco-Ethological Existential Analysis 89

Chapter 5: Totem and Animism, Wind and Fire Catalysts - Different Solutions 115

Chapter 6: Celebrating 150 Years of Queensland Policing and Aborigine Clan Unity 141

Chapter 7: Unveiling Peaks: Twilight Dimensions the Undulating Waves 165

Chapter 8: PPS-Complex PTSD: Complex Webs — Brain Matter 199

Epilogue 241

References 247

About the Authors 255

Foreword

Aboriginal Trail: Trials, Travail, and Triumph Using Psychology with Indigenous Police is an original book – launching what needs to be shared with the world of policing in particular, and to readers in general as a dream realized. For me having met a colleague and peer as an active Sgt. from Queensland Police Service and myself a New York born and bred Sgt. from the NYPD is special but not unheard of. To be able to have Sgt. Matt Moloney bridge gaps of a few thousand miles and to work my own theory and interventions with complex trauma layered in the land down under where coppers have to deal with the surreal strangeness of indigenous culture, tyranny of distance, the reality of isolation and other trials of nature that are at least as challenging as the criminals of the region is truly an awesome experience.

The pilot of all this work is truly Sgt. Moloney and his creative and inimitable style which is truly as Aussie as you get. His true edge does not mitigate what he would be shy of me underscoring as his own unique knowledge and wisdom with true street experience as a police officer with magnanimous kindness. I must say in all earnest frank certitude the credit of the work here lays in Sgt. Matthew's passion and reason to make a change as a pilot. My position and mission throughout has been his wing man and navigator. I am hopeful my colleague and scholar Sgt. Matt Moloney will be asked to make some policy changes as the wisdom of an evolving Australia and Queensland venture to meet new Vistas on the horizon of potentialities and change existentially. Existence and existential psychology are wed and issues that are social and psychological need to be placed squarely in the arena of ecology and ethology when a people are asked to police their own communities. Service implies stepping out of one's own ecological niche into a survival zone which will always lead to transcending one's own safety in ensuring others safety.

Service as in public safety entails actively enlarging one's circle of shapes and what is afforded as comfortable into what is unknown terrain. When the quantum intra-psychic moment of trauma hits it creates an original crater in communication and adaptation. Dissociative and grief patterns become recognizable to a cop doc tenured in the steppes and precipices that officers teeter on. In some cases, we will examine deeper and with sensitivity as to the cultural and existential issues. We will weave a trail that brings out the conversation of the original Australians, and the beauty and depth of their silent language which articulates in subtle tones needing to be heard. My colleague gaining leverage in doing his critically important work by modifying and using my perspective and integrating method into practical reality is about the best pay I could receive. This caveat is to deter anyone in thinking I have done this from a pure or altruistic motivation. I have done this work as a scientist and cop doc who truly resonates with the courage and determination of my fellow officers.

I in turn have been a guide throughout his exploration and together we are still journeying through rough bush and with the help of and wisdom that is authentically indigenous. That language is genuine as the language and wisdom of street wise, and smart public safety officers. It can wither in the complexities and simplistic squalls of modernity which prides itself on forcing change. I could not stomach or tolerate

Foreword

such an anti-scientific and existentially devoid pseudo-intellectual and impoverished ruse at being humane when one is force and infantilized.

Intellectual freedom includes being at liberty to present the reality of challenges and travails in the trail being tracked by aboriginals that are both trackers and street cops. That language of science can languish as much as the Aboriginal Australians if a melting pot of ethnicity washes away in a force that waves differences in the banner of respecting cultural differences, yet ignoring what makes each one different and sacred to their own banner.

That is room for pause. Let's pause and re-direct to the language of trauma and taking an approach I developed in the NYPD, I have called the Eco-Ethological Existential Analytic Approach to Complex Trauma. Having the distinct privilege to assist a brilliant colleague to co-author and develop this guide together for posterity and with the distinct gain of prosperity. Prosperity not in the mundane way of acquisitions, splits in stocks marketed in the streets where walls abound and ceilings descend upon those who may not have but investment in bringing to attention the importance of a people on the brink of a great period of cultural, spiritual, change and synthesis. The narrative delivered to you is enhanced by the existential dimension. My cop doc corner is placed as my method and idiopathic style as to how an eco-ethological existential analysis can add insight and gentle nudging of Sgt. Matt's work/efforts/contribution which uniquely targets responsibleness. It pauses, re-directs our attention to pressing dimensions that may otherwise be ignored, marginalized or shuffled away as stuff that can be dealt with by pretending 'It' does not exist: 'It' is exactly what we seek to understand. 'It' is likely to be the most important fulcrum toward change if articulating that it is not what it is, but what we seek to understand that adds sense to the bewildering experience of depression, anxiety, being cursed, or being jinxed with some spell cast on him/her in a world that ultimately fades away. That reality of curses, being jinxed and spell-bound for Aboriginal Officers is not alien to our own existential dilemmas.

One such dilemma is the grasping of the terminal condition of life. For all human's life itself fades like a dream as we age. Fading purpose in life is challenged by overwhelming trauma and losses in which all modes, means and methods of escape fail to work. Outside of commonalities to the human condition is contribution's to wisdom: Existence shifts in a paradigm quite unique as indigenous Officers can educate us well.

Dreams segue to open the conscious facades erected to censure a reality that embraces life, but paints such reality – opaque. Interpretation of dreams and artful coloring of what is invisible in the travails of life for the Aboriginal is made into pathways for the rest of us who are stuck in the chasms we have colored ourselves into -- Opaque. If we Stop, Pause, and actively listen to what is said. Dreams are the oracles and the steps to other sensibilities that draft the culling sonorous tunes away as reality is made palpable. Palpable as the trackers -- tracking the earthy scents and trails that become soothing and more familiar as our unconscious awareness is drawn taut and tightly wrapped into focus, as reality is made tangible in its complex simplicity we can bypass so easily from a tower of speculation, and the bastion of illusions comforting us in our complacency of superiority.

The applicability of police services that hail from two different continents to speak the same language of tolerance, service and vigorous efforts to temper justice with a sense of mercy -- is a hidden language of culture that is a lattice of compassion in policing, lacing the illusion of two worlds that are in reality one. As an author privileged to be invited to write three chapters' as a cop doc in Dr. Jack Kitaeff's, second edited edition of his, *Handbook of police psychology* (2019) the most original and passionate chapter is one where I described racism against police officers and their families in a way a cultural anthropologist, clinical psychologist/psychiatrist, and criminal justice scholar could understand scientifically – I titled this hatred and open attack on police as Centurioncide : It cannot go without saying an Aboriginal Officer has a two edged sword of racism to deal with.

Foreword

One is assimilating and accommodating to attempts to infantilize him/her and by marginalizing him/her as a police officer daring to step out of traditional culture – this racism comes from his own inner society. The larger society holds stereotypical and marginalizing ugly views of the Aboriginal citizen as little more than condescending stereotypes revamped and re-launched. It is paradoxical and yet sanguine to consider the frank solution lay in the police society which transcends both inner and outer larger society and belongs to none save its own – it is here he/she as Aboriginal Police Officer may find anchor, solution, chaos and order in process. You and I will peak in and explore heuristically and descriptively that process in the here and now.

The here and now is science at its best, nascent, and exploratory first. Spirituality framed in an existential analysis opens up the issues and puts laser focus on the most important clinical problems. One such problem is the great justice administration dilemma – that dilemma is how to prevent the loss of a human life. The aboriginal officer and the non-indigenous officer do realize to save a life is to save a world as the ancient Jewish Scribes suggest. This book itself holds the promise to be an ambulatory intervention that may save more than one life by valuing each life as a story and with its own myth to be told and lived. Description, classification, and research where realizing that reality which is that truth is not so self-evident. Truth is one of weight where balance between cultures yield mercy balanced by justice -- one individual at a time. This reality can only be dreamt whereas the aboriginal tracker can educate us by putting his head to the grind where understanding cannot be rushed under reductionistic, opportunistic, and global judgments that sweep away the varieties of humane experience for the sake of the winds of comfort that usher in convenience -- alone.

—Dr. Dan Rudofossi, Psy.D., Ph.D. Retired Sgt. NYPD , Licensed Psychologist NY and California and Police Surgeon, Amtrak Police and MTA, P.D.

Preface

Who would have thought that a rather serendipitous meeting in New York with Cop-Doc Dan Rudofossi would have highlighted such a clear path forward? I was in New York on a break from my Churchill Fellowship, where I was enquiring into the subject of the 'Police response to mental health crisis situations, with a focus on culturally effective responses for indigenous Australians' also known to the world as Aborigines. I had purposely left New York off the study itinerary because at the time I believed the circumstances between law enforcement in the precincts of New York in comparison to the bush stations in Queensland's Far North have little in common. Yet, when I learnt of Dr Rudofossi's Eco-Ethological Existential Analytic method I immediately recognized a framework that would succeed. Dr Rudofossi trained, guided, mentored, and tutored me in understanding and applying his method. I first used the methods outlined in his book *"Dealing with the Mentally Ill Person on the Street"*. I quickly realized that his framework accurately explained and therefore was equally applicable to so much of what was happening in the bush with Indigenous Queenslanders. The value of the framework doesn't just lie in its applicability to working with indigenous people as citizens. I used, and continue to use it when training and developing skills with indigenous police officers, including tracker police officers.

Trackers are people who see paths in seemingly impenetrable situations that others don't within indigenous culture. Trackers perceive and point the way forward as pioneers. It turned out that I went off the planned path and met a police tracker as retired Sgt NYPD, Dr. Rudofossi in NY showed me the way forward. We communicated a track forward.

Facilitating communication among indigenous and non-indigenous populations, problems emerge. Problems such as high stake risks, environmental triggers for disasters [man-made and natural], mediators between cultural identities and organisational sub cultures that are legitimate, and those that are illegal create large gaps: Gaps for anyone who's role requires management of expectations including: emergency situations and servicing such emergencies in First Nations, Front line Law Enforcement and Emergency Service Providers, Legal and Paralegal Professionals, Counsellors, Community Co-ordinators, Conciliators and Members of the Judiciary. In this regard the book offered to you is unique. The Eco-Ethological Existential Analytic framework works in complicated situations such as the Australian indigenous context. In my mind this is evidence that it will help to forge a new way forward for mental health interventions generally.

As the pilot in the field of service I present cases from the perspective of a current serving ranking officer. Dr Rudofossi provides clinical assessment as conduits that speak with the academic and the clinical world, and suggestions that assist the police officer indigenous and non-indigenous. My hope is that my perspective offers a view that most academics, researchers and clinicians would not be privy to and also demonstrates that Dr Rudofossi's principles are transferable and applicable in a wide variety of locations. If his principles work in Queensland's Far North with a group of people that Dr Rudofossi had not previously met, in circumstances he did not have in mind when writing, then they very well might work in many areas in need of his approach to trauma and grief and clashes of culture, ecology and its ethological roots. Consequently, while this book is academic in orientation, it encompasses many successes to be gauged at some future point. The case examples of my actual work are a presentation of true dialogue. My own narrative while edited and refined remains true to the colleagues as we say in Australia my mates who are proud indigenous people, proud law enforcement officers and me as a commander.

Qualifying this point is we have entrusted the navigation by one of our mates in NY as the tracker cop doc to edit our material and deliver palatable and useful dialogue without taking away the essence. Scientific boundaries qualitatively expanded are not discarded and hopefully this work will have relevance for the cultural anthropologist, evolutionary biologist, and clinical psychologist who will respectfully navigate through our field observations and ongoing experiment. I rely on Cop Doc Rudofossi to be the navigator as scientist, professor and clinician to underscore where research and insight can further my explorations and practical application in the field. Indeed, while I unashamedly rely on Dr Rudofossi's guidance and leadership, I encourage analysis and input from others including in other disciplines, as no discipline working in a silo will succeed. Even as a native-born Queenslander when I first dealt full time with indigenous issues, I didn't understand what was going on. I felt I was caught in a dream that while not quite a nightmare, had nightmarish elements to it. It was only when I started to understand indigenous people through what, thanks to Dr Rudofossi, I would later identify was their framework that I felt I was coming out of the dreaming. Dr Rudofossi is an insightful man. His insights gave me the framework to start making sense of what was previously too subjective and insubstantial to make sense of. A theory may be appealing and attractive, but it is of no use if it is inapplicable in the real world.

The practical applications of Dr. Rudofossi's Eco-Ethological Existential Analysis I have provided demonstrate its practical and effective impact. My work in this area remains, as I suspect it forever will, a work in progress. The more I find out about the indigenous framework, my framework, the police framework and how they all interact, I realise I have so much to learn about my indigenous countrymen, myself, the police, the human condition and the speciality of psychology that explores it. But as Dr. Rudofossi has convinced me what I have to say in my own words and the words of my mates is crucial toward understanding the solutions that rest on an Eco-Ethological Existential Analytic framework dynamically.

What started as an exciting collegiate meeting evolved into a professional association, which in turn blossomed into mateship, or as one can say friendship of him and me and my family and his. As much as we tried to narrow focus, the frameworks we discuss cover such a diverse range of subjects: investigations, justice administration, emergency response, effective communication, ancient spirituality, modern existential dilemmas of choice and responsibility, historic biases and challenges, indigenous culture, racial and cross-cultural relations that I could not help but raise them as topics. All these subjects emerge in an individual's ecology, influence ethology and shape each niche. In doing an Eco-Ethological Existential Analysis being a co-author of this book was challenging, invigorating and purposive to write with passion. I hope you find it challenging and enjoyable in the reading. We have each put our spirits into this story. Traditional indigenous Australians believe when a story has a spirt, it comes to life.

—Sgt. Matthew Moloney, Queensland Police, Churchill Fellow.

Acknowledgments

First, and in profound appreciation for my ability to have survived and grown in my faith in the Highest being – the highest spiritual force, G-d! I often reflect, as many greater folks than I have said, "There go I but for the grace of G-d, Go-I!" It has been my good fortune to have so many blessings that follow: But of all grace is my soulmate, who is my wife, entrepreneur, teacher, and botanist, Dongyu Brachah Rudofossi who is my best friend and lover -- my compass in stormy weather and tempestuous roads with her companionship, brilliance and compassion that lights my life everyday -- My Wife is the light of my life.

Thank you, Dr. Paul Richardson Editor, Teneo Press for your welcoming me as an author in a collegial style and encouraging creative expression in a professional guide: Your reputation for welcoming your authors and support in publishing I can attest to and with that offer a guide that I hope will assist many in public safety and mental health who work on the front lines of Aborigine Citizens and LEO's - indigenous and non-indigenous of Queensland Police, NYPD, FBI and DEA. Of Course, Sgt. Matt Moloney who stayed the course and piloted the track for all of us as a true-blue Commander and who also honored me with learning my method of assessment, intervention and application of the Eco-Ethological

Existential Analytic Method. Sgt Matt M is a hero with compassion and reason to become a leader for Queensland police and beyond as friend and brother in blue.

Tracker Barry Port my gratitude for what you have shared with us and the world for prosperity and peace. *In partnership with the finest officer–Patients I owe my education and wisdom still* learning from you all. Each journey hopefully enlightened your path as it did mine! To Cop Doc Peers Conroy, Kitaeff, Leenaars, King, Schlossberg and Gilmartin paving new roads without forgetting our own beaten paths! Chief Anthony Mercogliano of MTA PD and MTA Police. Lt. Jack Latorre, hero extraordinaire! NJ and NY Detectives Crime Clinic President Bobby Basso. Chief Vinny Mansfield, Chief Louis Vilenti, and Police Chaplin Shlomo Rizel. To my students at NYU, John Jay and St. John's University and NYPD the brightest and finest -- the best. In partnership with the finest officer–Patients I owe my education and wisdom still learning from you all. Each journey hopefully enlightened your path as it did mine! To Cop Doc Peers paving new roads without forgetting our own beaten paths! To my students and NYPD, the brightest and finest -- the best! Thanks to St. John's University especially Professor Commander Tom Creelman, Dr. Collinari Schlossberg and Dr. Harvey Schlossberg, and Dean Passarini Chair of Homeland Security, Law and Criminal Justice.

I thank my family: My Wife Dongyu Rudofossi my lady, mentor and best friend in the odyssey of this life my beauty and soulmate an inspiration to me in her abundance of lifelong love. My mother through thick and thin – who somehow understood with the wisdom of a mother and love. To my son Jonathan, USMC, who keeps me laughing with his humor, he is so much better at it than his Dad. To my daughter who is ever growing and my joy of sparkle in her youth, Emily R. Rudofossi. My grandmothers who loved wholeheartedly. To my sisters who are lifelong friends: Vicky and Mara. Spiritually – Biala Rebbe thank-you for your timeless noetic-wisdom and training a guy with my background into becoming a Rabbi to side saddle when needed along with being a Cop Doc

Acknowledgments

Memorial to my blue brothers laid to the haven of Heaven with the Almighty: Det. Giery; Det. Heidelberg; Lt. Seymour Jones; Captain R. Montgomery. Cop Doc Al Benner and many others I can't fit on this page. Memorial to Rabbi Moshe Hillel Sperber a true scholar who passed into the garden of Eden at 51 years young this year.! In beloved memory of the most courageous and compassionate writer violinist/poet my father, Harry Julius a combat veteran with 4 ribbons in WWII, USN who never tired of breakfasts every week and sharing war stories NYPD and USN. My grandfather Morris an infantryman in WWI, US Army who fought under General Pershing and brought warmth and love in my life and my grandmother Alto Bella whose beautiful soul was taken to early. To WWII decorated Veteran Pop, Mr. I Friedman I salute your courage, humanity and friendship! My Uncle Abe who was a USAF hero, so long, until…

Sgt Commander Matt Moloney Acknowledgment – thanks to my wife and family. To Dr. Dan Rudofossi, as mate and the Inversational man, navigator and heavy lifter. Thanks for taking the time to teach me. A man of your character, intellect and achievement reaching out and indulging me did not go unnoticed, unappreciated or taken for granted. Thanks to my wife and family, Police Tracker Barry Port, and the Churchill Trust for the opportunity. Robert Nelson, Jo-Ann Nelson, John Upton, Scott Templeton, Maureen Liddy for guidance, the Coen Men's Group; the Support Officers, Marilyn Kepple, Community Police and Liaison Officers in the Cape. Marilyn Kepple, Sergeant Jeff Tanswell of Croc Survivor Legend; and Allison Nerdedine Bernard – You have not been forgotten.

Aborigine Trail

Introduction

This book is written by two Police Sergeants with six decades of police experience. This book may be viewed as a histography of integrated insights and knowledge of what incorporates an ecological approach in part, it incorporates an ethological approach which indisputably frames what is neglected by most researchers and clinicians – survival motivation.

Based on one Sergeants expertise as a licensed clinician with double doctorates in Psychology [clinical and developmental] and post graduate studies in ethology- [biology and psychology] it would be compelling to read and learn about his approach. The other Sergeant has learned how to understand his colleagues approach known as the Eco-Ethological Existential Analytic Approach as a bonafide Peer Support Officer without portfolio for now. This is crucial because Dr. and Sgt. Rudofossi will for the most part be a navigator and as called in the blue culture. A navigator in the public safety eco-ethological approach is known as the Recorder. In the police dyad of patrol and investigations there is the Recorder who does just that – writes and narrates what is said and frames the dialogue and evidence gathered; the Operator is really the Pilot who does the actual on the ground and air events in the front line.

As Recorder and Navigator Dr. Rudofossi will begin each chapter with an Introduction section that will provide a landing area that offers a flow from one major area of description of a problem through the foundations of a solution including investigation into some possible options that layout a tentative solution. Depending on the content of the chapter itself, where possible a clinical perspective will also be delivered as, *Cop Doc Dan Rudofossi Corner.*

Sgt and Dr. Rudofossi has been dubbed a Cop Doc and it makes sense rather than alternating between Sgt. And Doc throughout the book. It stuck over two decades and is worthwhile to indicate he has traversed both the police world as a sworn police officer and also the clinical, research and academic world as a Practicing Psych Doc and Professor. **In an amenable and collaborative decision, it was given Cop Doc Rudofossi the task of being the scribe throughout this book as the author who has written this book based on the interviews and enormous field research shared between Sgt. Moloney and him.** *Areas of clinical, research and applied methods of forensic and police psychology/psychiatry are within the expert domain of Dr. Rudofossi and clearly was perforce necessary to be guided by his leadership in this area.*

Dr. Rudofossi acknowledges an abundant wealth as a gift from his co-author Sgt. Matt Moloney who labored while being in the field of very active and challenging service as a police commander and scholar and his time and dedication given to dialogue and corrections in the actual writing on technical informational material related to Australian and Queensland folklore and cultural nuances to mores! This will remain evident within the flowing pages of the actual book which is written within a lattice with flowering branches that spring veridical in shape and form.

As Pilot and on the ground, air and sea literally and metaphorically, Sgt. Matt Moloney who is pursuing a post baccalaureate from the generous beneficence of a Churchill Scholarship was able to visit and learn as well as stay in NY. In a stay over in the center of NYC and much continued dialogue with Sgt and Dr Rudofossi's approach he has succeeded with a unique perspective which includes more than a superficial acquaintance with one of the most complex and diverse of multiple urban communities known as the Big Apple. In NYC he has become a participant in Professor Rudofossi's classes whereby his wisdom about Aborigine culture and Policing is bound toward becoming a staple at St. John's University classes in forensic and police psychology on the undergraduate and graduate level.

In qualifying a limitation, although both police officers remain separated by oceans and the span of two continents their unique undertaking is truly sui generis – a novel approach tempered with conservation of culture, totems and taboos of the indigenous folk and the larger culture they perforce assimilated and accommodate too.

In reviewing much of the literature out there today readers can find interesting, purposive and excellent articles and chapters on the struggles and resolution of the aborigine's people as indigenous to Queensland and Australia. Sadly, it is not difficult to sieve through much bombast written as hardly veiled political discourses that have littered much of what passes as easy papers and even short guides proffered as panaceas. The result is discord and without a solution in-sight, or in mind.

The larger problem of indigenous folks who are left with identification of problems, solutions offered, and ultimately dilemmas are not given viable answers. Viable answers have become complacent where collisions of culture, and ecological-ethological niches conflicts are left unsolved, and violence and discord are accepted. The dilemma of integration of a minority community within an overall majority community of Australia has obvious historic disadvantages: Indigenous Australians have experienced what may be best viewed as disenfranchised losses in their assimilation and accommodations to the larger societal influences in an urbanized modern society. In fact, as the authors will argue the disenfranchised losses in some instances are internal fractures from their own tribal leadership. Disenfranchisement of Aborigine Officers from their own cultural identity, colonization and the explosion of the newest technological advances without time to assimilate and accommodate to such quantum moments intra-psychically from an unconscious and conscious level is a remarkably irresponsible move. While peoples are not pawns in a theoretical chess game when a collision of micro with macro-culture is done without respecting traditions and conservation of unique traditions – immeasurable chaos cannot be weighed.

Using an Eco-Ethological Existential framework to make this collision of cultures more understandable is one goal of this guide. It is a modest goal and even one that lays out a fragile boundary on what is chaotic but in doing so an attempt is made toward solution as focus and not undisciplined chaos.

Via dialogue rather than purist pedagogy the author hopes that eco-ethological niches that have and are shaping defenses of newly trained Aborigine Officers are made more noticeable and valued. Until recently, Police chosen from the dominant culture represented only a segment of the community policed, not the full 'Gestalt' of the communities that were policed. Solutions have been started to ameliorate glaring discrepancies, for example indigenous citizens have been recruited and trained as police. Yet indigenous and non-indigenous officers, especially those from remote, isolated communities face their own particular set of challenges. In our guide Sergeant Matthew Moloney of the Queensland Police Department who is a veteran police officer and highly experienced in delivering service to indigenous Australians provides an insider perspective!

His insider perspective has not ever been delivered in a book form and is sorely needed. In-deed the most remote, isolated indigenous communities of Cape York, is supervised by Sgt. Moloney as the officer in charge of Cape York stations. Amongst Sgt. Moloney experiences, is his facility in working side by side with indigenous law enforcement officers sworn and unsworn, including the last Aboriginal Police Tracker Barry Port on the cutting edge of policing. As of the finalization of this guide such a stalwart and fine Citizen of Queensland, the Queensland Police Service and one can say, citizen of the world Tracker Law Enforcement Officer [L.E.O.] Barry Port may find the power of eloquence in effigy with the publication of this work.

All of this rich information and truly mind opening apertures is completely the credit and initiative of Sgt. Moloney, not only a Churchill

Introduction 5

Fellow, but as a creative and dynamic shaker that is moving some pioneering insights to pass along to police and administrative supervisors and executive managers including elders and wise men and women within the Aborigine communities as distinct. Distinguished communities with their own eco-ethological niches that includes their cultural and geo-physical dynamics and problems. As to the problems and solutions that can be impactful in pioneering issues where minority officers and communities and majority officers and society can clash.

As for my own history within the police local, state and federal over decades as Cop Doc and police street cop and Sgt., including being a retired Police Sgt, NYPD, and director of the clinical and assessment domain of NYPD's MAP program as their first EAP now known as POPPA I have dealt with all sides of union, brass and line officers and the Executive and Mayoral Units of the Big Apple. As Chief Psychologist for HHSG-DEA EAP nationwide and other departments including the MTA PD my credibility owes much to pioneering collaboration in forging ahead with a digestible guide to better and more effectively deal with stress and strain newly recruited officers too veteran officers deal with including the awesome work of Chief Mercogliano. As a Cop Doc with over three decades of policing and police psychology experience, I have developed a theory, method and intervention with trauma, grief, mental and behavioral disorders this adds another dimension as to how it is delivered in this book. It is delivered in digestible format where Sgt. Moloney insightfully sifts with deft influence in working with the indigenous population cutting an edge into a barrier that like the Reef from down under. My paradigm of Eco-Ethological Existential niches gave him a solution in re-directing the impact on justice administration, and implications for indigenous culture in solving collisions of values, survival motivation and withdrawal into a new path of integration and cooperation.

The conclusive goals that are mindful of time and modesty includes the potential of our analysis which covers the multiple faceted layers of indigenous Eco-Ethological Existential niches not a singular linear model that provokes mindful recognition that Indigenous officers deserve to be considered and integrated into the Queensland Police Service with equal parity and respect.

Arguably a greater mission is also a truly historic model aligned with inspiration for other police and public safety/services. This insight recognizes that all voices need to be heard: Incorporating the Eco-Ethological Existential Analytic Approach will result in a respectful cultural synthesis and contribute to ongoing efforts to bridge the many gaps between indigenous and non-indigenous Queenslanders. Clinicians of many varied backgrounds will gain clinical insights. Meaning clinical professionals as much as Administrators from different countries worldwide can give audience to models that can be broadened to group therapy and narrowed to individual differences and therapeutic healing once learned and understood in psychotherapeutic approaches to all participants as defined in this book.

In both of our views we diverge from pop culture and even established trajectories by conserving the paradigm of classic anthropology and psychology as applied by reconfirming above all, the integrity of the Indigenous culture must be viewed in the context of individual differences and the reality of experiencing the trauma events in an ecology and ethological context of motivation to truly be impactful. Respecting the choice to depart from tradition as well as to embrace tradition are choices when done responsibly are valued and presented as such.

It is also important to note that Sgt. Moloney ought to be given not only an award but the support in his own recognition to apply my framework of the Eco-Ethological Existential Analytic approach to the Queensland dilemma of assimilation and accommodation to urbanization and city development. This includes complex trauma and grief insights that reap rewards for the police, Australia's first peoples, and especially those descended from the first Australians currently serving as law enforcement officers. Innovative measures are dire needs requiring harvesting

Introduction 7

for serving the Indigenous people's needs. While an Eco-Ethological Existential Analytic approach does not require full assimilation, it does require respecting the existence of indigenous folklore, mores and the wisdom uniquely prized in indigenous culture. Using the Eco-Ethological Existential Analytic approach will result in a strengthening of police legitimacy, and an improvement of the relationship between police and indigenous Queenslanders. This will have broader ripple effects for the wider community and state of Queensland. This has begun on a modest opening by Sgt. Moloney and in collaboration within his frame of outreach and practice.

The promise of what I have called the 'psychological imagination' to compliment what sociologist C.W. Mill called the 'sociological imagination' is to clarify, interpret and then confront the dilemma of collisions of cultures into a respectful synthesis. That synthesis includes a bio-psychosocial both/and an eco-ethological existential analytic approach: *Counter-intuitively, cultural competence is not about supporting a melting pot concept, but a hot potlatch. Allowed to grow naturally and organically, without being contrived or forced the potlatch will empower many different, but complimentary dishes without making a howling mess of each absent taste and style.*

Summing up you have dialogue that boldly attempts to imperfectly work out solutions that are best for all – perfection is not doable – pragmatic development is. This guide is sorely needed if you are among students to practitioners in forensic, police and general psychology; sociology; anthropology; history; homeland security/criminology professionals, and Law. Four cultures: Aborigine; Queensland; Police; and Civilian are in need of a humane approach which values cultural competence – to such a reader this guide is relevant, useful, and broad enough to clinically educate participants and observers of such struggles and challenges toward humane scientific solutions. This guide promises to deliver the difference where discrimination counts in delivering a reasoned and organized book that educates, motivates and offers solutions to the reader

CHAPTER 1

WITNESSING WISDOM IN ABORIGINE AND POLICE ECO-ETHOLOGICAL EXISTENTIAL NICHES

INTRODUCTION

The first chapter will give you as the reader a framework to gain an understanding of policing, indigenous culture, and Aborigine clans and communities: Each area of inquiry consists of different individuals with their own unique ecological niches and ethological motivations that are deliberate and conscious. In part, these individuals and communities are motivated by what can be expanded toward description and insight from a perspective that has been draped over by unconscious motivations. In my approach as the scribe amongst the two authors without neglecting the richest of experiences and wisdom of my peer Sergeant from Queensland we move into what I have created not ex-nihilio but sui-genesis from decades of experience and research as much as clinical interventions in what is called the Eco-Ethological Existential

Analytic Method of assessment, intervention and treatment of complex trauma, grief and dissociative disorders. However, for this book we will focus on insights that include the cultural and noetic aspects of what is defined as eco-ethological existential niches within the non-indigenous communities and indigenous communities. In order to achieve our goal, it was decided on by both authors that I would be responsible for the writing of each chapter in the form of dialogue. Dialogue conceptually means exploring and delivering some potential and actual solutions to real life dilemmas and enigmas.

Some problems are left unanswered to be sought through by readers and others that desire exploring beyond the scope of our immense respect for both the Aborigine and Non-indigenous human experience narrated in this book. This chapter begins on describing what is not a macro-cultural analysis, but is an eco-ethological existential analysis of individuals. These individual folks' gift us with their own experiences and the eco-ethological existential niches that have contextualized their lives and the impact each has recounted for us to understand.

In this analysis we will target the familiar and more so unfamiliar terrain for dynamic inter-relations and experiences of each participant who observes all the changes and their impact on his/her life-space and style of living and learning. Learning the varied hues and cast of emotions to enhance survival and all the way up the ladder of comfort toward the centre of existence and becoming one-self is respected as is the process without gilding the reality to a sparkle and shine. No apology will be given. Qualifications where needed will be proffered to the reader to include reasons, rationale, and honesty without prevarication. The dose of humility for the reader equally applies to the authors, especially the navigator tasked with writing the narrative for this guide. In my role as Navigator: Our maps, coordinates, velocity and altitude along with turbulence needing shaving and editorial razor cuts will not diminish weathering through the experiences the Commander of Matt Moloney

Witnessing Wisdom in Aborigine and Police

as Chief Uniformed active Sergeant here as he has and is going through in the Aussies land known as Queensland, Australia.

My neatly tucked packages for surviving the journey you are too embark on will begin shortly. You may find spills and stains that give you the near perfect imperfections that highlight what is real from sur-real. The real from sur-real and truth itself as reality as best expunged from a scatterplot of sur-realism is the package you will receive to work with in your own domain as researcher, administrator, clinician and student. Sur-realism has its place in the shelves of hung art in the brain's memories that are recorded and best understood for its nature as lived and experienced minus the mis-judgment and distortions all of us as imperfect persons are so subject too in recording and historiography as professionals or novices. It is the navigator as narrator and Cop Doc that is entrusted with this task and all the pitfalls and hardships of refinement and the errors that cannot be culled as oysters from its oblong shells is my ownership and not the pilot who has allowed our boarding his trade passage that is being worked on in 'the job' as done in Queensland Australia. His heroism is my appellation and not his own: Sgt Matt Moloney as many officer peers and officer patients of mine unduly brush off their courage and determination that is done and achieved in extraordinary ways and means to do their best in assisting other human beings individually and collectively. Hero is well earned in that Sgt. Commander Matt Moloney has a right dose of humility, temerity and poise in his dealing with the sundry vicissitudes of a complex and irate citizenry that transcend culture and as always whittle down to the foibles of 'doing the right thing'. Matt Moloney does and has done the right thing in a job tougher than most can tolerate, depict, narrate and walk – as a fellow Sgt. I tip my hat in the privilege of being allowed to walk the walk and listen actively with him. Having said what needs to be said, lets embark on this odyssey together.

CREDIBILITY: COP DOC AND SGT. COMMANDER 'ROOKIE ORIGINS'.

Cop Doc Dan R: "I am going to ask you Sgt and Commander Matt Moloney if you could highlight in your own words why you decided to become a copper or police officer in the first place?"

Commander Sgt Matt Moloney: [Pause and clearly reflective] "As a rookie I wanted to make things better for my countrymen and women. I wanted to play a part, however small in contributing to human kind's store of knowledge and insight. The ride was rough and the road still remains rocky. Credibility is a large vantage point that any serious reader desires cashing in on from the moment he/she picks up a book. At the time of our first interview and communications for this book which is mid-2017, I have twenty-six years service as a Queensland police officer and police sergeant. Hey, Dr. Rudofossi you were a street cop and Sgt and came on as a police officer rookie in the later mid-1980's and you've worked as a street cop, commanding officer, and Cop Doc now. You have never left your saddle for 30 years. That outweighs my years on the job."

Cop Doc Dan R: "I can remember like you recounted that I entered to learn, and left to serve. NYPD has the motto, 'Enter to learn, Exit to Serve'. It fits and it worked as a cop and now as a Cop Doc that is retired and getting some rusty spots in my limbering up in the morning haze when the dew falls and I yawn with my coffee to awaken to a new day. Well, I will say you have quite a lot of history behind you as I do and together: We have some 60 years together in policing and using police psychiatry and psychology."

Commander Sgt Matt Moloney: "Where I come from in Australia, we do not have any real municipal police services that function independently. This is unlike you Cop Doc Dan as my colleague in the standing Army of the NYPD which has over 40,000 police officers and more civilian professionals to boot."

Witnessing Wisdom in Aborigine and Police

Cop Doc Dan R: "Well this may be a true to life fact for the NYPD but truth be told each precinct captures a certain geographic area and the population within that require police assistance and our support to manage issues from criminal behaviour to traffic control to fires and medical emergency to name a few outside of the larger issues of terrorist and organized crime gangs and larger secret societies that target innocent civilians based on race, gender and ethnic and of course religious beliefs. But if it works, I am hopeful we can get to some core areas where the Ecological and Ethological Niches that make up the venue of policing in Australia exist and specifically in Queensland where you live and work."

Commander Sgt Matt Moloney: "If I am to describe he Eco-Ethological Niches of Queensland Policing to you I need to break it down in a way that makes sense. Criminal and traffic law enforcement services are delivered at the state level of administration. Each state has its own service that is responsible for law enforcement and the bulk of justice administration. To offer some comparative ratios and volume of people, let's start with Queensland as a bit larger in population than twice the size of Texas. The population of our state is about five million, with around two and a quarter million living in Brisbane, the State Capital. Our State Capital is in the South East corner of Queensland."

"Although the Capital holds two and a half million people, the population of Queenslanders includes another million souls who live in the built-up areas in the South East corner around the bulwark known as Brisbane. The remainder of the population is spread over the other eco-ethological niches of Queensland: These eco-ethological niches as you've called them are mainly on the thin, fertile, watered East Coast."

"The Outback, which fills the imagination of both Australians and Americans, is pretty much the rest of Queensland territory. Even that can broadly be divided into the West which is cattle and sheep country, and the far North part of Queensland. That far North region of Queensland encompasses Cape York and Torres Straits which is relatively undeveloped and disproportionally lived in by indigenous people. Remember that indigenous people are really Aboriginal clans' folk that are not one singular type of people over another."

Cop Doc Dan R: "Commander Matt Moloney as Police Sgt who has so much rich experience dealing with the varieties of local and diverse populations of indigenous people could you first give me some impressions that are general and even what we can call nomothetic. Nomothetic means the general picture within the populations we are looking at together. Not just a statistical compilation or some pattern that emerges but without mincing words and trying to correct your own perspective regardless of the way it may appear to the reader. After all, if we are to do our task right the reader will learn something new about not only indigenous folks and non-indigenous folks but the grey colour and iridescent hues that colour each culture. So, the more defined eco-ethological niches and finally the individual differences that shone within each interaction of two or more persons I believe will move on in our exploration if this makes sense to you my good Commander and Sgt?"

Commander Sgt Matt Moloney: "Yes, it does make sense as to my reasoning, interpretation of events, evidence and subsequent conclusions as I will own my experiences, my interactions with my fellow countrymen and women. What I will try my best is to present my own real, my own and authentic self and experiences of others. I will try to outline my interactions as they happened.":

Cop Doc Dan R: "Good than in your pause the focus will be expressing your own experiences and understanding together some direct and conscious motivation as well as unconscious possibilities as to motivation in your service history which is active and fluid in educating not only our reader, but in dialogue me as the recorder or scribe of this book."

Commander Sgt Matt Moloney: "Clearly they were strange experiences, but the more I am cognisant of whom I am and I become comfortable with myself, the more I realise how much of the indigenous framework I have incorporated into my way of thinking and being.

Witnessing Wisdom in Aborigine and Police

In becoming existentially aware in part as the focus of your approach to trauma and grief I have been able to reflect on how much the indigenous framework has in common with the police one: In my view it is the Aboriginals and I who has become the outsiders to the larger Queensland population. Let me explain what I mean. We are fringe dwellers on the outskirts of polite and acceptable society. Much of what is said in this book will be hardly palatable to those who have a world view that is different than mine and the Aboriginal folks-people."

"I am challenged by the viewpoint which has so many commonalities with mine that I have opened my mind to embrace. That perspective is the Aboriginal Officers, in a frame work with you as my fellow Sgt. and Cop Dr. Dan Rudofossi. Still, in an age when the culture of so many even those who are bandied as a culture but are really individuals banded together, no doubt attacks will come."

"It is important to talk about motivation when talking about one's own odyssey as I have chosen here. Dr. Rudofossi I know this is about me and my experiences but if I can pause as you always recommend before unleashing all in a wild flux, you've outlined a keystone of motivation in forming your theory and treatment of trauma and grief by allowing defences of law enforcement and other emergency services officers often under attack from various quarters to understand their own varied responses. Responses disfavoured by the public and even within so called police and public safety circles and larger culture may be more of those who have gotten on the band wagon of being police cult followers and buffs who snugly fit in and then criticize innovators as outsiders. We have roots in being sensible from an eco-ethological existential paradigm as you discovered and created in your method of assessment and intervention with us. With the recent spate of police shootings in the USA, some justified, some lawful but awful, others as a result of fear or panic and less defensible, this has become particularly relevant. Predictably but still strangely, there have been protests in Queensland linked to and inspired by these movements in the US."

"It's true that I want to counterbalance the disproportionally negative, unfair focus on the failings of police now and in the past. I make no apology for that. All this is said as a brief to offer my own perspective and that is as I have learned so much can be misinterpreted when saying one's own mind for others to view."

"To make it clear, I want to contribute to a just society and a safe community as you Dr. Rudofossi point out in many books and chapters you've written whereby you've defined anti-police actions as trauma, grief and dissociative fractures in our communities and our families numbering in the millions worldwide as worth combating."

Cop Doc Dan R: "Thank you for your very thoughtful gifting me of your own use and modifications in understanding my approach so eloquently. I would like to know what in my approach you can elaborate on and within your own framework that is so specifically so significant in impressing you so strongly?"

Commander Sgt Matt Moloney: "Dr. Rudofossi it is one of three chapters you've contributed and I peer-reviewed in US Army Major Professor Dr. Jack Kitaeff's second edition of the *Handbook on Police Psychology* (Kitaeff, 2019) whereby you have called racism against police officers and their families first and then elegantly changed it to a sticking term that fits so well where racism against police officers, is re-titled **Centurioncide** *by you Dr. Rudofossi. I agree in your choice of your* term. I have to resay, I wholeheartedly agree with you in your estimation that captures harm, baseless hatred and attacks that have ranged from psychological injuries to homicide of way too many officers worldwide as Centurioncide."

Commander Sgt Matt Moloney: "It is liberating to know one from our own culture and ranks has given his life to answering a calling to stand up for police and public safety officers as a population that collectively and individually are worthy of being noticed and acknowledged as fellow human beings with the rest of humanity and not distanced from being humane beings who often give the greatest of sacrifices in mental and physical health with very little voice of the impact such sacrifices really have both on an unconscious and conscious level of experience with the rest of academia, clinicians and the intelligent population of fellow human beings we share this planet earth with."

"With that said, your gift is profound and helps in developing credibility as a currency we both share regardless of continent shifts and differences [smile and shared laugh]. If we could for now go back to as we had to the geographic regions of your turf and venue as a police commander for our readers in the region of Queensland my fellow Centurion?"

Commander Sgt Matt Moloney: "I have been tackling the fact that most of the land north of Cooktown on Cape York has become indigenously owned. This is a newer development as the indigenous people of Queensland cover a broad geographical, social and cultural range. The Great Dividing Range, a mountain range which stretches pretty much from Cape York South to Southern Victoria divides the fertile, urban east coast from the outback."

"The Northern most point of Queensland is Saibai Island, which is about two kilometres from the mainland of Papua New Guinea. The people who populate Saibai are Torres Strait Islanders who share much in common with the Papua New Guineans. Heading out West, Queensland covers a lot of dry, semi and full desert country: This region includes the unique skills which have become rare in Australia such as shepherding sheep and cattle in farms containing these domesticated mammals. People North of Cooktown are rural and colloquially known as country folk, much like people in Colorado or New Mexico. In the south corner of the State is Brisbane the capital of the state which is like most large cities of its size. If you go further south of Brisbane you can see the surf beaches of the Gold Coast, which to me share much in common with the beaches of California."

"I have and still serve mainly in the regional service centres, out West in the outback and disproportionally in Cape York and Torres Straits. Each of these broad delineations has its own distinct framework. Having done my tours of duty in each I will share with you what I can bring to life for you as we move on in our journey Cop Doc Dan."

Cop Doc Dan R: "I am all big ears" (I accentuate listening well by leaning to my left side and frame my ear in a clasped hand to hear fully and attune to my colleague's narrative) Could you begin with that first framework as to where you learnt and were initiated into becoming a police officer?"

Commander Sgt Matt Moloney: "The first framework I learnt was the police one, it was the most challenging, and I can say meaningful. Everyone thinks they know the police framework. Those outside of the police, even those who deal with police quite often, for example, prosecuting attorneys, criminal defence lawyers, the magistracy and the judiciary although they know the police framework they are exposed too, they don't know what lies under the surface of their many assumptions about many of us. They don't know alot that is subtle and explicit among police in our individual units. *They deal with us a lot and have some idea of our inner culture and ecological-ethological niches and some superficial aspects of our culture, but they don't get the whole picture.* I am not making a value judgement against any of these hardworking professionals, but they simply don't move in our framework. In fact, it is true to say when I have interviewed both indigenous and non-indigenous officers the joint consensus is many who know a tangential aspect of police culture have tried to minimise and devalue our framework looking more towards abstractions and theory."

"In the same way, I have dealt a lot with indigenous people, lived in their communities, worked with indigenous officers, resolved and sometimes inadvertently caused disputes, delivered justice administration, sometimes delivered legalism, but I cannot make justice happen for indigenous people."

"Dr Dan, frankly speaking, I work with, and in the indigenous framework. I respect and value much of what I have learned from the indigenous culture and wisdom. I will share with you the deeper umbrella of what covers the eco-ethological niche[s] and the existential issues."

Witnessing Wisdom in Aborigine and Police

"It is respecting not only the folks who are more than capable of autonomous governance, but the different individuals I have met and have interacted with. I don't subscribe to identity politics. To me this view like all that narrow an entire people into a neat category just doesn't make sense. It's true that the best people to give insight from the indigenous framework are indigenous people who are themselves police officers, and you will hear their voices in this book."

"I have learnt a lot about indigenous frameworks, how they relate to police frameworks, and as I intimated are police frameworks and models within police work itself. The simple fact is that some tough lessons were learnt the hard way and relatively recently. I now know as with all of us, I still have much to learn. I will illustrate some of my experience by showcasing my mistakes, as well as many more successes. In not succeeding at first, my mistakes help me learn taboos in culture and interactions that can hopefully fuel your desire to learn about Aboriginal Officer's and our shared culture."

Cop Doc Dan R: "Stop; Pause and Reflect for A Moment: Please, Sgt. Moloney you may have much to learn, as we all do and much more to offer all of us – we need to learn from you! In your first few moments with me, you've admitted to the reader that as a street level peer support officer you humbly move forward, and have made some mistakes. Sgt. Matt your connection to other officers and the citizens you serve developed in your own eco-ethological niche through hard-won skills and abilities you've developed as a police officer, investigator and what we would call street cop, but you Aussies, call Copper."

"Sgt. Matt your point that police can understand the myriads of possibilities, limitations, and frustrations including traumatic losses and grief with appropriate and culturally competent leadership from within police circles is not well taken in United States academic and professional clinical groups is I will affirm true in some circles but not all. In forging forward with apparent simplicity your thoughts are quite complex to process. Let me elaborate, the fact that you have a keen ear to facilitate the verbal and non-verbal descriptions you've gained as an understanding and insight into Aborigine Officers experiences within a larger police culture is very well worth listening to for me as clinician, Professor and Cop Doc. You are challenging each officer to accommodate to a new framework of eco-ethological niches as they emerge as you value my approach for the Aborigine Police and perhaps civilian population impacted by police collectively and individually. I believe in some way thus far, your nascent shared experiences are qualitatively and descriptive anthropologically progressive, even without portfolio in a linear academic sense. Let's keep in mind that Dr. Margaret Meads, classic work *Coming of Age in Samoa* (Boas and Mead, 1973) was such a classic study in its own time and milieu. You, Sgt. Moloney's as participant observer status as a police commander are challenged by your own macro-culture where you live within an eco-ethological niche of trauma and losses in Queensland. You, in fact, as a police officer facing an existential vacuum looming over indigenous people sucked into forces larger than their own is perhaps a raw study, a beginning toward what Dr. Mead did in her own ingenuity and time frame?"

Commander Sgt Matt Moloney: "I can't see us exactly as Dr. Margret Mead was but I can see your point as being part of the community in Queensland and sorting through the developmental conflicts that keep turning up in the police domain and on the assimilation of Aborigine people into the larger communities they meld into and adapt too."

Cop Doc Dan R: "Your challenge adds a lot to tackle as far as what we both intended at first. Fortunately, the grass-roots interventions you singlehandedly are unfurling Sgt. Commander Matt Moloney is one that leaves more than a popular leafing interest but a growing underbrush that can withstand the fanning of negative and bias attacks on the two cultures you live in. That is the Aboriginal and the Police and Public Safety cultures."

"I would like to quote to you, Professor Margret Mead (1973) who articulated a very kindred challenge, "There is hope, I believe, in seeing the human adventure as a whole and in the shared trust that knowledge about mankind, sought in reverence for life, can bring life."

"Sgt. Moloney you and I also share a deep antipathy toward those who stoke hatred that harms police. Such hate is spawn out of ignorance, racism, and deep-rooted drives of aggression, destruction and self-loathing. The term that best captures the attempt to marginalize society's most ardent citizens with hatred, and blatant attacks which harm officers and their family members I first titled in the Handbook of Police Psychology (2012 & 2018) which my long-term colleague Dr. Kitaeff invited me to write. Rather than Racism against police – '**Centurioncide**' is my term that best fits, perfidious sedition against guardians of law and order servicing the public trust. You suggested a bit earlier in our interview that this impacted on your motivation to gain a foothold on my approach which you are mastering very nicely!

Commander Sgt Matt Moloney: "How can I actually help explain Centurioncide to the indigenous members of Queensland and the non-indigenous members as well without watering down the bias and racism we experience as police and public safety officers and our families who are cast in blue?"

Cop Doc Dan R: "*Centurioncide* is the intentional and willful wanton destruction by force against the social, existential and purposive empowerment given civic self-governance and service by sworn law enforcement officers: Wanton destruction by hateful and destructive forceful attacks of a social, academic, moral, physical and psychological nature against a police officer, his/her family members and society can be viewed on a continuum as Centurioncide (Rudofossi. 2018). We will return to this concept of Centurioncide and operationalize it within the scope of this book as it has been operationalized in other formats. Centurioncide was first used in the second edition of Dr. Jack Kitaeff's Handbook of Police Psychology (2019)."

"Centurioncide is the term I wrestled with and came up with in capturing the legal, social and psycho-physical maladies uniquely circling the encampment of police and public safety officers and their families, notwithstanding an attack against society as well. Cide is an end: Endings as in homicide, suicide, the endings of peace, life and resistance in the flow and ebbs encircling life itself. Cide is a negative and forceful uprooting of social and civil life when appended to a creative root as Centurion. Centurions are both the ancient and modern equivalent of public service and safety officers as the front line serving and protecting all societies."

"One can say at the best levels of performance and existence, the final line of the Pax Romana of society as civilization is the Centurion: Centurion's guard the front perimeter to the deepest inner circle at the nadir to zenith that represents society at its lowest point and highest. The trigger finger stopping a terrorist from wiping out innocent civilians to the Oratory genius of President Teddy Roosevelt as NYPD Commissioner encompasses the public safety official known as the Centurion (Lorant;1959)."

"The reduction and marginalization of police and the aboriginal folk and the larger folklore of the Aussies all contribute toward Centurioncide and ignorance: Pausing and re-direction of our attention with solution may focus a generative insight responsibly rather than degenerative criticism with no solution save not emptying out the baby water of novelty with the bath water of tradition."

"I have Stopped to pause for a long moment good Sgt. Moloney and now want to hear your tenured and challenging situations as a Police Commander on Cape York, Queensland, the Outback in Winton; and Thursday Island in the Torres Straits as you promised. Is that good with you, Sgt, Commander Matt Moloney?"

Commander Sgt Matt Moloney: "That was one large return to my perspective Doc Dan but I am game on! I will start by sharing with you my shark duty on Thursday Island: I served in regional centres on the coast in central Queensland, far west in the outback in Winton, in Thursday Island in the Torres Straits and indigenous communities on mainland Cape York. The Torres Strait Islander people are indigenous

Witnessing Wisdom in Aborigine and Police 23

Australians, but are a distinct people from mainland aboriginal people. I don't really do big city policing. If you asked me to define myself, I'd call myself a 'T.I. Baidam' and a 'Cape Bullyman'. T.I. is short for Thursday Island, the main island that is the service centre of the Torres Straits, and 'Baidam' is T.I. Creole for shark, which is what the Islanders call coppers. In their culture, sharks are not all bad. Being called a Baidam is not an insult like 'pig' or 'filth'."

Cop Doc Dan R: "Well, then let's examine what is possibly meant when shark is used for a copper by a Torres Strait Islander?

Commander Sgt Matt Moloney: "There is a degree of ambivalence towards sharks because they can take you and eat you, but they are not all that bad. Sharks fall into the dinner menu by some and in traditional culture and legend sharks had an important role with mystical significance. In a competition for a woman's affection two brothers, one named Baidam (Shark) and his competing brother Avati lived on either side of the Torres Strait Island."

"Both brothers vied for their idealized feminine Poniponi flew off into the sky as her umbilical cord envelops the starry night. The point is that the coppers can be even seen as brothers with the indigenous people of the Island in this perspective. Potential is always awaiting possibilities of which one is hatching, the other is strangulation in birth. Think about it for a moment. Stifling of one culture by control without letting go is one end; the other is sharing the space in the light of birthing respect for each culture."

"As for Cape Bullyman, Aboriginals have had a lot more negative history with the police than Islanders. Cape is the geographical area, and Bullyman is not too friendly an aboriginal parlance for policeman."

Cop Doc Dan R: "Sgt. Matt let me ask you, Why? If you could explain to me, how did the name Bullyman stick for a while within the slang language?"

Commander Sgt Matt Moloney: "Bullying of the mainland aboriginal people was perceived and perhaps to a degree was somewhat true, that is, when comparison to the earlier days of policing are made."

"Baidam have sharp jaws with snapping teeth. Exposure of such teeth was seldom exposed in the context of Bullying with the Islanders, but sadly it happened. Bifurcation between two indigenous groups such as the Torres Islanders and the Aboriginal folks and their relations with police became the mould from which further divisions became more pronounced.

Cop Doc Dan R: "Using an eco-ethological existential framework, it seems like it wasn't just the quite large distinctions between Torres Strait Islander and mainland aboriginal culture but the history between police and the two groups, while it shares much in common, is different. Is that a correct inference?"

Commander Sgt Matt Moloney: "Differences abound in both the Torres Strait Islanders and Aboriginal Folks and police from an Eco-Ethological layout. Yet a lot more commonality lay potent and ready for creating bridges. The Bridge between life and death is a hard span to travel for most mortals: Mortal as I am, I tried to work on my case as larger than life itself. It is hard to come up with a proper title of this case." (Silence).

Cop Doc Dan R: "That sounds like a life altering experience existentially speaking Sgt. Mate Matt Moloney, please continue and give this case a name to wrestle it to being expressed if you could?"

Commander Sgt Matt Moloney: "It was life altering from a centre-point of my own existence. I would say this case can be called 'My Big Casket: Death and Dying at a Time - No Funeral Director Existed! Well it began like this Dr. Dan; the span of time had blown in for me to sail as the Coen Police Commander. I had learnt a lot about the culture of my aboriginal and Torres Strait Islander countrymen and women in many preceding years. My understanding included a few steps forward, a few back, then some more to be gained. It appears each time I started to think

I knew the culture well; perplexing outcomes curved way off trajectories as outlines in operational guides. I had a lot to learn from indigenous citizens as a police official. That learning could only be done in practice. One such challenge was a particular job I was confronted with in Coen. While this job fits nicely in jobs that are challenging – 'It' still haunts me from time to time."

"I was 'on the job' as a copper who was 'becoming an investigator'. I was involved in the investigation of a young indigenous woman who went missing in rather suspicious circumstances. Appropriately, I had contemplated the cultural impact of how much death and the spirit world pulled at the centre of this particular job: 'It' all started at a funeral."

"That fact was, I couldn't find any funeral director in Coen. *I struggled with this fact which rattled my expectations with amusement, startled my sensibilities, I was lost.* In the Catholic, Christian, Hindu, Buddhist, Muslim and Jewish faith I always could get hold of a funeral director."

"I was used to having men and sometimes women in black respond to my calls. No quiet, black clad looking professionals were present and organising everything in need of being ordered in the ensuing chaos of a funeral."

"Where had all the allied and front line of the funeral directors gone? They too were painfully absent. No ditch-digger? No stout chaps in overalls that wait to fill the grave were anywhere to be had; Dr. Dan I will never forget the fact you were told when you were a young fellow that if you didn't buckle down and study hard you would become a 'ditch-digger'. Well we can call the grave diggers 'ditch-diggers' but they couldn't be of assistance here, regardless of any name – none were around. In the United States undertakers await the funeral itself as the liaisons of the dead. My first identified problem laid its way around death without a funeral."

Cop Doc Dan R: "I get your point and that was a dig, (grin) but, why is neither funeral director, nor ditch digging undertakers being on leave such a problem?"

Commander Sgt Matt Moloney: "The answer is clear, for after any funeral service most family members are so emotionally exhausted, they simply don't have the strength to lift a shovel. But the grave won't fill itself. In Coen this has resulted in a custom developing to fill the need of 'how?'; 'when?' and 'where?' to get the actual deceased person buried in the long line of plots."

"In Coen, when services conclude and everyone has paid their last respects to the dead person as he is laid to rest in the coffin the rest of the family and friends come forward to assist in filling the grave with soil. Usually it's the young or at least not old men who do the shovelling of dirt into the grave."

Cop Doc Dan R: "Shovelling dirt into the grave of the dead in Coen as in other cultural groups and their unique eco-ethological niches may be among their Rites of Passage: Well what happened in terms of your own unique interpretation of this practice as you experienced it?"

Commander Sgt Matt Moloney: "Being able to shovel dirt into the graves final resting place is demonstrative. The behaviour of re-placing the newly tilled earth as a consecration by the concerned visitor: as family member; close friend; co-worker, clergy and in my case police officer is to share the displacement that the passed dead person has left in their wake. The sense of loss is no longer left empty as the officer is allowed to doing something."

"A way of expressing solidarity with the family is to assist in this giving to the dead person and family members a concrete action that ventilates an active empathy as a token to the living that the significant participants still care. When I observed this ritual and the shared symbolic significance offered to each participant, I felt compelled to partake as a participant-observer. Yet, I was inhibited. Being a police officer

Witnessing Wisdom in Aborigine and Police

is an existential state whereby boundaries surround my own culture of policing. Both Queensland Coppers and NYPD beat cops are most sanguine and aloof in being uninvolved in people's personal lives as long as the style of life they are living is not disruptive to other people's lives and living space. So being a good copper I was taught and practiced good manners. Those manners included not becoming intrusive in personal matters related to the traditions and customs of each indigenous family as they observe their own religious practices and customs."

"The challenge was becoming aware of an ill-defined invitation to participate in shovelling the earth for the member of this family who passed in an untimely manner. My dilemma was his death provoked my own passion to participate in the mores as uniquely practiced within his familial rites. I was held back. I halted at the door of action by not wanting to violate the mores and customs of being a proper copper who remained present, but also uninvolved on a personal level of experience."

Cop Doc Dan R: "This dilemma is one that seems as a challenge to you and perhaps each officer. On one hand, where does the officer draw that line in an uneasy balance of duties, boundaries, and desires to fit into the community without overstepping being a copper? Relationships develop within a specific family and the officer. Sharing rituals as invitations appear may become moments existentially taken, or lost as Rites are bridges whereby one becomes a viable member of that community, or not, that is if I am reading you right?"

Commander Sgt Matt Moloney: "In this case that officer facing the dilemma of swapping dirt or not to swap dirt was me! The swapping of dirt is one dirty business here.

Cop Doc Dan R: "Yes, swapping dirt is quite a messy business, how did you ditch this dig and move forward or sally far away? I am listening to the context of what sounds like an invitation you pressed on with yourself."

Commander Sgt Matt Moloney: "In a way this was an invite. This was not my first funeral in Coen. My first had been that of a severely disabled little girl. We had to investigate her death. Her death may have been natural as in cases of SIDs death but we had to check all leads and ensure no foul play had hastened her short life to a complete - 'Halt'!

Cop Doc Dan R: "Halt! That is a real pause where you just had a re-direct to this young girl's death. Could you kindly continue?" (Silence).

Commander Sgt Matt Moloney: "I moved very diplomatically as my enquiry delicately led the way. At my intentionally slowest pace I moved with caution – methodically and rationally. During the course of our investigations, a good relationship with the parents in its slow process was forming. I had been invited to some of the family gatherings and to the after-funeral feast which is when as in most other faiths a ceremonial meal given for the survivors. This feast ensures the bereaved will eat. It serves as a way of socializing and bonding with others present for the funeral. At the time of this little girl's funeral I figured that it would likely have been appropriate for me to assist and wield a shovel at the burial as a nice deed without much thought being put into it. Being a rookie copper, I was not familiar enough with the do's and don'ts in Coen culturally and as a copper. I held back my boldness to step up to the ditch and dig in to the soil. With vehemence and declarative enunciation,

"In lieu of a shovel I reflected with no added trouble sitting on the side lines quietly. No one took me, for any more or less of a copper. No more or less a copper, than any of my non-indigenous predecessors. No one knew of my internal conflict and challenges."

Cop Doc Dan R: "It seems like you had some heavy balancing to do as being caught between the rock of neutrality and the hard place of jumping in with full emotion and passion. Some dilemma of the heart and soul and due diligence and boundaries laid out in concrete, huh?"

Commander Sgt Matt Moloney: "My conflict lay in the centre core of my soul. I wondered if I dug in the soil along with family and friends of the newly dead, I could be overstepping my boundaries. Yet, I felt there wouldn't be any harm in my assisting this young couple and extended family member by joining the funeral rites and ritual as a community copper. My own contemplations were disrupted when a colleague police tracker, and indigenous community member educated me and befriended me. Right on time came, Barry Port the Tracker. In the chaos and solemnity of the funeral, a relationship between the deceased and our police tracker sprung in developing a lead and motive. As in all death investigations all was more complicated than just finding out the 'what's?' and 'when's?' of a death case. I can't help but interject on the point that a truth emerges, "there go I, but for the grace of G-d, go I." That Lionhearted leader that led so well has helped me make and had made and continues to make sense of the seemingly senseless. For me Barry Port as tracker has led the way with my navigating through the maze of finding cultural competence with the Aborigine clan members."

Cop Doc Dan R: "Your use of Sir Winston Churchill. offered a powerful interjection of a deep reflection that what is at the centre of existence is not the mundane core for everyone and applicable to no one in particular, but the existential core which is hardly ever prescribed and almost always responsive to the individual. That being so, if I am correct Barry Port is a Law Enforcement Officer, Queensland Aborigine Police – Tracker. That being the essential correct title that precedes the name Barry Port?"

Commander Sgt Matt Moloney: "Yes, you can correctly say that Tracker Barry Port was the last Aborigine clan members with specialized expertise employed by the Queensland Police Department. Barry Port remember was a full-time police tracker. He is not as sometimes characterized and labelled, the Liaison Officer."

Cop Doc Dan R: "Why is the label Liaison Officer not a good fit for Barry Port?"

Commander Sgt Matt Moloney: "First, Officer Barry Port doesn't really like performing that task of doing liaison work. Second, he is not a diplomat and resents being placed in a placard on a desk or chart with a title that hardly captures the essence of what he does, how he goes about doing what he does, and marginalizes the depth and grasp of his professional skill."

"Tracker Barry Port is both Aboriginal and Tracker and is justifiably proud of what both titles mean. Barry Port did not emerge out of the legendary bog, a descending fog, but was born under a tree on the banks of the Coen River on, or around the 6th day of October 1942. During World War II, Barry's father held the heritage and traditions of being a member of the Lama Lama tribe from Port Stewart."

"Barry Port's mother had her own original roots traceable to the Ayapathu tribe from Ebagoolah. Sadly, Ebagoolah is a whisper nowadays in a town that has buckled under the large wave of assimilations that swallowed smaller cultural identities. Ebagoolah no longer exists in practice and is kept alive via anthologies, biographies and historiographic monographs by the few anthropologists, psychologists/psychiatrists and historians."

Cop Doc Dan R: "It appears you hold it in your own stored memories and have share this history with me with may become a linchpin for others with such interest and passion to uncover and perhaps one day in some way revive. Many communities in Europe of Jewish and Gypsy origin could not be returned to what glory it held in its heyday but nonetheless the rare tomes and collective unwritten and oral histories revived the soulful essence to be revived nowadays or in the future, perhaps?"

Commander Sgt Matt Moloney: "For those who know we hold it in our own stored memories. That stored memory of what Ebagoolah is nowadays as ghost-town is juxtaposed against its rich history and what forced change without adequate assimilation and accommodation can do. Barry Port accordingly did not get swept under the Act in Queensland. For our purposes the Act also offered much to the participants in terms of monetary and other benefits. But, in equal measure the Act swept the youth away with much ado with little substance to absorb and connect with their original roots."

Witnessing Wisdom in Aborigine and Police   31

Cop Doc Dan R: "That sounds familiar with some social programs meant to help homeless people and yet many have shared with me and others they are scared to go to centres because they feel the predatory homeless rule and also sabotage those who earnestly are seeking shelter and some assistance to get back on their toes. The same is true of substance abuse patients and repeat offenders of illegal drug use where instead of offering true rehabilitation and detoxification they are offered safe syringes and lesser synthetic drugs that are now given safely. Well, it appears here on one hand a better solution is reached and with the best of intentions but on the other hand the results are often an even more entrenched drug and homeless problem for the folks most in need of shelter and detoxification are now scaffolded to deeper issues of victimization and deleterious drug addiction. The Act sounds like it had the best of intentions by most but some worse effects to still tackle for the participants impacted by this well-meaning legislation. Did Barry Port as an individual feel impacted by this Act and how so and why?"

Commander Sgt Matt Moloney: "First, Doc as Barry Port was being educated in Coen, he went through the usual educational system of schooling most kids did. However, at twelve years of age he started work at Mount Croll station where he was a ringer, and worked mustering the domestic animals. He learnt his tracking there under the direct tutelage of his father who, I have been told, could track a Goanna across bare rock. This background was indispensible to not only Barry Port who became tenured in the skills and learned traditions of his fathers and forefathers where traditions and culture was not hidden, corrected, or swept under larger jingoisms as multi-cultural but accepted as the culture of being part of the Lama Lama Tribe of Port Stewart."

"With a number of decades under his belt of being a cattleman, tracker and a tenured musterer and a refreshing acceptance by the Queensland Police Barry Port became a Tracker on "the Job"."

"Uniquely in the century that has passed, Barry Port joined the Queensland Police as a forty-year old. The years were the rocking and rolling

1980's. The 1980's were historic and full with Discos while the young adults to middle age folks were trying to recapture youth, Barry at 40 years of age was captured in the label they gave him, "living-history of an indigenous tracker. Indigenous Tracker is the term used but even that respectful title hardly captures the legend of Officer Barry Port. It is quite possible that I have had the privilege of working with as depicted in the media light, the Last tracker as Barry Port."

"In the culture of policing not all, but many officers hold reporters, journalists and editorial boards as leaning far too much to the left of political honesty. In the written word they may in reality be way too limited in really and honestly saying things straight and from the hip. The coverage and attention paid to Officer Barry Port is not much different to me and for that matter him, as we spoke frankly and opening up to you, as a fellow police officer and Cop Doc, Dr. Dan Rudofossi, I feel you as well."

Cop Doc Dan R: "Well, I will say I have tried my best to sally far away from the politicization of science including Psychology as a premiere science, practice clinically including as an Expert Witness and Police Cop Doc and of course as Professor. But I would not waive off and consider it trite to say I too have felt the brunt of political manoeuvring to silence me at times and in subtle and sometimes more explicit and hostile ways and means. In returning to Barry Port as LEO and tracker extraordinaire I had two points to share with both you and he."

"My first point is above all the iatrogenic impact of well-meaning clinicians to educators and reformers of all ilk is that in being all too human any one can err by believing they have the grasp on the definitive truth and that includes you, I and Tracker LEO Barry Port. Taking a heuristic approach which expands boundaries one is most likely to endure many hostile responses and yet to not do so is a negligence existentially where one is centred. Iatrogenic intervention applies to both sides of the political and scientific spectrum when politicized and stances become howlingly one sided. Is it better as Iatrogenic is operationalized to not have tried an intervention due to the cure being worse in side effects

Witnessing Wisdom in Aborigine and Police 33

than not having any intervention whatsoever? This is hard to prove and beyond our dialogue here but is something that is worth the while to consider in sweeping programs of reform which often tout the individual but rarely in reality even consider the dissenting individual or group including for example listening to the fundamentalist perspective, or conservative participant (s). This is equally egregious when labelling any intervention and those supporting such reforms as 'left leaning misguided liberals"

"The second point is that regarding Barry Port being reduced to the austere and so broad title of a titular head Liaison is right on point and I remember when I was director of clinical and education branches among others for Membership Assistance Program of the NYPD, I too felt the weight of such attempts by a politically appointed Guru as an attempt to usurp all credit for enormous work and success. Suffice to say this is larger then the scope of our conversation but it is well worth the while to explore in other venues as to the use of words to minimize and marginalize the impact of reformers and folks who press the boundaries of both the left and right polarities for the sake of genuine compassionate interventions. In Barry Ports case his was the compassionate intervention of tracking down criminals that preyed on his own fellows within his own community. For me it was in similar vein doing and establishing real crisis and ambulatory methods to combat suicide, severe and debilitating addictive behaviours and mental illness of a severe and decompensating isolating effect from mushrooming to premature death and anguish. Having said this parallel and offering some context to my own responses of yours with Barry Port aka Tracker and LEO. I wonder if some more historic context may be useful to give even richer context?"

Commander Sgt Matt Moloney: "Cheers to what you shared Dr Dan and to your own connections as I think of the historic background of Barry Port as he has shared with me. The life and historic tales of the Tracker Officer fits in a humorous way with tracking the truth of the trails of progress, evolution and the pitfalls of de-evolution without diverting too much as we return to my point. So, my point is that most media coverage focuses on the idea that Barry's skills as a tracker are redundant, along the lines of 'who needs a tracker when you have a chopper?' In other words, for those who are not from police culture the chopper is a euphemism for a helicopter and other contrivances that can effectively sweep large terrains and find the bad guy/gal without as much labour-intensive and costly tracking skills as Barry Port yields. The real splash into economics and policing is that Barry's Tracking skills were still used by the Coen coppers when I was there."

"As recently as 2011 he located a sentenced offender who fled the Coen court house after a two-hour track. As a direct result of having Barry on staff, the Coen coppers had an unofficial 'no foot chase' policy. This is not out of any sense of concern for consequences if we run people down. We have a tracker. Police do not need to run anyone down in a pursuit. For example, suspects can run as fast and as far as they want, but they cannot hide from the skilled and highly effective Officer Barry Port who has indeed tracked down fleeing felons. Barry Port tracking is at a lesser speed, some skills he possesses has not been as swift as to immediately break a fleeing felon, but he breaks the impoverished myth of being antiquated by outwitting and outsmarting the brazen foolhardy who to try to outrun and outsmart him to this day. I mean this is sensible is it not?"

Cop Doc Dan R: "It is superbly sensible and clear that Ageism or the bias against folks that are aging is extant in force here as much as old score racism. That is, he is biased against.

"The crux of the issue is the idea of Barry Port being swifter then the perpetrators razor slice to the dice of the gamble, he/she can escape the sleuth who runs the gambit of the perp, and more than just a sprint down an alleyway."

"Forgive me being playful and not wistful (pause) about Barry Ports situation but clearly the sensibility and eco-ethological ingenuity and alacrity of his tracking is crucial and has helped save not only perpetrators lives, the witnesses he has given some sense of succorance and justice

Witnessing Wisdom in Aborigine and Police

too, but his gifting hi fellow LEO's too. How LEO's are gifted may not be as apparent. You and I as Sgt.'s with many decades of street experience both know how dangerous pursuits are. For the last Tracker and LEO Barry Port to possess his unique skills and track down wanted felons with violent records rather than enter into hot vehicular pursuits definitively saves fellow officers from invariably crashing and burning – from a literal and metaphorical perspective. If I can suggest Barry Port's awesome ingenuity being brought to me, and re-directed to you and to our reader's attention is worthy of a great noetic, Cheers!"

Commander Sgt Matt Moloney: "Cheers! Right on target Doc. Barry is a bright law enforcement officer: Alacrity to find lost people, criminals in flight, and establish the unfurling ugly truth at crime scenes is the core at Barry Port's skills at observation. Observing things that even trained observers like forensic investigators and scientists miss are things that this unique last tracker knows how to uncover."

"An example, is a car crash where Barry looked at marks in the dirt and described exactly what happened. He used his method to ferret out who, how and which drivers were at fault and where the line in the bifurcated highway crossed the legal limit of speed. His powers of observation imply something extraordinary about individuals who possess clarity of perception; this ability is true of Barry Port. Barry Port again had the unique skillful control over his powers of perception. It was at this funeral that I was at, was the defacto of the tracker's brother. One could be forgiven for thinking that this would make relations easy, but as with most things in Coen, it was complicated. Prior to 1966, Barry's family were not under the Act. They were declared citizens. This was because they had earned it."

"In a current stance of entitlement which is almost epidemic among all people and their claims including the many narcissistic personality types in the United Kingdom and for that matter the United States, often the worthiest as those with humility and in need are sometimes forgotten. To me this is true of language. Especially the core roots of languages spoken at one point by Aborigine Clan members, and now let go of. The Port family were among the most reliable and hardworking people ever in their own district. They weren't just declared full citizens in Coen, they earned that status regardless of their wits, energy and charisma without apologetics and bitter water in their cup. The Port family allowed expressing their hard work with all that entailed - including being able to attend the pub, sit at the bar, and drink a beer."

"Indeed, Barry Port is given esteem and respect by most of the non-indigenous community: Some, but not all the Queensland Aboriginals, Murries as folks of this cultural background call themselves in a polite manner hold Officer Barry Port as a legend even when he was working and for his own times. To some degree, again not all but many Murries hold Office Barry Port as a legend for all time. A legend for breaking through barriers to achieve a level of competence and stay inside his culture of origin as a Tracker. However unconventional, Barry Ports legendary tracking skills used adroitly in hunting down known felons and missing people in danger with balance and facility make him the rear participant observer. One foot in his Aboriginal culture and one foot out while almost always circumnavigating outside his own culture. I reflect how my own odyssey has also taken me to the same crossroads and bifurcated tracks as Barry Port."

I struggled with my desire to join in and participate fully in the Murries culture rituals and rites at times but with the admonition in my own mind was actually of you Doc, as my Cop Doc advisor toward maintaining boundaries. I took a quote from you Dr. Dan Rudofossi as you put it well."

Cop Doc Dan R: "Are you referring to my saying to you, "getting down and clean: Success is multiplied by sweat, skill, and sedulous achievement that no one gave you on a silver platter of dross. You earned your reward in the hard field of dedication, commitment and faith larger than you and I."

Commander Sgt Matt Moloney: "No, but I sure use that perspective but it is written down here and you told me and I recorded it as follows:

Witnessing Wisdom in Aborigine and Police   37

"The ideal and real have huge gaps that can wrap around and at times bite you hard and fast. Always have some second and third options available to wiggle away from when investigating and assessing new terrain – all terrain begins with the mind and its vistas are boundless. So, chart off what you can navigate, and pilot onward with your navigator in the wings -- as you fly, onward and forward and ever so rare, even in reverse to move forward."

Cop Doc Dan R: "Thank you for your recording my quotes as a gift I cherish and will try to remember myself when the times get tough as well. If I can pause for a moment, at the time all that you were describing was happening back then, who did you rely on, that is, if anyone to help navigate through the turbulent tides and vicissitudes?"

Commander Sgt Matt Moloney: "While at the time this was happening, I had no real navigator and no real advisor. I had used my street smarts as a compass, and my moral fibre as a needle in a chaotic haystack. It worked because my friend and colleague was Barry Port, the Tracker. Barry Port's tribe is Lama Lama as disclosed earlier and he is recognised by his members as a respectable person and an elder. *An elder is a wise advisor.* Elder is not a title given away by some superficial sense of entitlement. It is not through privilege unearned, elitism, or given away titles done so easily nowadays but Elder is earned over time. Elder is evidenced by one area of proof whereby the person tested is capable of handling tough situations with effective, and decent outcomes."

"Elder Barry Port gave and still gives his focus and direction toward a lifetime of service among his own indigenous lands and people of Queensland. Barry can be said to be a tightrope walker as a tracker for the Queensland Police - hardly stable tightropes make tracks in the air that have always landed him on his feet. Some very harsh judges have mislabelled him as a Judas, others as an opportunistic 'sell-out'. Other inter-tribal members have pointed him out as an Uncle Tom, meaning not a participant observer but a hired gun that blows the whistle of the highest bidder."

Cop Doc Dan R: "Those judges sound quite bias in their triumvirate blows at him from top down and all-around Commander Moloney. What do you think of such aspersions? Any merit at all?"

Commander Sgt Matt Moloney: "I vote no merit and nay to their say! It is an injustice and also blatantly false slander. This vision of indigenousness, whereby a vision of pure victim hood and subsequent entitlement all but defines modern discussions of indigenous issues is imbalanced and unjust. At the root you often find everyone but indigenous people at the core of this instigation which leave the real indigenous folks as dependents of those who believe they like childlike imps need special protection. Self-governance and squabbles are all violent because they include real debates and hard-core transitions."

Cop Doc Dan R: "The his-story of Officer Barry Port is one of sweat, skill, effort and achievement often sidelined or ignored. Sedulous commitment does work and is anything but selling out; it is cop-ing in with true humane intervention for all and not all for one group or another – divisively as Tracker, Elder Barry Port shares with you and us. That is if you and I are putting the tracks that line both sides and a centre for last Tracker Barry Port to be placed historically and as a pioneer of all Aborigine culture and specifically of merit as a son of the Murries and inclusion within Queensland Police and society for his enormous contributions from an eco-ethological existential perspective. He was and is a pioneer and in doing so he has achieved success again within his own level of inner-sight. That is if I am tracking our tracker correctly?"

Commander Sgt Matt Moloney: "I agree you've gotten down with Barry Port and I to describe what you heard as the word smith you've been called. It is true that most but not all of his cohorts agree in this inner-sight which gives an expectable evidence of his gifts to all: His vision of befriending all fellow human beings, indigenous and non-indigenous Queenslanders, preserves the inner culture of policing and becoming and being a true-blue trooper. Officer Barry Port also lives up to the standards of being an Elder Murries and tracker." Let me give you more of the context of the his-story behind Barry Port's, brother. The brother of Tracker Barry Port. Barry's Brother, Phillip Port is a respected traditional owner of property and domestic cattle. Although a member of the Lama Lama Phillip did not foreclose his own initiative and thought and at times acted outside the box. For example, in issues regarding cattle and land he sometimes sided with another Clan, the Kanju. Some of the key leaders and players in the Kanju Clan looked favourably on Barry's example and legacy, a substantive portion did not."

"The majority of the Kanju are made up by one clan, the Creek family. This alliance caused some friction between Barry and his brother on at least one occasion I know of personally, between Phillip and others in the Lama Lama Clan."

"I have been told, but have never confirmed that ironically, the previous elder of the Creek family Tom Creek was also not under the Act either. Like the Port family they had to earn what they received in the face of harsh demands and biases as obstacles to overcome. The previous Elder had a reputation among all that knew him as a hardworking, decent, likable, highly respected and very tough man. The local non-indigenous police also concurred with this viewpoint. Barry did not get along and had some issues with some members of the Creek family."

"Now prior to saying anything else, there were members of the Kanju and Creeks with whom I got on quite well with. Some members of both the Kanju and Creek I didn't synchronize and connect with well, either. You see, there was great tension between the Kanju, Creeks and Lama Lama Tribes not withstanding other tribal/language groups and clans in Coen that competed and feuded for tribal rights and other benefits. Barry as disclosed quite openly was born on the banks of the Coen River."

"Barry Port on a trip we took together guided me to his actual place of birth. As I sat and resonated with him as he disclosed to me, the fact was that but for that parcel of land, he is still not recognised as a traditional owner of land."

"Understandably some tension and friction arose as the Creeks are now the owners of this property. Although, as a participant observer watching the inheritance claims and squabbles, I kept my own firm boundary in place and that it is not for me to say traditionally who did, or did not own that parcel of sacred land. On the other hand, I felt Barry Port's pain and also his struggle as well. Its complicated."

Cop Doc Dan R: "It seems on an unconscious level of awareness we can pull the fact you identify greatly and deeply with Barry Port as one of your own heroes and in some ways may reflect back on you and your own struggles eco-ethologically and existentially as you've experienced similar challenges as a police officer in communities that treat you at times as if you are the invisible man?"

Commander Sgt Matt Moloney: "Looking at my feelings as being motivated unconsciously is interesting. Barry Port is my extended mate, or as you say in policing in America and especially the five points of NYC, "brother in blue", further I realize in a different way you are my cop doc brother Dr. Dan R., and coloured blue as I am and he is,

"I felt not only for Barry Port, but with empathy and identification with him!"

"The hard fact is that Police Tracker Barry Port is not welcome on Kanju land and can only go there when he is in the execution of his duty. Any other time although he is not only an officer of the law, an Elder in his own Lama Lama Clan, and also is a first responder legend he is told in no uncertain manner and very distinctly with the same message at heart,

"Barry Port you don't have permission to go here, except in the performance of your duty!"

"It is important to understand the gravity of this admonition if not warning to my copper bro and mate, just because you were born at this location and you are a bona fide Murri does not automatically mean traditionally you have any claim to this land from which you were conceived. If you are here in the performance of serving us in the community then you have a pass to come and go as you please. If you are here for personal reasons or entertainment and religious purposes stay in your own home town and territory as we define it for you!"

"That is a very complicated topic and I definitely will not make a judgement either way, but I can raise the point to give some context as to why Barry doesn't get on with most of the Kanju clan. Indigenous culture is complicated and there are different claims and points of view to gain perspective, it is clear that Barry Port was hurt emotionally by being disregarded and his viewpoint marginalized which he must suck up too as an officer and tracker."

Cop Doc Dan R: "It is truly challenging for you and how could you stay objective or neutral in the centre of your soul and being in dealing with the issue of contradictions and inequity to those who view this dilemma including myself. A dilemma of being thrust in the centre of Barry Port as yourself too being an Invisible Public Servant and being given the sign and warning No Entry to Men and Women in Blue. How can you not feel somewhat blue and even if you don't act on that anger – not hurt from the losses of being disenfranchised and having no voice as our brother in Blue here Barry Port?"

"In regard to the invisible grey wall of indifference to public safety officers you and Barry Port are not that different from your brother and sisters in Blue in the NYPD who also suffer losses that are disenfranchised: Perhaps another point for research and solutions to sort through as we are quite connected across great oceans of divide. Our connection is the bridge offered via our joint suffering and losses now being given some ventilation and expression. What do you think good Commander Sgt Matt Moloney?"

Commander Sgt Matt Moloney: "I can't agree more Doc Dan as brother and fellow Sgt and your crew over in NYC and the NYPD. Ironically, it is European guilt that has caused this situation because it is Europeans who decided to hand the land back and European anthropologists who decided where the boundaries were. When his birthplace was a cattle property owned by whites, he could go there. But now, he can't as his birthplace is now owned by Kanju and Creek Clan members. Twisted irony the so-called oppressive force is not by non-indigenous individuals but by competing indigenous clan members."

"Equity and parity are not always in Barry Ports view and my own found in your own culture and race but in those who embrace the whole human race as humane, perhaps. As Barry's brother Phil Port associated with the Kanju and Creeks for amicable business ventures and his survival economically: Barry's blue culture and its rules did not. In taking a moment to process this inter-familial dispute they were not quite Cain and Able, but they left much unspoken for years. In fact, as Barry Port shared with me, they had not exchanged a pleasant word in years. Incidentally and for complete clarity, there's no doubt that the Creek clan are traditional owners of land and big swathes of it: The twisted irony is that with the rush to hand everything back indiscriminately to clans who had the loudest clamour, there is contention as to whether or not the specific clans were given their own rightful places, or were usurped by others opportunistically."

"Again, to qualify my own view, and for complete clarity I am not able to say who owned what myself. I have heard varying reports from different clan people who adamantly claimed they were informed by their ancestors that the land on and around Coen was theirs. I spoke to the recognised elder of the Creeks, Alan Creek whom I found a reasonable person to get on with and he is adamant that the land is theirs. Then again on the other hand other individuals are as adamant as some of the people making counter claims."

"Thankfully, I can add in truth, it's not for me to say who actually owned what? What it did mean for me is that I had to understand and take into account that emotions around land possession and concomitant claims to rights for some and not others ran deep as to ownership, or not being entitled to ownership. These conflicts are tied up with identity and power of not only the clans but the elders as well.

Witnessing Wisdom in Aborigine and Police

Cop Doc Dan R: "How did these conflicts get resolved if at all for you as apparently being placed in the middle of them due to your allegiance to Barry Port and his professional skill and legendary abilities and your service as a Police Sergeant?"

Commander Sgt Matt Moloney: "These conflicts became the energy to fuel the dynamics whereby they had a great impact on the framework I was working with for the Kanju, the Creeks, the Lama Lama and Ports and my own journey with each clan and with Barry Port who was the guide and tracker for my education and edification I could and did trust."

"Another fact is that indigenous people were displaced, often with extreme violence from their traditional lands by European settlers and the police. No-one who has any sense of history denies this injustice and painful history as well."

"As a consequence of the recognition of the fact of violent displacement at the hands of European Settlers who are really squatters, a land mark court case handed vast swathes of land back to indigenous people for ownership. Now large swathes of land are no longer Crown land. They are owned by indigenous people. But precisely who owns what causes some friction between the various indigenous tribal, language and clan groups."

"Further, there are still some non-indigenous families who hold onto their leases and are effectively small, isolated islands of white graziers surrounded by seas of indigenous land. A very complicated framework indeed."

"For me, I quite like Barry's brother. He has a good relationship with the police. I'd never even had cause to deal with him officially except as a witness to events. He has helped me with some things and given me critically important advice on cultural matters. He is a good bloke. Even if I didn't like him in situations like funerals, all bets were off. He had suddenly lost 'his missus'. She died just like that. I felt compassion for him. I wanted to demonstrate my support of him in this sad time. However, I was concerned that my empathy for his brother, would annoy Barry, as he may see me as taking sides with his brother and thereby the Creeks."

Cop Doc Dan R: "So the dilemma was the fact that you had an allegiance that was primary with Barry Port as colleague and peer LEO and tracker and even mentor amongst the Aborigine Clans and his brother Phillip although a 'bloke' at times was a pretty decent fellow too – although brothers they both vied at very different levels for your understanding and empathy. The loss of Phillip Port's wife triggered an affinity and empathy as a married fellow yourself and you felt empathic beyond any political or cultural differences you may have somewhat unconsciously sided with due to being brothers in blue with Barry Port?"

Commander Sgt Matt Moloney: "Yes, you can say that and I will not debate the dynamics of my own identification and affiliation here as likely being correct and on point Doc. Remember my dilemma earlier with shovelling at the funeral and burial without funeral director and ditch diggers: Save us, including Phillip, other family members, friends, and me – without courage to push the boundary well and apropos they would be without help and support really needed."

"My dilemma was I greatly respected Barry. Although Barry preferred to stay shy of Creeks and equated many as thugs and bullies not to be trusted I could not."

"It is true while there are some thugs and bullies in the Creek Clan, there are thugs and bullies everywhere, including rare as it is in police as well; but not all members can possibly be all such bullies and thugs. Being in the police taught me to respect all other peoples as human, not based on racial or cultural characteristics. But, in truth it's not that simple. There are some really excellent people in that clan. Of course, Barry knew this but it was hard and I did not want to disrespect Barry's need to be an individual and as human as the rest of us and stay off in this touchy situation between brothers."

Witnessing Wisdom in Aborigine and Police

"For me, I get on with many Kanju and quite a few, but I could not say all of the Creek clan. One of the Creek women actually married a police officer who is a competent, capable chap. It's true that at times as a group, they could be very difficult to get on with but I personally admired them. They are making real efforts to move forward. Even if I didn't have that admiration, they too are citizens of the state and as subjects of Her Majesty the Queen deserve impartial, professional, fair law enforcement first and foremost as a sworn officer I will try my best and did my best!"

"All of this was actually turning over in my mind at the funeral. I'd been thinking hard about the quandary of whether or not to help with the burial, but couldn't work it out because there were just too many variables and considerations. My framework was overwhelmed by the other competing frameworks."

"I came to the conclusion that I should just ask Barry. The problem being is that Barry is a reticent chap who keeps his thoughts and opinions to himself. But I was hoping that he could put aside his dislikes of the past and the Clan members that showed their antipathy toward him. I hoped he would overcome the attacks on himself, and tell me what he thought."

"The end result was we were able to resolve the rift. The burial and my soil covered over the conflict long enough to bridge the gap of distance and conflict within and without a decent family and two brothers by a third who had been related by blue blood."

Cop Doc Dan R: "A measured odyssey you began as a rookie and now as the peace maker you are as well Sgt. Commander and Scholar Matt Moloney! You built a reality and reliability by ingenuity through a dove and olive branch."

Cop Doc Dan Rudofossi Corner: Irreducible – Imprints Indelibly Laid Tracks

Queensland Police Tracker, Barry Port is not bifurcated into two separate personas and split on a tightrope balancing gimmick of two cultures dancing on the top of a pin-head: No pun intended. He is not on a collision course but has coursed well as a train on a track with parallel lines to bridge both cultures and the world he is forced to work within.

Barry Port is brought to life in his synergy of both cultures in a wise way. He is as any other adult man a person with a distinct identity that is well consolidated and coheres in a complex way in his own creative compromise. It is through Sgt. Matt's illustrative descriptions that we become keenly aware of the dynamic interplay of what would lull by as a howl and hoot rather than a measured understanding we are beginning to acquire.

Sgt Matt's shared experience of how lonely and disparaging a thought that the village of Ebagoolah wallowed into the abyss of disappearance between the throes of politics and coercion as the melting pot of assimilation churned culture and identity into unwitting change – unmade. The precipice of such subtle beneficence is a precipice in which change metamorphoses the inimitable Tracker Barry Port into an occluded port as his tracks leave a trace where his iconic legend pales into the foreground as he transforms into the ever illusive hidden and Invisible-man.

For Sgt Matt I observed, the reality of his experiences underscores his heart being and standing in the right place. Matt's soulful nature yearned existentially to pitch in with a shovel but he felt he had no strength to lift the shovel. This perhaps as an error, but one forgiven by the family as he had made up for with respect and empathy what was veiled by simply not knowing the right ritual to complete the gift. The gift as most police [indigenous and not indigenous] close the cases and the death for the bereaved. Each culture has its own rituals and most important each family may have a different way to bereaving and burial and so finding out what is acceptable and supportive may yield purposive closure for officer and the victim's family as well – if one is privileged to be invited to that funeral. I would suggest that the enquiry socratically will add power and poetic influence to a bond created rather than destroyed with indigenous and non-indigenous as well. He truly used his ingenuity and stopping, pausing and re-directing as my method and his own to win, rather than rue the Clans day and his own with further divisiveness.

I used an eco-ethological existential analytic approach with Sgt and colleague Matt Moloney which helped clear and heal some misconceptions held onto in his own return to a more healthful processing of trauma, as Matt said,

"I still at times remain haunted by some I know are part of my history as a copper. But my existential choices to accept and 'internally-witness' such reality."

The progress towards cure is minus self-recriminations in understanding the eco-ethological niche and demands as being beyond his ownership and ability to cure himself completely of as a mere mortal. The features of the cultural landscape was one which he realized now was a feature of the ecological-ethological niche that had a subtle but critically important impact for working on the case he was given. In his continuing work as we move forward in this book let's not forget Sgt. Matt Moloney has moved a forgotten language and culture into the vision of our existential beat as we press forward with him in uncharted territory within his eco-ethological niche in the Centre of his own existence as copper and pioneer. This privilege is not to be forgotten.

Unlike my own odyssey Sgt. Matt Moloney is still in the saddle as a uniformed police official. This is important information as his courage and determination is also a linchpin in my own motivation toward expanding the Eco-Ethological Existential Analysis to the Coast of Australia as I share consanguinity with my brother and sister L.E.O.'s: Sgt. Matt Moloney's roots lay in the bare bones that guarded and lived in penal colonies. Distinctions once held sacrosanct divided so many souls as the supernal glue that holds edifices of nations together. Australia as a Continental King and Queensland as matriarch are such examples of Yin and Yang: Humble beginnings we all share become bridges for generativity. The manna we all eat in common is perhaps best enjoyed by respecting the cultural and individual differences without trying to bake each portion into one for all, but in part – for each in his/her own way.

Psychological boundaries of respect of differences may re-assure balance amongst the people of Queensland and their heirs: The branches and leaves of Queensland extend interdependently to the rooted tree of Indigenous culture and people: Unique branching and roots that graft into each other by intervention and exogenous accommodation – regardless of asymmetry and even temporary chaos usually punctuate growth and development successfully. Progressing forward, Sergeant Matt Moloney proffers to us that you and I can navigate to an understanding and insights in his own Odyssey as shared wisdom.

CHAPTER 2

IN, BUT NOT OF: AN OBSERVING PARTICIPANT AMONGST THE FIRST AUSTRALIANS

INTRODUCTION

In this chapter I as a licensed psychologist, and Ret. Sgt. NYPD and Queensland Police Commander, Sgt Matthew Moloney and Churchill Scholar will explore the challenges of becoming a participant observer. Professor Margret Mead as a first-rate anthropologist discussed one of the critical challenges of any scientist is to live amongst and study the culture they become co-joined with. In our minor modification to Professor Meads caveat we also challenge the myth of pure objectivity as impossible for mere mortals: Critiques of 'pure reason' as Kant suggested are moral imperatives (Kant, 1929) are also not within our reach as practicing police supervisors and myself as also being called the NY Cop Doc: Replacing 'pure-objectivities with some novel points emerge when a clinician and police supervisor is tasked with describing complexities in interpersonal dynamics. Those dynamics are first with me and my esteemed police supervisor colleague working together and as suggested in the first chapter – our narrative. Although as a Cop Doc the writing tasked to me, in no way lessens my colleagues' hard core glib, material, and on point piloting through a maze of turbulence. Navigation through the maze of what is in need of shaping and palatable communication to you as reader is communicated with no easy brush, or primed pre-package delivery.

Dynamics also emerge in oscillating, static and fluid waves when cultures and their eco-ethological influences emerge in wild attempts to merge them into one amalgam too soon and rapidly. Finally, intra-personal dynamics and conflicts emerge in the experiences of Sgt. Moloney taxed as a police commander, scholar and humane family man with a highly energetic and creative artful style. Sgt. Commander Moloney as a pioneer deserving of the title *Observing-Participant* bridging the worlds of policing and culture in his own unique style has given me the privilege of entering his complex world as a trusted navigator and to that I vouched for him as he for me and our joint goal of enlightening the reader: You!

Cop Doc Dan Rudofossi Corner: Segue, Observing Participant – Not Participant Observer

Leaving off with some very challenging experiences Sgt Matt Moloney worked through as a police commander assigned to what the NYPD would call the Marine Corp of the real job, Patrol. In the NYPD as in Queensland PD the toughest job is doing "the job" – unexpectable situations and the tempo of the urban war zones is captured by the plight of the toughest of all service members the US Marines. Although Sgt Matt has had his share of doing the cavorting, cajoling and culling out of the mystery to qualify as an investigator without portfolio with humility he defers from being called what we give the honour and the hard sweat of being a detective supervisor. Sgt. Matt's experience as a Queensland Police Commander creates room for pause: Pausing as the complexities of his calling as a police supervisor become entangling with subtle affairs that bridge over his own personal identity; his identity within the police culture; the

An Observing Participant

influences of his own ecological ethological niche; and the centre of his existential struggles and purpose which underscore his true intelligence, toughness and clear-headed direction.

In the goal of 'interpolation of shared purpose at the crossroads of differences hardly established or known at the time of his own intervention and our own postvention we are called to the task of sifting through truth, rather then convenience. Salving our conscience awareness of troubling issues and clinically speaking – problems and their challenging solutions are not easy when neither are clearly spelled out. I remember as a graduate student in the pluralistic, parochially left and quite liberal ideology of my own education and the ideologues that at times taught courses at NYU that I felt at home in many instances and baffled and at times overwhelmed at the divide between reality and the ideal version of reality proffered. My doctoral team and as well as Professors at the time were unscathed by politics as legislated, as much as education corrected by the rim of politicking.

Liberal was also more than a concept and perhaps operationally placed in bold definition by the way it was lived by the Professors I met, and in all fairness supported my research, my outlook, and my clinically naïve but sharpening skills. Not all Professors were like that, some left leaning and some right leaning converged in their own odd personal idiosyncratic autocrat style and not only at the breakfast table where thorns coloured their acrimony and pith to dissuade me of my life-long work!

Fortuitously, I began connecting to real clinicians and their skilled clinical approaches: Dr.'s: Richard R. Ellis; Albert Ellis; Janet Wolfe; Ray DiGuiseppe; Nando Pelusi; Charles Brenner; Bob Scharf; Bob Barnes and Dorothy Barnes; and Ann Graber. Being idiosyncratic and quite stubborn in seeking not advocacy for police and public safety officers but educating and healing those peers impacted by horrid trauma and loss I was eager to learn and dismayed over the arrogate assumptions made about police officers as deindividuated heroes or corrupt ignoramuses of one cast and hue.

I was also shocked that people were writing about police culture I was living, but never donned a real police uniform and 'the job' as practiced. The same others always had some interjection, prevarication or injunction to share about my lifestyle or even more peculiar about myself of which they had no clue. It is easy to prevaricate if one is challenged to come up with problems and solutions and others are unaware of the realities of the culture enquired about. Being a police officer is not voluntary and not civilian it is uniform as our colleagues in the armed services of the Army, Navy, Marine Corps, Air Force, and Coast Guard. It is a culture with many layers and interactions where violence and trauma are interlaced with existence and the unique dimensions implied when we use the term existential – we will examine later in this chapter. Assumptions are speculative innocuous projectiles at best, and gravely harmful at worst.

On the other hand, assumptions about police culture and the individual police officer, can be quite well meaning, or malevolent in equal measure by accident. Regardless of intention assumptions impact similarly in there wake if it is negative and judgmental. An example is some ideas expected to be too foolhardy in its sweeping generalizations, in some politicized academic circles nowadays that circulate is the idea that a person is racist or misogynist simply because a person is born to one race, or religion. Such thinking is tragically flawed irrational thinking where blaming an entire population for insidious thinking in some is stereotyping in this most extreme manner. It is inherently blatant racism when used as a dictum with no substance to lend evidence to such a speculative theory, and worse legislating enforcing such a theory is tantamount to fascism on an intellectual playing field.

Like all speculative field experiments and ventures noted as such, these idealistic and misguided extremes are simply interesting anecdotes about humans: But when pejoratives are posited as truth, many dangers are sprung anew. The least danger, being intellectual fascism that can become reality and transform into virulent fascism.

An Observing Participant

Intellectual fascism is when without substance an entire argument is left out of an enquiry because it is viewed by a political pundit or group to be less then valid. This is exactly the arguments of the far left and right as exemplified by such historic monstrosities as the Nazi party exacted on humanity.

Burning out arguments by corrections that are based on force are nothing more than fascistic. The correction of science to frame what is considered nice and pleasant outcomes is not science but ascetic corrections to an aesthetic ideal. Although it is beyond the scope of this book to review the impact on art as an aesthetic practice it is not beyond the scope of this book to assert art as poetry and dialogue corrected as the late Professor Karl Popper did assert is the root and core of fascism regardless of semantic plays (Popper, 2002). Certainly, such corrections applied to culture, ecology and an ignorance of ethology and existential demands by humane beings cannot be touted as science, nor scientific practice – for me to do so is to acquiesce that forceful and authoritarian intellectual cleansing is acceptable to science. Agreeing to corrections based on any factor outside of a quest for truth is anathema to science, philosophical honesty and integrity as a humane healer and practitioner (Fromm-Reichmann, 1960). Perfidy replacing dialogue is junk science and science as an aesthetic dimension has all the facets of colour and passion wed to reason as effulgent (Kitaeff, 2007). So, let's move forward with an example and put light on the chiaroscuro of perspective.

Let me give an example that is personal as a Jewish police officer. Because someone shared with me a peculiar comment such as, "Jews like Pastrami on Club Bread, and therefore I liked Pastrami on Club Bread" was an assumption that was a non-sequitur, a mis-attribution bias – perhaps: However, in no way did that give evidence the speaker was anti-Semitic. I confirmed such predilection as a peer or supervisory police officer making such assumptions may be in a social psychological perspective biased, I was in no way offended and in fact it is no less or more then a fellow stating that because I am a police officer, I prefer coffee and donuts for breakfast rather than some food items more wholesome and nutritious. To wage a paper civil war against this officer because she was a boss on 'the Job' struck me not only as preposterous at best, but nefarious at worse.

This is not a light-hearted antidote to amuse you as a reader but to put some biases in perspective. Not every member of a specific culture and group wants to be assimilated or accommodated to a major cultural view – this includes the culture one is born into. In my view while the other officer was eager to see me strip the Supervisor of her authority, throw her under the bus – it would be mercurial at best to attempt to kill her sense of humour, and at worst I would be insidious if I complied with a co-religionist whose motivations were suspect to me.

I offer by this example an important lesson as a Cop Doc who tightropes between the culture of policing and law enforcement as retired LEO and clinician to police and public service and safety professionals. Hopefully, not woefully my examples are relevant to other minorities who also need not reduce all interactions to a divisive nature but rather to the superb humane qualities of becoming humane as a lifelong odyssey almost none of us achieve but some may come close to only through the hard work of self-introspection and motivation towards acceptance and tolerance of our innate fallibilities.

I also walk the tightrope of expectations and idealism at points of pontification and ivory tower glints that retract in the light of matted surfaces in daylight as a Professor in Academia. All spoken about different gear one wears as well as uniforms – I am a participant most of all and succorance is gained and inner-sight gleaned from observations of self, others in the culture of belonging and interest which is parsed out in the passion that calls me.

As a participant observer one is asked to participate with members of a different culture and pretend to interact 'as-if' one is a genuine member of that culture. If one is not a member of that culture from an ecological-ethologic niche then it makes sense to discriminate one-

An Observing Participant 55

self as a scientist and to clearly state one's teleological vantage point in gaining information.

Avoiding what Professor Postman who created the dynamic field of media ecology called the Triumph of Technique (1984) which focuses solely on 'Why?' we pursue research, clinical or administrative goals; or conversely the query as to 'How?' exclusively leaves us reduced to bureau-pathology, Bureau-pathology lies over the artificial crossroad of exclusive focus on 'How Too?' Or, just philosophic meandering of Just Do 'It!' without including 'Why?' we are supposed to do 'It?' is not neglecting the 'Why?' one is seeking information that is accessible to participants allowed into more limited circles of protected mores, rituals and totems.

Umberto Ecco understood well enough, words and the wordsmiths who iron out the subtle persuasion of semantic differentials are the conceptual constructors or de-constructors of our application of ideas into the field of reality (Eco, 1979). Hence the hypothetical construct of the Participant Observer, may be better placed as the Observing Participant.

Nowadays concepts are stretched or reduced into fads and their progeny of echoing-encores, and hence the active observer who is compelled to become a participant to overcome a ceiling or watershed in intelligence gathering of science that is kept dry by the umbrella of psychological science requires straight terms that are semantically sound. I prefer the term an **observing-participant** where many gains are far from purely objective. Altruistic ideals at the heart of such allowances may honestly allow one observing participant to gain the time within one's space to observe, self, others and the world in which they uniquely occupy as a guest in a new culture without prevaricating and pontificating as if they are one with that new culture. Being frank is crucial for credibility: Being disingenuous and staying within a frame that conspires to delimit truth as it emerges is easy street. To pound a beat in NYC as much as in Queensland in this way is equidistant and parallel as one gains that experience by living, breathing and doing the job. All others as even welcome observers are guests.

In this chapter Sgt. Matt Moloney and I will parse out some dialogue in which we together conspire to aspire to the grind of 'the Job' and distil the wisdom to you as reader and co-participant seeking to learn from our observations to apply to your own academic, pragmatic and ideal goals you seek from our field of experience. This dialogue is not literal but constructed out of our real conversations and communication so you can sip the results as sanguine without dealing with the mess. So, it follows:

Commander Sgt Matt Moloney: "You know Dr. Dan I see you as seeing things I have missed and I can relate to your view, I am like a US Marine as you put it well. I mean in dealing with the colliding of cultures and the individual person lost in the sea of politicization of policing and peoples I am given the task of making peace among the parties involved. Large words as cultural inclusion and diversity held so much promise but it forgets the language and meaning of the individual behind the myths, both constructively and in a deconstructed way. All parties, including, or perhaps especially those claiming neutrality and objectivity being the worst offenders. I mean when I pause as you ask us to do and think about it. Will a value judgment on the idea of whether or not colonialism, even with all the bloodshed, disruption, injustices, in the end result in a good and defensible process? Perhaps, colonialism is indefensible, disastrous, and a setback to indigenous Australian citizens but can it also stand as part of the human story. That is humans progressing to a future that has much to offer all its citizens. Don't mistake what I am saying which clearly points out that colonialism itself as a cultural disaster. It is a major disruption to the social, political and psychological lifestyle of all involved– especially impacting on indigenous Australian communities. It is crucial to realize the indigenous folks, and those people who did industrialize the country all have their own wisdom. Treating people as if they don't have the capacity to understand the process of being pulled to the front or back of the bus"

"Passengers as well as a bus driver are needed in this process, 'ay' Mate? So, hearing their point of view is critical: Right?"

Cop Doc Dan R: "It is right if you are truly exploring reality not fictions created in one's own Chimera. It is interesting [pausing] good Commander Sgt. Moloney that you choose to tackle such a large philosophic issue with the clarity of practice as your counter-point. If I am getting it right it seems to be your wish to clarify some politicization of social issues in the context of culture clashes which continue in our ongoing dialogue that broadens with indigenous police professionals and indigenous citizens and the larger groupings of citizens. If I am hearing you correctly Sgt. Matt, it is resistance to the idea of invalidated concepts parried around as if they are facts that pains you deeply. Students curiosity and mindfulness is crucial but reality is not created in wishful desires of a narcissistic perspective of one's own ideal as culture. Culture is not one's own idiosyncratic ideals but what is developed within the space of time and in a community setting. Perhaps door stops left partially opened, become more likely closed when division is applied. If integration is the sought-after prize patience and active listening comes first not feet on the ground radical change. Evolution is not reversed by revolution. Revolutions are not peaceful changes and evolution is eclipsed, at least momentarily by 'It's' force against dynamic stasis. That stasis is oscillating equilibrium which holds as much stability as a roller coaster. The shape of inclusion as we discussed earlier includes truly respecting the fact that in part resisting the melting pot for some of us, is the clearest way of maintaining one's own cultural identity, and for others it is not. For Barry Port he found a middle ground and for others they remain on either pointed side of the divide. You have walked the mind of both sides and stayed on course. Does this make sense to you?"

Commander Sgt Matt Moloney: [Pause and clearly reflective] "Mate, Dr. Dan it does make sense to me. It is perhaps the cop in you and the fact you understand my meaning which is that there is a middle ground of the diecast hardened in the battlegrounds where some 'militants' whose motives I suspect and whose world view and subsequent interpretation of events results in a misdiagnosis of the problem and consequently solutions that are positively harmful.' If this is the case than perhaps saboteurs are moving within the conflict to politicize it as left or right lines but not solution oriented in figuring out how to solve the problems of the meetings of the mind and settling the problem of objectivity because as you've presented many times in your books and conversations the myth of objectivity is as erroneous in human beings as the myth of perfection as you point out in dealing with the mentally ill (Rudofossi, 2015). For me to be straight shooting and clear for the indigenous people are not only one people but groups of cultural niches and in fact your conceptual framework of eco-ethological niches make sense by speaking about the aspects of indigenous society that bridges differences which is the spirituality and ritualistic aspect of society which has its own ethical framework and not that of larger huge societal structures and morals of politically correcting the culture one allegedly has chosen to rescue as outside its framework. But truthfully, victory for civilization and cultural progress for the developing country of Australia is partially achieved. There is no real neutrality on the subject of colonialism and mostly those being colonized."

Cop Doc Dan R: "The rich elegance of Indigenous society is coloured by organic interactions that shape and model 'Organic' growth, regression, and atrophy. I say organic to be slightly playful and in a balanced and serious manner too provoke critical thinking. The misuse of the word Organic and the attempt to operationally define organic as unnaturally applied for example, by placing all cultures and peoples as homogenous 'Australians'; or conversely as Indigenous Australians and Non-Indigenous Australians in too serious a manner is a fixed concept without differentiation and therefore made inert. Straining the meaning of the word Organic by staining people to forcefully follow power pointed ideals."

"Power pointed ideals applied by forceful change is non-organic because life is not reducible too linear discrete moments ideally presented as static and subject to change. Life as cultural evolution is dynamic. Frankly speaking, it is better to say inorganic as it resembles artificial concepts."

"As we have discussed and worked on issues and problems the foundations of humane interaction include being aware and non-apologetic of the ethological motivations that shape and are shaped in the individual existence of each person within an ecological niche. Culture is a result of such shaping and speciation in valued skills, habits, thinking patterns [schema], and interactions and cannot sustain itself without the individual imprint that can create violent breaches in progress and in betterment of development can bulwark the changes needed to grow."

"In fact, we are seeing the results of trying to wrap formulas around groups as a disaster in the making. Applied psychology, anthropology and medicine as mental and physical health was never meant to be dictums of forceable change but like a compost heap allowed to percolate, deteriorate and provoke growth. The fiction that any group is represented in theory and in laws is not another myth – it is deconstruction of social life as it is and will always be."

"For example, our tracker who is a law enforcement officer is a unique individual who has expressed his ingenuity and his gift by also working within a society that is organic. This fundamental of the individual cannot be changed even in the most illusory social thinking. So where does this lead us as scientists? Holding onto the fact that politics is not science and correcting society toward one ideal or another is coercion and so-called movements that are anti-fascist may be the most fascistic. Provided humane beings hubris never reaches so high that consideration of such truths such as nature and nurture are not opposites but dynamic and fluid compounds. The individual and the society in which he/she must adapt is reality and the participant will not topple over if living organically is not genetically or socially modified to the degree social norms and mores are cherished and intact."

"The allure of amusement and amusing our lives away is much more of a threat in a society that is becoming more global, artificial and amusing as an introspective journey without others let in to the sacred circle at the heart of existence, (Postman,1985). Selfish individuality is reclusive and avoidant but holding onto one's sacred sense of values including religious and spiritual beliefs is the cornerstone of civilization and civility in a social sense. This is worth while preserving and I believe you are in your unique style do just that – fairness and compassion are a hard-balancing act you imperfectly achieve so well. Agreed good Sgt Commander Matt M?"

Commander Sgt Matt Moloney: [In a serious tone]. "Dr. Dan balancing this act was reflected in my very first contacts with the raw reality I faced in dealing with the indigenous culture in Aurukun. While it is true that colonization was a cultural disaster it was not a complete disaster: Cohesion of traditional indigenous societies has been disrupted. The so-called community of Indigenous people are in reality many various micro-communities within the large continents of Australia and Queensland itself. The Potlatch between Australian settlers and Indigenous folks was framed as a big rescue operation. In most big rescue operations without laying the groundwork for reconnaissance to establish the boundaries of support in a culturally competent style. That said the rescue operation did increase the respect and the overall understanding of the ethics and doctrines regarding Indigenous people. In my experience the ethics and doctrines of guides for patrol to integration are delimited to – the 'Abstract' without taking into account individual differences and the different niches that exist in the real peopling of communities."

"As you point out and have emphatically addressed in all your books and guides on trauma and grief the individual is crucial. I resonate deeply with this admonition and as you clearly put it a proscription against a global prescription. For example, what cuts to the core is cultic practices and indigenous spirituality is not understood and hardly respected in a cultural program of diversity agendas without understanding diversity means respecting the fact that Indigenous culture does not match well with Aborigine clans. In fact, when Indigenous clans are thrown into the porridge of so called 'diversity' which is a natural organic process and not forced divestment of growth and potential decreases as his/her centre of existence is stripped of purpose."

"Dr. Dan R. for me it appears that songs and ceremonies are ways in which many individual Indigenous folks reach their own spiritual path. That path is crucial for mental health and healing from traumatic losses and gaining competence in the individuals own societal structure. Facebook and other social media memes are destroying the indigenous cultural advantage and overall benefits within eons of cultural evolution by forcefully pushing agendas such as the weak are of equal value to the warriors within Indigenous society. Who has made the outside near do well the engineer of the society of Indigenous folks? It is ironic that the issues of individual rights versus the one individual empowered to lead the clan is devastating to the Indigenous clans that create the threads within each society established. In saying the cultural motif of the Indigenous world is changeable by large dictums of contemporary society is much more damaging then the colonization process. Those who initiated the colonialization project started out with an attempt to respect some aspects that were sacred to some Indigenous clans: What we do now is continue with what I can sadly call – 'Cultural Incompetence'. The difference being the initial interventions overthrew the customs long entrenched with somethings that were believed to be of value to the indigenous clans, including what was believed to be the best of Queensland society. Now we trade the worse aspects of majority society that translates into – 'endless-victimhood' and 'insatiable entitlement'. The new vanguard is taking, usurping and re-defining indigenous culture and the eco-ethological niches with post-modernism and 'relativism'. Both ideals are empty and devoid when placed in the context of indigenous clans. We are not gifting anything in return for the vacuum used in a taking away the rich cultural heritage of the variations in Indigenous clans throughout Queensland. In interfering via interventions into each clan's cultural centres within the recent once again well-meaning agendas of total equality and equalitarian philosophical movements the cultural centring of each clan appears to be not only threatened but under siege. The perpetual victimhood, empty relativism and meaningless post-modern anti-culture in the name of culture has placed its tentacles around a dying society of Indigenous culture."

Cop Doc Dan R: "It is of more then semantic acrobatics to say as you do so well Sgt. Commander Matt Moloney that 'each clan appears to be threatened' and I like your use of 'threatened and under siege'. The idea you bring up was a cornerstone of science and applied science whether behavioural, psychophysiological, cultural anthropological; medical-psychology or psychiatry to not in the name of progress force change on any people but to allow evolution to co-occur with knowledge and choice including the response of saying "no" to certain interventions. Since much of the reform is allegedly shaped and motivated by psychology, anthropology both cultural and physical it stands to reason as in individual interventions the only time force is allowable and even considered quite humane is if danger to self or other exists."

"Somehow in a world that aspires to human rights and respect for all cultures it is a legitimate point that not all members of any culture aspire to the same focal point of change that you are suggesting may be coerced and cogitated into one amorphous body of what is deemed 'politically-correct'? If, I am right, your honesty as an educated Churchill scholar who is also a ranking police supervisor on the front lines is remarkably astute and insightful. [pausing and emphatically with vehemence toward my colleague in policing] Well, for two decades if I got you right Commander Moloney you've summed up what I wrote about in healing from Complex Trauma where terrorism is the ultimate capacity for in-human evil 'playing god with a small 'g' is the first refuge of the terrorists haven as mere mortals when any of us collectively or individually try to *correct a culture to fit a notion* – we become stuck and shaped by all humanity as a nightmare of neon rainbows – an organic rainbow is not cast in a hue that demands all cultures and religions are the same and all-inclusive of conformity (Rudofossi, 2013). That dictum binds and blinds creativity with blinders that occlude vision in myopic dystopias without recourse to respecting differences, non-

An Observing Participant 63

violent dissent and real growth. Diversity is self-evolving and not to be politically commanded in corrections that sanitize traditions and mores of each culture to fit global 'notions' of what each culture must do to conform. Even in organic diversity conflict and compromise form the shapes of what that very culture in reality suggests and is expressed by each individual's response to what each dimension means in his/her appreciation of space he/she will use in time. Does that somewhat capture the position you are asserting as well, or better yet would agree with good Commander Maloney? Is there an example you could provide if so that can help those who are lowering their third ear to actively listen to two Sgts who are continents apart but giving fifty years of front-line experience as Cop Doc and Police Commander intersect?"

Commander Sgt Matt Moloney: [Reflective and sombre toned]. "Dr. Dan. You are a keen observer of humankind and a man of real insight. You've hit in on the head. I am stunned by our synchrony. Let me explain with offering my own experiences and affinity, coveting and repulsion of some aspects of a smaller eco-ethological niche to use my new frame work of looking at different cultures within a too large macrocosm of culture. That culture is the indigenous citizens of Aurukun, Queensland. Notice, to individuals that group in Aurukun the reality is they are not the indigenous people of Queensland but the members of Aurukun's indigenous community which is sufficient in and of itself in description and reality. On one side of my experience with many citizens of Aurukun's community I have met kind, generous, caring and soft-spoken citizens with a truly very real earthy sense of humour and healthiness."

"Another side of my experience with more than a few citizens of the Aurukun community is the more than average occurrences of behaviour. That can be expressed as riotous outrages where murder; clan violence; and domestic disjuncture and conflict is dragged out into the streets from homes that are disrupted by sweeping policies to rescue Aurukun Citizens: Are we really rescuing Aurukun citizens from their 'backward ways? It appears to me that the need to create a more so-called civil integration into a politically corrected contemporary culture has been failing as an intervention that is supposed to be moving the indigenous citizens forward."

"It also at first appeared to me as I shared earlier that the sophisticates who pontificate about the citizen, they save have no clue as to the real-feeling of the family nucleus as practiced by Aurukun community. Again, as in my earlier discussion with you Doc, the problem for me is how does a police officer reconcile the fact that we do not know the reality of the nuances in the Aurukun culture as it has progressed and where our demands to assist and act impartially are not in some ways damaging?

Cop Doc Dan R: "That is a tough series of questions so please pause and incline your ear to actively listen to what my response is to your wonderful and deep questions and resolve as both an insightful and perceptive law enforcement officer. I think we can understand the damaging impact of so-called progress better by looking at the phenomenon of what is known from a clinical and ethological perspective as emotional contagion amongst the Aurukun community. The critical importance is that in an eco-ethological niche which is framed family to family and the larger shaping of evolutionary patterns of adaptation is that if the method of intervention is to rescue you as you put it so well by Pontificating Sophisticates: The sophistry increases exponentially as agendas replace discretion."

Commander Sgt Matt Moloney: [Inquisitive]. "How and why is that emotional contagion really so easily a susceptible phenomenon? I know myself from a historical level it has happened on major scales and smaller ones, I also agree as to your take on my perspective I am sharing with you, but how and why does this take place within cultures from your own Eco-Ethological Existential Paradigm. For me personally and professionally, although the larger world of academia and politicians the Aurukun community is just a dot on the map of Australia – these people are a lot more to me. My brother and sister officers truly serve and try to improve our law enforcement services to them but we see

An Observing Participant

the really ugly stuff: I think if I am able to get a grasp theoretically, I can effect a better change for me and my brother and sister officers via presentations, or papers we write or I write using your method of assessment and intervention to create understanding that just may work as your method is bringing some better results. So please explain that 'how' and 'why' from your perspective as to the mess the well-meaning changes that are very in line with Political Correctness are having on the citizens of the Aurukun community?"

Cop Doc Dan R: [Passionate and with vehemence]. "How and why is a very good question to guide our answer. Sideways not forward, and lateral not horizontal inroads into closed corners are what is likely to be the result when the idea is to change a culture rather than work on establishing a trusting and respectful valuing of traditions, mores, and totems and taboos within each culture and family."

"Family and traditions as practiced within each nuclear, and extended family which have evolved and been shaped over centuries. Such mores are not creations made in a day but honed to adaptation through the customs within the Aurukun community over millennium. Attempts to sweep away traditions bolstered by the glue of layers of mores and their values uniquely prized within the community and specific in use to each family clan cannot be flash fired away by new ones re-inserted by contemporary thinkers. Such insertions cannot do much help: Insertions enflame rebellion and conflict within each community as eco-ethological *mal*-adaptation with a violent repercussion. The facts stand that each family mores are uniquely practiced and understood within their own eco-ethological niche. The overall community provides each families niche as to what is valued and prized on a cultural and purposive level of satisfaction. In understanding the emotional, and one can say psychological space of each family – a different pathway is possible as an eco-ethological approach captures the trauma and grief of abrupt changes without neglecting the most critical natural motivation as existential. Existential is the reason we collectively and as individuals place our lives on the front line to save others without reducing our motivations to drives or their derivatives as causes for heroic behaviour. Like other words 'existential' is hardly understood by most and is used as the word trauma and grief with many pre-fixes and suffixes without history as to its foundation.

"The premiere thinker among others is the real deal Dr. Professor Viktor Frankl whose work, Mans search for Meaning and Ultimate Meaning (Frankl, 2000) was inscribed in his brain and written after he survived Auschwitz not as a doctor, and a professor of clinical psychiatry/psychology alone."

Commander Sgt Matt Moloney: [Questioning in piqued and curious mannerism]. "Doc Dan R I am with you, forgive my brief interruption to ask you, 'why emphasize Professor and Dr. as being so important to emphasize Viktor Frankl as Dr. and Professor?" I mean he is as you always emphasize a human being regardless of credentials. Is there any reason I can wrap my head around?"

Cop Doc Dan R: "No interruption at all, it is crucial to ask questions that are sensibly placed in our Socratic dialogue. Well, one reason I say Professor Dr. Frankl is tradition. Professor Dr. Frankl's healing and scholarship were truly legendary. He was a humane being of faith whose un-swavering faith in a higher being than the narcissistic equivalent of me, myself and I such as Hitler, and Mussolini who felt along with Ramses that the highest achievement in life is to become a god with a small 'g' and many statutes in their own image, rather than a humane being such as Professor Dr. Frankl whose victory was in being and becoming 'decent' as a humane-being. It is the de-emphasizing by those who felt insecure over his credentials that reinforce the value as to his achievements professionally, but not humanely. I believe they are important to cherish and give him the title he most genuinely earned. Does that make sense to you?

Commander Sgt Matt Moloney: "It does make sense! In fact, I see the point very clearly as to why you emphasize the credentials for Professor

Dr. Frankl! Those with hatred would call him 'kike' and 'scum of the earth' but in reality, he upheld his calling both as a professor and doctor with integrity and decency as his model for all to learn from."

"Hitler as Fuhrer-Father, or Mussolini as Caesar pushed humanity apart in their destructive and violent methods where the bottom line was being worshipped and idealized as you put it, 'gods with the small 'g' force. Dividing the world into black and white rather than grey in their radicalized nationalized democratic socialism with the agenda of one race, one culture and one voice for all I with anxiety say is what PC sounds like."

Cop Doc Dan R: "Echoing each other in some ways – I think your response added much and is superb in insight and understanding. Thank you, Commander, Sgt for that wisdom worthy of sharing with others who are readers of this book. Echoes and narcissism go well together for the reflection of a leader is often refractions of that leaders self-ideal and even idealization. Let us get back to the question of 'how' and 'why?' the interventions and forceful changes to Indigenous society devolve rapidly. The existential framework is necessary to revisit. Dr. Professor Viktor Frankl's definition of existential in the context of the tragic was coined 'tragic-optimism'. Optimism is when you don't lose faith even when you are challenged with the harshest of circumstances." In a very relevant way Dr. Frankl in substance educated the world that a death camp, that systematically set murder as its endpoint: the players being the entire population of Europe's Jews, and the exclusive means towards death and destruction would occlude meaning to most. It is exactly the fact that death and destruction provoked meaning by those who grappled with life and death is at the core of existential struggle and survival. Behind the concept of existential analysis is the centre of one's existence is the power within to overcome the forces from within and without that conspire intentionally or accidentally to destroy the essential value of each humane being qua decency"

"This implies a healthy narcissism as a balance to unhealthy narcissism. Existential as an operating definition suggests core values that empower a humane being to transcend his/her culture, religion, personal psychology and physical self as soma. Paradoxically rooted in all dimensions and not relative to any-one is the conservation of the family. Family existentially includes not only talking of tradition but centring one's own personal existence as purposive. From a cultural level of understanding in approaches that theoretically assert without saying so explicitly we are left with the thought that each family in a community are clones of one another. The damage within a community that forces individuals to be educated and follow agendas to correct their own cultural beliefs is akin to giving dosages of change imposed from without the community, or from those within that have been reinforced in surrendering their traditions and mores to larger so-called common core dictums."

Commander Sgt Matt Moloney: "It is those so-called common core dictums that pressure an officer to act impartially and be a participant observer while those rules and enforcement dictums tell us to intervene aggressively while remaining passive. The very Australian value that we are going to effect change is an intellectual value not a cultural value. We are perhaps afraid of freedom for ourselves and it seems even more scared of it for our indigenous citizens. It is also a hard fact of reality that it is the overall culture of Indigenous peoples that when personal responsibility is thrown at them as a core directive, it is shunned. This seems true for the Aurukun and other clans that our love and perhaps obsession with freedom itself is not accepted from a historic and cultural perspective. Traditional indigenous culture holds there is no such thing as natural death. What I learnt is that within indigenous culture one's human death is always caused and determined by another human agency and not accidental or even in reality self-inflicted it is always shadowed by this belief that what is called black magic is at the centre of such destruction and ends. The riots and clan wars where young folk and sometimes tenured members of the Aurukun citizenry are hurt and killed are attributed to black magic. The belief that women also are sexualized

An Observing Participant

in male culture is not chauvinism to the Aurukun but shared sexuality and desire and not to be messed with as competition within and between males for the affection of women is looked at as natural. Concepts as chauvinism and forced mannerisms from the larger Queensland society is taken as coercion and force is met with counterforce as the whole structure of Aurukun society is thrown in chaos. This is not the full picture yet but a strong factor of the collisions with larger versus smaller culture in eco-ethological niches."

Cop Doc Dan R: "Your incisive points are rich in understanding. First, your underscoring passion in expressing contradictory directives and the reality for an officer as a participant in, but not of, as I suggested earlier with you in defining what is real as playing a Catch 22 and subsequent Experimental Traumatic Neurosis in Police and Public Safety Complex PTSD. If we could move back to later in our ongoing dialogues. In your second brilliant point you spell out the fear and denial of death which is the fear of freedom and sadly as Dr. Erich Fromm pointed out in his forgotten tomes, the forgotten language, escape from freedom and the sane society a significant point that converges on what your police wisdom pivots on. That wisdom existentially is the reality that life demands we live in the here and now as best as we could with a desire to embrace the differences each life and lives, we live among with and amongst converge with. The harsh reality is in our human desire which transcends indigenous and non-indigenous peoples; the occidental and non-occidental world of people lies the distance scale of existence we all try to control and understand or by accepting the demands of freedom and the impact of choice and responsibleness on the very human awareness of death. This awareness is either buried within the psychodynamic unconscious layers and defences along the deeper layer of existential unconscious and conscious struggles."

"The fascination and drive toward a battle whereby destruction and creativity linger in our bosoms depths till our last breath draws on the crossbows of life and death is not settled until the day of our last exhalations. Each community cannot exist without the traditions and mores of each family in a dynamic that is organically shaped by the interaction with each other and within each family unit. Attention is necessary as to the types of family that range in terms of personality dynamics as insulated, conforming, rebellious, gregarious in style and tone and other permutation without judgment and stigma necessarily added to an already strained formula. Attempts to correct a society on a global level as some radicals suggest, is imposing an occupational force on a limited culture by a macro-culture. But so is trying to correct a microcosmic culture to fit a political idealism suggests one revise and re-constructs that society as a whole to conform to the macro-culture."

"The idea that death is never visited on any one including riots that bring crushing death and mayhem as being caused by 'black-magic' is sensible to the individual Aurukun as he/she sorts through the imprint of horror and violence. Don't we see this when we look for the malevolent forces that drive our clashes such as the Charlie Manson gangs who press for white supremacy and race wars; and the Symbionese Liberation Army's Donald Defreeze who murdered Dr. Foster an African American pioneer as an instrument of the pig class of imperialists. In bright contrast of clashes between law enforcement units as cultural groups eco-ethologically and the gangs fought on American and European soil, we again see an almost mystical and magical attribution of cause and effect. The struggle against death and the drive that motivates violence is as old as the entire human species."

"It is important to acknowledge as you suggest if I have gotten your very insightful point correctly that the beliefs of Aurukun while paradoxical are no less so then other cultures and more so understanding such cultural differences is crucial rather than needing to educate each member by forceful dictums to re-educate. Did I get your point down well?"

Commander Sgt Matt Moloney: "You did and added some clarity to my own as well. I like the directions we are going as you support me as a real commander in the saddle of policing and add colour to what

An Observing Participant

is viewed as you put it black and white rather than red, yellow, black, brown and white, apricot and tan to mention a few colours including the colourful personalities you've interwoven for me. It is the lack of real understanding as to the collisions of cultures and their respective multiple layers of ecology and ethology so crucial for any discussion of Queensland and Australia that really strike me as misinformed as to the real plight we deal with and have been dealt."

Cop Doc Dan R: [Empathically with passion tempered by reason collegially] "Misinformed is apt as a term to describe the collision of cultures as you put it well, Commander Moloney." (Pausing) "The micro-culture and macro-culture clash and implode and explode with such myopic planning anthropomorphically: Anthropomorphic control although possessing the root or idiom of Anthropos is anything but Anthropology, or the study of, and one can extend that study to love of humankind."

"By identifying all species and animals as if they all are human, leaves the observer participating in a fictionalizing vista of animal life and the variations that exist at peace, war, neutrality, and any such combination as being one single state of mind and behaviour of one caricatured pathetic animal."

"The ridiculous notion that animal differences across species is directly comparable with our own may be legitimately extended to cultures wiped out without attention to the needs of each culture within a larger cultural framework. Further, each family's inner-structure and needs forced to conform to outside agencies forced compliance to an ideal static viewpoint is better conceptualized as *fitting all families into a Procrustean Bed to sleep in*: In other words, the destination is a state of no respect of any differences in an Anthropomorphic sense: The entire program focus on supporting differences in reality is washed away as all are viewed as being and becoming one and the same. Reality pressures us to understand that individual differences exist and are centred in a family dynamic. This is clearly so for the Aurukun citizens and within each unique Aurukun family's eco-ethological existential dynamic framework individually and collectively. To ignore this is not only ignorance but tragic-optimism without comic but tragic relief in tow."

"In connecting the membrane of community living on a conscious level of understanding it is the needs of the community as multiple families of individuals adapting and sharing very important centres of living and prosperity in unique adaptations. These unique adaptations serve survival needs that are now thrust with radical changes that bring not sweeping changes toward a goal of mutual respect, valuing and assimilation and accommodation that works but sadly, dissolution of families and tradition's – devastatingly! To effect change time and patience done with calm equanimity must win, or the rushed and harried forceful change will only rue the day away."

"These devastating losses are not only one trauma events but multiple events as experienced and embedded in one ongoing event but viewed by most as one static event in the space of time. The most chilling aspect is that without understanding the eco-ethological existential glue that coheres each family as one the traumas laid out by affordances that seem plausible impacting radical and devastating quality of life changes is largely – *unintentionally done without a clue!*"

"In my view point it is critical and sober conservation that is needed in the world of academia and technology, although the fuel of such human endeavour is financed and motivated by fiscal and hence political forces. The police who are on the even playing ground of indigenous and non-indigenous citizens can be the stabilizing power to empower our own unique individual officers and families by inner-sights and impact on sobering radical intrusions in communities by exploration and vision sharing for each community as service oriented are better prepared by looking at the family units of the Indigenous and Non-Indigenous populations. The existential motivation is a powerful motivator to counter-forceful insertions into the distinct and unique communities. Violating boundaries by a purity of merger and forceful changes including laws, law-enforcement, and heavy taxing that are interpreted as confrontation

An Observing Participant

will fail and engender conflict within and targeted to the group trying to effect such change as invasive."

Commander Sgt Matt Moloney: [Introspective and Collegial Assertiveness]. "You've answered a lot as a Cop-Doc: For me in my practice it is hardest when I process the daily struggles. I have day in and out whereby I have gradually allowed myself to filter my caring toward understanding more and more of each family which are Aurukun within Queensland. In my attempt to understand I view the individual as separate and distinct not just as an Indigenous person to be baby fed and spoon fed but as a complex human being like me. I also think I am beginning to view myself more charitably as it helps to think of each different culture in a dynamic influence and the value of each unique adaptation. I can now capture some unique wisdoms in the changing adaptations to each eco-ethological niche whereby I abide by the dictums of law but I have perhaps in some larger way accommodated to being part of each indigenous and non-indigenous persons lives and living. Still, I find the hardest part the idea to be impartial as Queensland Police Directives command me to follow. I realize the discretion is more and more limiting in many challenging ways, but in trying to do the right thing and find my perspective it helps most in practice to really live among and with Aurukun individuals who in their individual way live with me as well. I in my identity modes as a police supervisor and all of its changes and they in their respective identity modes create conflict organically which takes a lot of compromise to work through. The hard work is nothing to fear but look at as a template to ensure quality as well as the effort to iron out differences, understand how to move within this community, and finally as a map to guide me. It is hard and at time confusing but is clear as day when the soot and dust of conflict settle. (Pause) I think map is a good term."

Cop Doc Dan R: "Map is a grand term Commander and Scholar Matt Moloney! It is such flashes of your brilliant observation that allows me the liberal notion to conserve the gifts your intellect provides and share with you as with the reader – barring no edits- 'Brilliant'! This is no side bar on your own insight into your-self as we return mapping out our course. [Matt smiles reluctantly]. The map is not only metaphor but your own cognitive, behavioural, emotional, ecological and ethological reality. Map as metaphor is alive and dynamic with oscillations and static moments as standoffs and existentially moving forward together as you pilot and I navigate through rough shoddy terrain: The Outback as ventral and dorsal regions of Queensland leave me struck with the momentum of your energy and challenges you face with courage – 'It' belies a smooth easy path and is surely anything but orderly and clear: In our own map as dynamic and interactive, moving on to cross the messy interaction of two continents let us re-convene in our next discussion of trauma and loss. In our next dialogue we can bring texture, detail, corridors, straits and obstacles into focus as boundaries of what our map entails in its full colour, hues, and shape develops and boldly envelopes what awaits you, I and our readers."

CHAPTER 3

PRIMER FOR TRAINING AND LEARNING AS CONDUITS WITH INDIGENOUS OFFICERS

INTRODUCTION

We left off in an attempt to theoretically operationalize living and dynamic coordinates of an Eco-Ethological Map that Sgt. Commander Matt Moloney pilots and I navigate in Chapter 2. Un-impeachable to our work is the realization our Map as with others is not static but fluid, it is not oscillating and to re-create for our use metaphor becomes coloured in with cognitive, behavioural, emotional, ecological and ethological reality. Fleshing out interactions recounted with Sgt. Matt and me an entire world of indigenous and non-indigenous police, trackers, perpetrators, and community come alive. Analysis from an existential, ecological, and ethological dimensional Vista is anything but simple: Complexity unavoidably is the fluid centre of existence laying out the trellis of individual's and their own persona – displayed as communities and within indigenous societies as clan communities. The actual trellis has a hidden support beam which is under the public persona of community lay each individual and his/her private sensibilities. This insight lead to understanding in our police and clinical mapping of the reality of cultural change are forced aggressive interventions given in the nicest of words as a semantic trellis of sorts that hides the reality, shadows the conflict and offers no real compromise that will last the test of time and practice for life, living and that elusive term of acculturation and adaptation for the indigenous and non-indigenous police officers and trackers and communities of clans that are shunted in a constricting word called 'inclusion' which excludes dissent and conservation of a balanced and dynamic equilibrium. We believe this is not the trajectory that must be and hope a rational and existential analysis will provide some options better placed in a map we are developing in our dialogue which expands to invite you to expand, contract, accept or reject – in any option you will join by engaging and participating. Let's participate together – now: Be-Aware, Vista ahead.

From an inner-sight as to that perplexing term organic and multicultural we both dissented with in part and to a degree in whole is not born of discontent but of reality and expressing at times unpopular but significant views. Such views are that the forgotten language of mutual respect, discourse which is historic and empathic, and a dialectical sense of progress cannot be amorphic dictums applied to the entire sea of humanity and dried up into an editorial post that dressed in hubris tries to self-righteously correct different and distinct traditions of each culture until it fits the procrustean bed of Ancient Sodom measures and scales. We have chosen together to dip into the messy and fluid well of tradition while keeping abreast by conservation. Conserving the values of classic anthropology and clinical psychiatry-existential and psychoanalytic as well as rational emotive and behavioural lattices. Dynamic boundaries help the different clans of indigenous Australian and Queensland people dance well as did traditional community policing. Community policing was strongest in the United States when both community leaders and police leaders at the executive level also curtseyed by allowing real ground to ground connections to take place on grass root levels. The different

Primer for Training and Learning 77

priests, rabbis and ministers connecting with the officers by name and not global idealizations, or demonization of police. Polite effigies of police and community leaders lead to closed doors and sealed shut windows. Personalities come in many colours, textures, hard and soft personalities of health and wellness and illness as does the entire human species so by reductionistic agendas an administrator is bound to harvest disquietude at best and war zones at worst. How and when does this transformation for human destruction occur and the chaos that follows?

The moment legislation and intervention departed all too seriously the result was division of what was balance into oscillations of myopia transformed into dystopia. How this is so being that the individual and his/her odyssey is lost in the translation where ideal trajectories are supplanted with real programs that force change and hence create extreme resistance and suppression of reality. But that suppression of reality is conscious at first. As time and forceful resentment replaces shared optimism a cloud of pessimism and repression which is largely unconscious emerges. Often the heroism of those who want to stave the dam of turbulence and catalytic friction from becoming catastrophic are left with attempts to impact on others through the map of learning and training. This is so in the cases throughout this book which is illustrative of Sgt. Commanders ingenuity, respect, love and disdain, unity and fracture within his own community which includes non-indigenous police and indigenous police/trackers and individual persons each with their own unique imprint of personality. The interactions are fluid, almost always bi-directional, and in a developmental context alive within each map that is centred within an ecological niche and ethological motivation of survival. Mapping the context of our trail is now the shift into the trials that demand learning the lesson that training is best achieved via learning the 'eco-ethological existential niche' that embraces. This eco-ethological niche embraces the broad concept of a cultural context by setting culture within the dimension of ethology [survival as individuals in a cohesive dyad - enlarged]. Motivation within an ecological context adds the dimension specific to each officer and unit and the larger society one operates within. How to ferret out with sensitivity as to what is and what is not relevant and impactful requires 'specificity', Specificity means what that eco-ethological niche provides existentially to the individual officer via their cognitions, behaviour, emotions and feelings in a way that not only makes sense but in makes superb sense as to he/she feeling good about being the driver in own saddle-back – forward. Passion fuels one's state existentially from a motivational perspective and creates a direction to exist in an evolving or devolving process of interaction. Let's explore the elasticity and potential of this process as dialogue unfolds.

Commander Sgt Matt Moloney: "Dr. Dan, I have been struggling with the idea of MAP, because it seems like the map in place in administrative offices often seem like fixed points, and not real points. But I like the concept as we have been operationalizing. I mean going back to Barry Port as tracker and his skills in tracing a traffic accident by looking at an observing his craft makes sense. It is unlike reading some text about his craft. In this context the point with training and education to me and my peers, both indigenous and non-indigenous is as you wrote in your survival guide when you spoke about dealing with what officer's call "pencil neck" thinking. Justice is one huge word and unless you look at all sides of an issue, what do you have? I think as you put it well, you have one sided and sloppy advocates!"

Justice is a common goal that the image of colonial police-officer and tracker have in common and not in a maligned way. Nowadays it is true that fascism is most prolific in the circles calling out different perspectives not fitting ones own as stupid, backward and racist without any knowledge of the specificity of what these words mean. Someone's lack of couth and complete sensitivity doesn't mean he/she is not caring or empathic but that one is simply blunt and forward to add all kinds of other pejoratives is itself offensive and cuts dialogue in two. I think truly colonial police officer and tracker are useful archetypes and paths to choose which open up a way of thinking and being that is humane.

Primer for Training and Learning 79

In fact, the *un-interrupted aboriginal tracker and colonial police officer* contribute and value each other's unique gifts. Learning and exchange is as I've come to see bi-directional and without an assumption given by the newer wave advocates who in their openness hide disdain by not honestly saying what is implied to indigenous officers and for example to Barry Port as tracker that they are pouring their pristine wisdom from a full vessel to an empty one as a pontificating teacher to a dull-witted student. In applying the eco-ethological existential method, I feel there is no direct prescription. If I am correct, I think that is part of the solution. Am I right Doc D.R.?"

Cop Doc Dan R: "You are in my opinion right on track and in fact I really enjoyed your witticism of implying the 'interrupted tracker and colonial police officer' of nowadays. Organic is not fabricated, embellished, and interrupted or like the concept trauma it becomes endangered as a yet an overused, abused and distorted play in words in which value as unique and different is made inert, passionless and painlessly anaesthetized. Selfless as a concept parallels less-then-self: Some say this is the right way to go. I beg to differ and ask to defer to Hillel the Sage who as Socrates born slightly later in recorded history liked to challenge his friend's way of thinking by poising questions to her/him such as follows":

"If I am only for my-self whom am I?"

"If I am only for my-self what am I?

"If not now, then when?"

Let's add one more poignant question before I synthesize Hillel with one additional question to answer in part your complex and priceless question with one of my own as follows:

"If I make my-self-less and lose essentially-me: Meaning if I do not appreciate my own moral compass – and my own ability to navigate my terrain, who will I be able to trust?"

"If I do not value my own moral compass which is correctable by those who have not been in my sandals or Camel's back, then who will guide my track back to Port?"

Commander Sgt Matt Moloney: [Passionately] "Doc, your play on words is serious as you are: Sometimes you kid with me and sometimes you're on target dead serious, but your questions are effective. Put in context for me, Barry Port and the other so-called colonial police are given their own compass within their own world. They are asked to navigate and track in the least mapped eco-ethological niches. Further it is often that the larger than life pressures prevail for a moment while the underlying storms settle. Often when it is turbulent as hell, and it is an officer, an aborigine citizen, or another in need desperately with their ship out of Port and it is then that a tracker maybe just what is needed is Barry Port to fit the bill. Perhaps the colonial police officer is needed to quell the riots so the tracker can track the villain and wisdom can prevail. Does that make sense to your interpretation?"

Cop Doc Dan R: "You make superb sense and your keying in on our sharing a developing evolution of navigation to guide our approach to colonial police and trackers as being two different and yet important and unique individuals as much as larger members of the culture. What counts in resolution of conflict is the integration and solution focus of what is pressing the motivation to get ones needs met and not step on the rights of others at the same time. By pontification and supercilious prescriptions that try to capture all members of a clan for example in one typed way on the stereo of description the actual interaction that begins with a shared dialogue as you and I are having is lost in translation. Does that make sense to you as a primer to approaching the cases you are presenting to me?"

Commander Sgt Matt Moloney: [Reflectively] "Yes, it does make sense to me as a primer toward training and learning because there is no one fits all prescription. [Silence reverberates].

Primer for Training and Learning 81

Cop Doc Dan R: [Introspective and analytic active listening in long pause]. "Silence is power and connection. You get my point. Pointedly and collaboratively, holding back from the tendency to be reactive and impulsive – prescriptions without looking at the individual does not fit a community of pluralistic and different citizens. By proscribing a general prescription, we make it harder to figure out a strategy up-front but the front line does not bottom-up and out in the longer running. Stop, pause and let's re-direct as our major framework. By not forcing an overall prescription we allow a path, direction, and development using our navigational tools to actively listen. Active listening demands using our emotional and active direct empathy with our colleagues. Colleagues being defined as other individuals trying to communicate needs behind the rhetoric and defence not only he/she uses, but we do our-selves in response to theirs, or on our own biases as well. By listening to our own defences, we increase the likelihood of actively opening up our minds to others views, even if those views are rejected. By consciously re-directing a compulsion to prescribe agendas by proscribing most prescriptions as panaceas you and I have narrowed the path to smaller more doable goals and actual effectiveness. By greater focus on modest goals the success is increased in the longer run, mistakes are not so massive and in fact durable change for the better is less resisted and likely to affect some real good for the families impacted. So, proscribing the need to prescribe for entire communities which are never the sum of their parts in mind and soulfulness as very human dimensions of culture and personality. However, admittedly in body and material dimensions such large prescriptions may in-deed work. Boundary setting is an important distinction to draw in the myriad sand crystals a beach may hold as a port of life and multiple directions of ebb and flow."

"For example, by building series of Dam's to ameliorate the impact of a Tsunami is at least in theory one physical material geologic solution for a community where the culprit is a natural dynamic force. Still many variables and confounds will exist including a unified front of many specialists coordinating a response. It is doable in theory because although individual differences exist the solution impacts on a community physically in response to a physical challenge to life. In forcing non-indigenous officers and citizens to follow directives or else be threatened and enforce immediate change only marginalizes individuals, collectively squeezing individuals and accountability into one mind set and creating walls of resistance and defence. By forcing change within the indigenous clan by creating legislation toward progress when the individuals in the community have been prescribed such change without real consent respectful of the cultural and personal differences of each family and its unique mind and soulful dimensions again resistance and defensive walls emerge. The metaphor of Tsunami is a rich one to contemplate as the forceful change which can only be done with physical challenges but not with mind and soul as the dimensions to consider. I know of no cultural group that is not influenced, shaped and developed in a healthy way without taking into account the need, very real need to respect the boundary of gradual change and only when that change includes healthier and more meaningful results reached in consensus, respecting the varieties of differences among Aborigine's and amongst Aborigine as a gestalt culture and the non-Aborigine culture, (Elkin, 1964; Howells, 1963; Oliver & Oliver, 1961; Turnbull, 1962; Williamson & Harrison, 2004). Conservation oft balances change in a way as an ebb and flow of tides, when the entire floor of stability is challenged without time to process and truly deliberate on consequences the shift is devastating oscillations and surges that do Tsunami like damage. [Pausing and allowing serious mindful deliberation.] Sgt. Commander and colleague Matt Moloney, did I make sense to you in this aspect of an eco-ethological existential approach toward conflict? Do you think my proposal for different Dam's that undergird, stave, and sieve forceful spiritless Tsunamis actually stand a chance by existentially centering each eco-ethological niche of each Aborigine Clan considering the complexity of differences in personality better then massive agendas of forced change? Finally, admittedly, I am suggesting using terms that respect complexity and differences by keeping terms such as Aborigine clans rather than a sloppy impoverished

Primer for Training and Learning 83

term Umbrella of – 'Indigenous culture' (Elkin, 1964). By using indigenous nowadays, the sum of the clans differing collage of colour, shine, texture, and form are speared by the arrow of reductionism into a unidimensional caricature. It appears a rich and gifted people are sacrificed for the sake of convenience. A convenience lazily destroying solutions for all parties involved – simplicity for complexity is sometimes quite daft, is it not?"

Commander Sgt Matt Moloney: "It is daft as a brush! It asks me to ignore the differences of clans, the reality of getting beyond not only stereotypes but to express the truth, that is reality. Before we move into a major situation that comes to mind. I want to give you some examples that may suffice in answering your questions in my own style." [Nodding assent, I actively listen]. "First, I want to return to an experience as a police commander, Sgt when assigned to Coen. Well, as you asked my stance as a police sergeant is to again keep strong blue walls up so the Murries Clan members: so, there is a divide between police and the policed. I am asked to if you want it straight infantilize the entire group although not in malice but in-kind co-dependency by simply not challenging any of the individuals with a more purposive relationship but with what you chap's in the NYPD call the patrol guide. Well our specifications and guidelines although different in some ways parallel yours as you explained. We are to always be courteous and professional and not getting into the corrective business of changing folks and yet folks ask me many questions either straight forward or implicitly. Also, for me I had a strong resistance toward just plain old fun and comfy type of interactions. I don't mean meandering and such as a married man beside being an officer and a dad of a few kids as you well know Dr. Dan. I mean having a desire to rescue this orphan Wallaby which is like the Kangaroo but a bit smaller and in need. Well, this little gal Wallaby was a trooper and she adapted well with many anecdotes I can share and did in the social media circuit. To get to the point and to spare using names right now some of the elders looked quizzical at first for me as a police officer taking a Wallaby as a mascot around with me. Even taking the notches up in an embarrassingly window unexplored as of yet I invited my kids to get in on the interactions with the other kids who were part of the Murries clan. The resistance by some of the Murries and antipathy lay under the surface of our day to day interactions with my spontaneous introduction of her-self as majestic, Miss Wallaby. This was countered by many Murries at differing levels of enquiry and curiosity embracing my offering my new orphan mascot as friend and amusing partner on the other hand. The little gal let's call Pauline aka Miss Wallaby was as exciting as the American perils of Pauline. She was quite fun, and although not so hot and heavy an addition to the police service she created a real bridge. She truly was loved by many, not all the Murries and was not part and parcel of community police relations yet she clinched the deal: As you Yanks say, 'Real-Deal!' I myself need to fill in some gaps as to her fate for me, my kids and I who fell I love with her and couldn't believe she literally hopped away one night. As I learnt later from Barry Port on the QT [meaning not disclosed openly at the time-but it is fine to disclose now];

While walking around with a Wallaby in a bag around my neck, I heard blokes, mostly local Murri people making jokes. I recall hearing one fella say, "Hey Sarge, I don't know why you're working so hard to keep something alive that will only end up as bush tucker for someone." That got a few laughs from the crowd. The chaps were making jokes, but like most jokes there was probably a degree of truth behind them. It is not uncommon for Wallabies to be eaten and indeed, I've eaten them on more than one occasion. Anyhow Doc the group of individuals that were standoffish and not embracing Pauline had the idea she would be dressed up quite nicely as a braised Wallaby as you may dress up a Peking Duck with some sweet and sour sauce. Her real name was 'Twyler' the Wallaby. I am calling her Pauline after you shared with me when I was in NYC the tale behind that name and your own grandma's name: Of course, in deference (Matt giggles in his inimitable style with a genuine heartful style). Finally, I realize the investment emotionally and my own protective nature as a police officer and service oriented humane being was only part of the picture I really missed her. As I recount this story to

Primer for Training and Learning 85

you, I still miss her and think of her often and unexpectedly worried she may have become food for a croc or any one imagining her as a fancy dressed up dish. I often go back and also think about her as assisting me better than any directive in passing by some obtuse rule against patronizing and bolstering a real interaction in an eco-ethological niche which would without my unwitting intervention simply be a caught Wallaby and dinner for a small family. I like to think Pauline aka 'Twyler the Wallaby' helped establish that connection with my help.

Cop Doc Dan R: [Pausing for more than a moment] "I reflect on my colleagues' spirit, action and emotional empathy as a Cop-Doc and fellow Sgt] Commander Matt Moloney you answered my question in part as metaphor, and in part in recounting your experiences within your own hard-won circumference of tolerance and acceptance without infantilizing and pandering to the Murri individuals you've intuit correctly in knowing better. Your taking in Miss Wallaby aka Pauline enlarged the circle of tolerance, courage and what is called the noetic dimension. First, you reached out to of the box of constricted rules and regulations without violating any laws and stretched them rather then shrink them which is brilliant! Second you created a potlach of emotions and compassion in which the type of a Wallaby as food item was transcended with you as a real authority figure offering by modelling kind and loving behaviour another dimension of you as an individual copper unabashed at being you as you are. In other words, the Murries were given an offering to engage with you in assisting raising Pauline and many stepped up to the mound where only Wallaby orphans dare to tread. This is exactly the noetic dimension whereby existentially you scaffolded across false barriers a frontier of mutual respect and continuity where those in the Murrie clan could cross over. The noetic dimension being that which transcends the material alone as soma and psyche holds the body and mind (Frankl, 1978) and all the nomothetic based rules that are only guidepost as best with real human soulfulness and shared relational interactions at the heart and soul of community. Finally, you offered what Donald Winnicott called a transitional object (1981, 1985 & 1987) as the tangible memories to call up in a 'warm, cosy and durable way' in which members of the Murrie clan can come to you not as another competitive elder, but as the elders do as a good enough figure of nurturing as father. You are as the elder being existentially a member of the community who may be always one step in the fringe and outer-fence; but on the other you are centred in the hub of their lives – meaningfully and quite real: In Judaism we say another word for truth is reality and you established in this wonderful gift once again a reality for me and all scholars and practitioners to embrace as a better way of developing bridges with the Aborigine clans is not by rushing in with co-dependent mutually distant interventions but in gradual steps together toward mutual respect and joint growth via respecting differences not trying to white wash them away."

"Finally, you brought attention to the variation in personalities of fellow humane beings and their soulful and mindful dimensions to encompass the circumference of any attempt to assist by being slow and effective change by being real! In our next series of interviews, I hope we can share that experience you hinted at when in the Big Apple about transcending the need to treat the Aborigine Clan members as helpless people and create overt dependency. I like the creative proscription we are discussing against limited prescriptions! Prescriptions are centred when all the dynamics are best known and the delimitations of scripts are acknowledged upfront."

"Fleshing out real cases, large and small, in which resilience and interdependence stokes the template of tranquil potlach where affection and affinity is shared nicely and with poetic brushes for all. Such as the sharing and raising of your own beloved orphan Wallaby, Twyler aka Pauline who in her young life was left in the unknown throes of peril as you last were with her before her mysterious disappearance. Yet, if I can suggest, the tense peace wreathes within and without each community and clan and non-clan members are tickled by the fires dint, lit and ever close to metamorphosis into warring clans – burial, tracking, and mating skills that convene the rituals that enflame or unite the different individuals with one another. You brought peace even if transitional and based on a subject that at times is objectified such as our unique and wild Pauline who has flown into the perils of another day – this time on her own lonesome journey..."

Commander Sgt Matt Moloney: [Grinning] "Doc Dan you've said it again, quite well. I thought about a case I have briefly and only on the surface shared with you in NYC. It is not just a crocodile and shark story. I know these shark stories fascinate many of my Yankee associates. I know my misses and I are quite fond of you, so, I think we can share a real situation I experienced with a shark which is centred within Torres Islanders eco-ethological niches and may be of some real educational value for understanding Torres Straits behaviours in a way that can help ensure educational and cultural competence without 'reductionism' so prolific nowadays. I was almost torn apart but was not, it is truly funny in a way. What do you say Cop Doc Dan? Does it fancy your directional pull if we first get this shark event out and in the open? Can we dry out by analysis the mistakes made and break into parts the whole situation to solve as we have done with the other events? I am curious as to doing an eco-ethological existential analysis over this event which is not particularly my best moment but it may help understand a similar event for scholars, police professionals here or abroad or mostly for Aborigine clan's citizens."

Cop Doc Dan R: "I say let's move where our unified associations take us in keeping in synch with psychodynamic and existential analysis in an eco-ethological existential framework. While we have agreed in most of our dialogue, I have become the trusted navigator and you the keen and adept trusted pilot we can switch our input when needed and best illustrates for our readers some wisdom that may be taken from sallow pale to resplendently useful."

"Yes, let's move into untranquil waters as we open new dialogue as to your intimated shark story where the joint response of tackling a Queensland Blue Shark has no distinction between a delectable fish; irascible Chap; or stalwart Mate as her choice meal. Her meal if I remember correctly forces a Tarantella by bumping her pray as she sizes him up as her quarry. Her quarry gets bumped, as she shimmies through the depths of the fishing coast to the surface as an unconscious demon to you, me and the Torres Straits Islanders who may take her as a guardian spirit, or deceptive marauder!?!"

"So, goes the Torres Straits fishermen, and Torres Straits divers moving ashore to the turbulent waters as Queensland Police and Torres Straits Islander Police patrol waterways from dusk to dawn. In this experience you've promised to share, perhaps you and I can unravel the chaotic turn of events you've hinted at through our eco-ethological existential analysis. This perhaps is not so different from the centre of conflict, resolution and compromise in unconscious waves of possession, obsession and right and wrong rites amongst indigenous people who sharing and raising your beloved orphan Wallaby, Pauline aka Twyler benefited from your ingenuity. Ingenuity by ensuring they too became subjects transitioning from spaces apart – now bridged – and ever so close to you without the spectre of stereotypes tearing apart what is evidence of unity and potlach once again. But another large experience of division may threaten the addition and multiplication of affinity and compassion."

"Nevertheless, not in spite of being torn apart but in the face of being maligned, move forward and upward."

"This leads me to suggest we fly to the Case of Blue Casts where teeth cast the dye of reddened waters and where as a Churchill fellow, we can both agree he said it best, "there go I but for the grace of G-d – Go I!"

Chapter 4

Torres Straits Island Police and the Thwarted Shark Attack – An Eco-Ethological Existential Analysis

Introduction

In this chapter it would serve us well to place our minds-eye toward the ever-narrowing view of Pauline the Wallaby, and her perils. We hope she eventually is able to find some reprieve as she maybe lost to our sight, but not from our heart.

The perils of Pauline the Wallaby, left all who heard of her – a less complete and even more so those who knew her – including Sgt. Commander Matt while hidden in loss initially, peace of mind has been re-discovered.

As Commander Matt knows well in his own 'internal-witnessing' in an eco-ethological existential framework is ever present. Pauline is in mind a wilful strike away from a cherished memory when he desires her closeness.

We learned in many challenging ways that affection encountered by that wall of losses sunk in suffering without meaning - becomes despair, as Dr. Viktor Frankl suggested to us all, (Frankl, 1988).

The antidote in part lays in the sufferer who is able to intertwine the lacing of loving memories around tracks that move our tears of remorse back to the strands of our thoughts holding optimism. Not a glowing all glossy optimism, but a sobriety in the face of the tragic – *tragic optimism* where we can re-gain meaning in our life's darkest moments.

Sometimes those moments are near misses where the tragic loss of life is left on the rock of security where fragility of life is made all the more vivid as the loss of our own life is teasingly close to being swept away but alas, thankfully, is not. It is here we gain meaning and purpose in the directions you and I may take.

This is all too relevant. Relevant, not only to the Torres Strait Citizens, Torres Strait Islander Support Police and the Queensland non-Indigenous citizen and Police officer but to all readers. Readers stepped in the quarry of enforcing and serving the law enforcement community from officers to civilians alike may pause and actively listen to all said and shared here: All different save one regard of being human, all too human and error bound. That error bound is not flaws but fallibility we are all subjects too and open to learning. Being educatable from different perspectives aligned with the humane being of being human, alas.

Foremost is this chapter underscores heroism and courage of one powerful not forceful Sgt and Commander Matthew Moloney. It is in this chapter which recounts what Sgt. Moloney without our joint existential analysis of the eco-ethological niche in which he faced a quantum moment of the breach in his invariant trajectory of security and the assumptions almost all of us take for granted but is far from granted without grace. That is a life and death struggle imminently upon Sgt. Matt Moloney without time to think as humans do in complex decision-making charts, graphs, and decision analysis but in the harbor of being novice-prey, apex- predator, or apex-survivor where action pre-cognitively surfaces in the space of existence.

Exquisite lessons are catalysts from Sgt. Matt's experience as fighter pilot in this chapter and myself as his Cop Doc narrator. Sgt. Matt's resilience and ingenuity on another level of experience is underscored as emerging from the noetic dimension. The noetic dimension is the region in our conscious awareness that doing the right thing may require going way beyond the threshold of our comfort and centre of existence as we know it to serve another distressed human being needs (Frankl, 1978).

I qualify this chapter again as one in which the dynamic flow of narrative is one that was not rehearsed, nor embellished but one in which Sgt. Commander Matt Moloney does what I assert almost all heroes and heroines do – downplay their heroism and unique adaptations: I refused here and in my hardnosed adamant stance convincingly, cajolingly, and with some imploring for Sgt. Matt to accept and internally witness his own unique ingenuity on an eco-ethological level. In this chapter I work through with Sgt. Matt an illustration of how my Eco-Ethological Existential Analysis is done in a professional and peer connected style.

Torres Strait Police are not distanced but made more universal and culturally connected as the Eco-Ethological Existential Analysis illustrates. All participants are quite human and humane. But as I am known to do, I will not apologize for the buoyancy that kept Sgt. Matt afloat physically, but in my own view was not addressed psychiatrically or in other words in a real psychological sense at first. I was privileged of not only working this out with Matt but sharing this for posterity for you as reader as well.

The poignant threat of being devoured alive is an ever-provocative threat for all humans and animals as anyone who has witnessed the noble wildebeest grabbed by a salt water crocodile along the Mara River of West Africa. Not too far away from the intense drama of animal ethological apex survival events of West Africa lay the Torres Island Straits of

Australia. Sharks with as much audacity as the salt water crocodile surreptitiously patrol the straits. They are not alone as the police and fishermen whose eyes open wide can't compete with the heat sensors aligning the sharks ampullae of Lorenzo. The scent of fear and struggle against death in the throes of life's preserve cut the surface waters to the depths of the unconscious throes all at once and the challenge to one's existence is never just academic or intellectual it includes all of that and much more.

Let's, Stop, and before you are taken too far ahead - pause and listen as Sgt. Commander Matt Moloney's encounter with a deadly man-eating shark in the waters of the Torres Strait: First we will garner some context of his experience with being on the Torres Strait Island.

Commander Sgt Matt Moloney: "Dr. Dan I am unsure if you know what it is like being on an Island where you work and form an attitude where diving is a necessary skill and if you don't know how to do it, you're sunk! No pun intended here too as you are fond of saying. I mean 'it'! You really have to swim and learn how to dive in an island. Life is surrounded by water on the Island of the Torres Strait. I became keen on learning how to dive and was still filled with excitement when I got to this assignment and locale. I had not dived before getting here."

Cop Doc Dan R: "Well, the Island of Manhattan is about the farthest Island I ever lived on, I lived in Long Island and Staten Island too for short stints. But I am sure as I have discovered and you have educated me – my experiences of living and surviving not only as a citizen but a police officer on an Island is limited to my active listening abilities and my sense of empathy which is in full active auditory reception. Please continue good Sgt Commander Moloney."

Commander Sgt Matt Moloney: "I remember from the start a first sense of trepidation when I actually went out to sea. I had journeyed to a reef between the Islands in the relatively speaking – open Ocean. It was a very mixed feeling. I had different senses and sensations of being in the ocean."

The Thwarted Shark Attack 93

Cop Doc Dan R: "Specifically, Sgt. Matt, could you go on and talk about your thoughts that come to mind about those mixed feeling and different senses and sensation of being on the Open Ocean?"

Commander Sgt Matt Moloney: [Reflective and emotionally evocative] "Yes, I remember my first sense of trepidation when I actually began to see the boat moving away from the shore and feeling the salty sea spray on my face. A mist of sorts that felt nice but also somewhat rough. It was also a feeling of exhilaration to be out in the open ocean. It was both feelings at almost the same time. It would move back and forth."

Cop Doc Dan R: "Where were you heading as you moved back and forth with the waves of the ocean?"

Commander Sgt Matt Moloney: "I was heading to a reef between the Islands in what could be said to be the open ocean."

Cop Doc Dan R: "What comes to mind as you visualize yourself heading to the reef?"

Commander Sgt Matt Moloney: "A lot comes to mind then but now what I am remembering I could see land in the distance but it was not close at all. In fact, the land was far away, at least a considerable distance away. Not an easy swim at all if I needed to get back to real solid ground."

Cop Doc Dan R: "What do you remember doing next?"

Commander Sgt Matt Moloney: "Well, I geared up and was very excited at the prospect of doing some real diving in the open ocean. But again, I was filled with passion but also with some hesitation I couldn't quite put my finger on 'it'. It is what it is you know! You, know what I mean? [Gesturing in equivalent manner, "I am with you Sgt. Matt" as I remain silent and riveting my attention to absorb 'It- all'.] So now I pulled on my borrowed gear knowing it was not mine but was given in trust I would listen and use it well and in a disciplined way. You know Doc I have somewhat of the hyper-excited officer style you write about in your survival guide for police officers but I also possess some hyper-intuitive personality style as well. It was a bit strange but then again you are similar to Dr. Strange, mate and ought to get my point." [Nervous smile, genuine but contrived as anxiety is more etched on Sgt Matt's face].

Cop Doc Dan R: [Slightly amused at the quip and humour, delivered as dry ice but in good spirits]. "I gotcha, now and let's hold off for some time before we type you in my categories of personality although I see how and why you've seen the common ground with my personality dynamics as related to defences as they emerge in different ways in officers. If you can good Sgt. Commander continue."

Commander Sgt Matt Moloney: "I geared up from toe to head. I turned around to the side of the boat and felt a sudden feeling rise in me. I hadn't touched the water yet. I was prepping up and couldn't pin point that exact feeling and what it meant but it was definitely within me. I looked at the water and saw the blue colour and it struck me while I could see quite a distance above the water, I wondered how my vision would be with the mask on and undersea water? I remember now what I had felt at the time. I had tried to ignore it and did not want to acknowledge it but it was not good. It was fear. I guess it was fear of the unknown. Like you as a copper in NY say, "it is what it is and that's all it is."

Cop Doc Dan R: [Abruptly and passionately] "Sgt. Commander Matt, as you know in police culture in the land down under and in the streets of asphalt and blue rock in the Big Apple 'It' is exactly what you and I are likely to be hiding away. Your use and my use of words and the concepts behind each word we choose is of major importance. 'It' is not what 'it-is' but what you and I can try to with much work, sweat and labour eventually allow to tear up and seek to understand. Understand in the context of your own experience of ecology and survival motivation. So, if 'It' creates some fear; some anxiety as a signal of what we fear; and some anger at having gotten scared let's not wash 'It' away. Your very legitimate feelings and ideas about 'It' is worth understanding. So, if it makes sense let's pause and reflect respectfully on your own genuine feelings as legitimate first. Forgive my interrupting your flow

The Thwarted Shark Attack

and pointing this out but you and I need to straighten out my approach to this understandable washing away of what 'It' may be that is so painful and scary and the fact is when we explore the 'It' you and I ought to use a slow and gentle approach. I would say it makes sense that valuing our need to listen to all that emerges to gain some perspective as to why collaboratively can help others understand but first and foremost you count as much as anyone else. Does this make sense as a desired goal for us to move forward with together on, or do you think what I have just said is quite strange and distant from you?" [Easy grin but straight on track to engage cop doc to cop commander honest and forward together.]

Commander Sgt Matt Moloney: "Hey, Mate, I like what you said and you did share this with me in NY when I was with enjoying and also in some measure weary of the city that never sleeps as to some seedy characters who were around. I guess I did forget some of this important insight and it is really necessary to remind me as I do realize as you were reminding me, I did feel fear. It was fear I did not want to sit with so I pushed that emotion aside. I was in total silence and asking myself some really tough questions. I also just remembered the films I had seen of Jacques Cousteau as a kid. It was for me a trip as if I was travelling to another world as you say often a different dimension of existence. I was with Jacques Cousteau as he was the coolest dude, Mate. The reef as I remember was full of life and colour and like him I was bent on exploration besides all the copper stuff I was excited and in fact I can say exhilarated."

Cop Doc Dan R: "Go on good mate Commander Matthew Moloney at star board, please go on."

Commander Sgt Matt Moloney: "Well, I was asking myself what precisely was under the boat that protected us as coppers and what if any monsters were living in the water? Silly in part but curiosity and desire to get wet was itching inside my gear all ready to jump in and get to experience the Reef from the ocean perspective. Very quickly as I was in the ocean in gear for the first time as an adult and not on a beach but in the ocean off this boat I slid into the water and it was exhilarating! I did see the colour and the sea animals and coral formations. I felt the confidence rising in me the first dive in and had enjoyed my experience which was not too long but fulfilling. I my own accomplishment at taking the risk and surviving. My fears were not in mind when I got into my dive which almost went way down south. I mean almost to the endpoint, my own that is."

Cop Doc Dan R: "It sounds like your first go at this free diving business went well and you did as you were instructed and felt really good about your dive and the sea animals you experienced sharing some space in the moment of time you all were conversing together in silence and peaceful co-existence. I would have loved the idea of fishing myself as nothing tastes better than a freshly caught and filleted fish from the sea. But that's me. So, go on..."

Commander Sgt Matt Moloney: "Well, I'm not a big one for fishing myself. To be perfectly honest I don't have the patience and I don't like the randomness of it. I felt for me better to go under one more time although like yourself Dr. Dan the day I went out the Torres Strait Islander Police Support Officers took me out again. I had been building up my confidence and objectively speaking I am a decent swimmer and at times quite good. I had decided to go out with them doing what was line fishing and diving for crayfish to eat."

Cop Doc Dan R: "I am aware of crayfish being those small lobster type of fish. Sounds like you all were looking forward to sharing again as in Potlach we have been discussing and were ready to have some fun in a sporty way."

Commander Sgt Matt Moloney: "Well, yes we were looking forward to doing some serious cray fishing but with some fun added on as a bonus. I became over confident as I sometimes do. I had established some competence and had decided rather than just fish with a pole and line and bait I was going to go down into the sea again and check out the crayfish myself. Cray diving is known as free diving and while I would not in an

The Thwarted Shark Attack 97

unsporting way fish them out: I would go after sighting them in their own turf. Fishing with a pole and lures is challenging and sporty, but the poor beasts have no chance if you go down and capture them while on tanks."

Cop Doc Dan: "You accented the prospects of survival for these poor beasts, that is the crayfish if you go down free diving for them but it sounds like you really want to emphasize to me that you did the right thing by going down and communing with them which sounds exciting and also quite educational at once. Can you describe the ecology of this area along with any thoughts that come to mind in terms of your own assessment of the survival needs you felt at the time you did this dive?"

Commander Sgt Matt Moloney: "Thursday Island is a small island directly to the North West of the Torres Straits. Hammond Island and the channel between the islands are only a few kilometres, if that at best. The channel is narrow in width as you move between the islands but this is nature's way of being quite deceptive to the uninitiate and the newbies at diving or swimming across that channel if you are considering doing that swim. In fact, that channel is so deep, I mean so very deep it is deemed an international shipping lane. To complicate the ecology of this island in the centre of the Island, almost squarely in the middle of the channel is a large bare stone. This stone culminates with a large protruding pinnacle. Bare stone and barren this stone sticks right out of the water: Hammond Rock is what it has been dubbed. I am unsure if it was dubbed in a Queensland Pub when some coppers and locals had too much to drink or as legend has it -the rock formation was created from movement and settling of Stoney mountain. Local legend amongst the Torres Straits Islanders has its origin mythically as a metamorphism of sorts. That metamorphosis was the wife of Waubin of Muralag who was a great warrior that hailed from Prince of Wales Island became petrified and of course immortalized as a stone. It also evolved over time to become the tidal stream reference point it is used for to this very day. The channel forms a link that is active and fluid oceans. The narrowness forms a strong tidal area with currents that whip around the rock formation with speed and force at times that are overwhelming to the uninitiate. All this said, Hammond Rock serves as an excellent fishing hub for the Torres Straits Islanders including their citizens in Blue, my police brothers and sisters, the Torres Strait Islander Support Police. As explained to me the coral reef and pelagic fish are abundant in this hub. Because of this abundance we went there first."

Cop Doc Dan: "Well, so far so good, what happened next?"

Commander Sgt Matt Moloney: "As I shared I do not like line fishing as much as the idea to view and explore the crayfish below. I had hoped the opportunity may happen to dive again. For me it was murphy's law that is what happened. Let me explain to me you how this sequence of events happened to me. I decided if I could dive, I could grab some cray fish for my mates to dine on. So, my reasoning at his point was I knew I had not been diving long and was at a stage where I even knew I was perhaps getting over-confident in my skills but something me was itching to get into the water and explore. The boat mind you Dr. Dan was in the hands of adept Torres Strait Islander Support Police Peers and the fishermen were nearby. Well my peers manoeuvring around the rock and behind the major current set out of the current and dropped drogue anchors as they are called to get the boat steady in unsteady waters. It was too deep for conventional anchors and drogue anchors were working well this day. The officers began to talk quite vociferously about the fishing for cray fish and this site being one of the best in the Torres Strait. I heard the deep water and good flowing current was protected by sharks. My ears rang with enthusiasm and I felt I could handle this with my copper peers right here with me. I asked the Senior Torres Strait Islander Support Police Officer, "Really?" "It's true Muterro" said Officer Willie Wigness, one of the Island Coppers who was along on the voyage with me. I said to myself, it is better to go in to the water as I did earlier. I had a new opportunity to find what I want: I can observe and if I fit to grab a cray fish or two and take it for food, or my copper mates –

The Thwarted Shark Attack

why not?" Part of me knew well it was dangerous and I felt that real apprehension arising, but I put my fear in perspective."

Cop Doc Dan: [Interrupting to not lose the moment in time] "Good Sgt. Commander Matt well if I heard correctly the Senior Torres Strait Islander Support Police Commander and your mate, Willie Wigness mentioned sharks as the native patrol team of those waters and being international waterways Sharks of all types could visit. As you and I know, Bull Sharks, Hammerhead, Blue, Mako, Oceanic White Tip Sharks and the large Tiger Shark all can be a great hazard to your health and mine if they mistake you for an animal in distress or even some odd fish that is challenging their food source and sense of territory? I say that because it seems you overrode that warning and intuitive sense.

Commander Sgt Matt Moloney: "I did and I grabbed hold of my flippers, mask and weight belt to hold me down. I also grabbed hold of my spear to catch cray, or other fish and of course if necessary, as my first and last line of defence."

"As Willie saw me putting on my gear in this spot he was not as amused as I was and made it clear. He paused and told me, "Which way, and where are you going Muterro?" I said, "Willie, I am going to dive in to get my eyes and if I am lucky and you too maybe some of those crays for our dining." I was thinking at that time isn't evident I am going to dive in and try my new skills as an underwater naturalist. At that point in a very different expression Officer Willie seemed concerned and said to me with his eyes opened wide, "" Bula Muterro. Listen. Those crays are protected by really big biadems (sharks). I no lie bula: Don't dive there!" I felt a twinge of concern as if I caught his feelings along with mine. I know the brain cells in the back of my head were setting off alarms at his warning and further I did know he cared about my well-being but it was the rush of getting this done and bringing home some cray as well as seeing the coral reef first hand that kept me going on. I had looked at Willie before I had come close to the edge of the boat geared up and my brain was screaming somewhere inside, "No! For G-d's sake NO! Don't do it! At the last moment Doc, I ignored Willie's warning and my own sense. I guess it was my own pride. I told myself as I did Willie, "No Mate. I'll be alright". I waved goodbye to Willie. It was as if to prove to myself I'm okay to do the dive. At the same time, I did what was inevitable I took one big step in. Don't forget Dr. Dan, we are coppers."

Cop Doc Dan: [I nod assent] "I am with you, Sgt. Matt I know we are coppers."

Commander Sgt Matt Moloney: "Doc, as I hit the water itself, I went under the surface and adjusted my mask. I felt the mask slip slightly off its mark and adjusted it. You know your mask moves a bit off centre due to water hitting it at first. I adjusted my eyes to the underwater light. I then floated to the surface quite naturally and blew some water out of my snorkel. It took a few moments, perhaps seconds to orientate myself. After those initial seconds maybe ten or so, I gained my bearing and was adjusting to the depth of the waters surrounding me. The sea had an indigo blue colour. That colour indicated to me I had entered into very deep water. I floated up, re-adjusted my mask and blew my snorkel free of any excess water and air. As I was blowing the air out, I looked out of the sides of my eyes. At first, I viewed the rock as reassuring, but I thought I noticed some movement around the rock. I realized as I was swimming at an easy pace a large fish was coming toward me. I hoped it was a dolphin, perhaps some baby minke whale, but not what it was."

"Without any doubt a large and heavy built shark was moving in my direction. I was and still am not sure what type of shark it was, but of being large, very powerful and coming directly toward me along with the movement of the swiftly running tide – I am sure. If I could use an analogy it was like a freight train. Doc, I need to modify my analogy and metaphor. Meaning the freight train as a moving inexorably powerful train that is not going to back off or be stopped if it is coming at you and it was coming directly toward me, but not particularly fast. (Silent).

Cop Doc Dan: "Take your time, cop to cop and cop to cop doc I am listening and here with you."

Commander Sgt Matt Moloney: "This sea going beast was coming at me like a grey missile and was not veering off for something or someone else. I felt a sense of adrenalin surge in my body and my breathing change as I became very concerned and fast without thinking much except, I am dealing with something very primal. I got primal too. My body language must have signalled to this shark whom I felt was reading me as I was trying to read him. Luckily visibility was good today, that was the day we were out by Hammond Rock. I realized calming down only a little that I was still twenty Metres way. Not much but at least not in mouth bite radius from the shark. I also realized this was a very real man-eater and being a man, I was no equal to his size and strength as he was moving with the current toward me. I had my now seemingly powerful spear weapon turn into a crazy spear toy like object with a Hawaiian sling on which it was attached. I also realized I had little to protect me and to fight against this large predator. I do remember thinking in seconds if that long he was over two plus meters and pure muscle and had three layers of teeth and I had my toy weapon that was of course not a toy but against him that's all it was. I nevertheless decided I would fight back and raised the spear toward him. I knew from my police experience that all animals want is a good meal as easily taken as possible and not a fight. I also felt assured if he felt I would not be an easy kill then he may leave me alone. I could escape – possibly?!?"

Cop Doc Dan: "I imagine at this point you felt you were going to be eaten alive. Interesting even though for most folks what you've been through is almost indescribable – you've described this well to me. What do you remember happening next?"

Commander Sgt Matt Moloney: "I had looked at the shark and as true as I am recounting this to you the shark looked back at me it realized I had taken a view of it and was ready to strike with my cray spear and was slightly over 6 feet tall so I was of comparable size and not so easy of a prey. It slowed and went a metre or so passed me and looked back at me as it passed me bye. We made eye contact and was making an emotionless assessment of me as food. It was doing an appraisal, an evaluation. How much effort would it take to kill me and devour me and how much energy and nutrition would I provide. I knew that I had been sized up as a potential meal and it decided to let me go. I realized if it had gotten me by total surprise underneath and I did not notice it and change my direction or my attention it would have struck and taken me by stealth successfully knocking me unconscious and devouring me before other sharks could feed off me. Knocking me senseless is the first step and I am not even considering teeth sinking in to me. I did not know if it was going to go deep and perhaps have another try by coming up from the depths. I was not going to hang around to find out. The tide was strong and had taken me a good twenty metres away from the boat and coming back to the boat against the strong current would have made that a slow and hard swim for me. I was only about fifteen metres away from the rock and that was in the lee of the currents direction so I made a hard choice and went straight for the rock. I can say with some confidence that I covered that distance in a quicker time than any Olympic swimmer could have. The problem was that the face of the rock was actually pretty sheer and steep. Coming up to it I realized there was a ledge at, or about sea level. It would have been twenty centimetres wide but that was enough for me to stand up on. Heading towards the rock, I built up enough speed to launch myself out of the water and onto the ledge I did it and managed to hoist myself up and land on solid rock."

Cop Doc Dan: "Sgt Matt how long did it take for your peer support to rescue you out of this nightmare, or is it better to say daymare of horror?"

Commander Sgt Matt Moloney: "The whole incident from me hitting the water itself to dive to getting onto the rock as my shelter was no more then three minutes at the most. I stood on the small ledge on the rock and looked over toward the boat. I saw Willie and that Sr. Torres Strait Islander Support Police commander looking back toward me. I realized quickly they must have seen the drama unfold. Willie looked at me. He saw how white and pale I was and knew what had happened.

The Thwarted Shark Attack 103

He knew without being told by me directly. He immediately said, "I told you Muterro". There are big biadems there. They protect those cray fish." He shook his head at me and said, "Next time, you go and listen to me when I speak to you!" the other coppers were rocking with mirth. The laughter wasn't suppressed for long. I realized I was in pretty good shape having survived but my bladder was full. I knew from classes it was the fight or flight syndrome kicking in. I had to within minutes turn around as my peers were there and empty my bladder, further adding to my humiliation. Having had all the big adrenalin hits themselves at some point or another also realized when I turned my back and urinated what was the trigger. The boat we were on belonged to the water police Sergeant. He too was snickering, but I could tell he was angry at me for ignoring Willies advice, he told me. "Well, Muterro" he said using my Island nickname, "too help you remember this lesson, you can now wait on this rock until we all have finished fishing." They spent a half hour fishing while I stood on the rock. Let me tell you Doc, I never again ignore advice from Torres Straits Police and when local people tell me things to look out for again."

Cop Doc Dan: "Although we are co-authors and as you know if you were my patient, we would not be disclosing this but in educating the public about trauma and loss if it is okay, I would like to pause and for us to do a bit more in our own unified work on your encounter with this shark near the Hammond Rock. I say encounter because this is one of the very close encounters with death you've likely been through with making it past the attack without being scathed physically. I am also taking more than a moment pause. I need to take pause because I find nothing mirthful or worthy of laughter by fellow officers here. You did as you intimated in gifting me your own unique experience of almost being killed by an Apex Predator in his/her own domain and the fact you did in-deed take a risk in trying to master diving before receiving more instruction. On the other hand, you were allowed to gear up and to try the untested waters where probably from the grey posterior and tips of the dorsal if white were a transatlantic oceanic shark the same that ate the sailors of the USS Indianapolis in 1945 (Lech, 1991). It may more likely be the notorious Bull Shark which co-habits fresh and sea water. The Bull Shark was the likely culprit on the NJ Shore 1916 that 'Jaws' by Peter Benchley was based on, as you shared earlier Great Whites are not apt to swim in such warm waters (Benchley, 1974; Kennington, 2014). You survived a major man-eating killer shark: You and I can return at a later time in placing these very forceful trauma events in perspective and each in its own place as you prefer to share and work through with me." If I could be so privileged as I consider you remarkably stoic and brave Sgt Commander Matt without barring any censuring: Can this work for you Commander Matt Moloney?"

Commander Sgt Matt Moloney: "Yes, I am open to this eco-ethological existential analysis with you. To be honest I felt this was a challenging event, but as I am thinking about the experience it is much more then I imagined it was at the time."

Cop Doc Dan: "As your insight was adept as to the flight and fight response: Hans Selye as you know came up with his theory as to positive anxiety known as Eu-Stress and Distress or dis-stress if you care to do an analysis of the word and break it down to its roots (Selye, 1976). You were on full throttle and a freight train was a wonderful analogy. What I am concerned with now is how did you feel when you were left on the ledge of the small rock for a half hour?"

Commander Sgt Matt Moloney: "Honestly, I was relieved as the fight part was over and now, I was waiting to be pulled up and taking aboard my peers police boat. Don't get me wrong Doc, I was the one who made the error here. I own my responsibility and the consequences which was a learning curve for me. No harm was intended by the Sgt and other coppers, both Torres Strait Islander Support and Non-Indigenous Police. I felt it was a good experience to share as I survived as the main point here. I also felt much good can be seen in how the coppers on both sides were united in this lesson I learnt. Do you see my point?

The Thwarted Shark Attack

Cop Doc Dan: I believe from a conscious level the great lessons learned and the comraderies among the Torres Strait Islander Support Police and Queensland Police here in effecting a rescue was superb. But once realizing you were okay – in my experience and training nothing is okay, was okay, and will not remain okay until a lesson is navigated on a compass that transcends the indigenous/non-indigenous; intra-clan conflicts; and what waters down the straight channel to the fact hubris over teaching you a lesson could have risked your life and limb regardless of how much you admire and share affinities with your coppers along the Torres Strait.

Commander Sgt Matt Moloney: [Light-heartedly, but tension leaking out with some contagious laughing]. "Doc, it really was my bad, my screw up and the other Sgt was close enough in his police boat to retrieve me if he needed too. I learnt my lesson and it was a good one to learn, you know it was not done to really test or let me fall into harm's way as my mates were right there with me after the event."

Cop Doc Dan: "I hear you and I agree your fellow Torres Strait Islander Support Police and Sgt figured he needed to teach you a lesson for your taking a bold, brash and risk laden move by free diving off the Channel. If we can contextualize your move first, I think it would make sense." [Matt nods assent to me]. "I recall you shared with me the excitement of watching Jacque's Cousteau and seeing his dives and exploration throughout the world continents and shelves where waterways intersect and are bountiful along with the wonderful mysteries of the Sea (Cousteau & Cousteau, 1970). You had shared with me many times the excitement of your Dad loving the fact you are a LEO and also his love of the adventure and Ocean in a more tempered and sanguine style. But the rub is that while you may have gotten carried away in a moment of hyper-excitement and leaped where others dare not dive – you are a commander and also did nothing more than Captain Cook the explorer, and Lt. Fletcher Christian did (Cook. 1773; Nordoff and Hall, 1948): There cadre of fellows who explored with them stayed with them to the end and as we know also repopulated the land with non-indigenous folks and immigrated and migrated from different geographic regions of origin. In your case it was understandable how a young man could believe he was somewhat invulnerable to the challenges of the deep blue and counter-intuitively would act on an unconscious means of overcoming his phobia which appears in part to have motivated you without your conscious awareness to dive with all the risks involved. It seems like the fantasy to do what you and Dad shared watching Jacques Cousteau, although you more than a man who is mature and has achieved goals aspired too, by peeking into your desire to feel the mastery over the taboo unknown sea the fulcrum lay under the surface of doing the dive: You did it!"

Commander Sgt Matt Moloney: "It does make sense on a psychoanalytic level and maybe existential but I am way over that level of development now as a grown man although I appreciate the interpretation as making sense on some level as to what I considered my bad and foolish action here. It may feel difficult now, but I do get the point of Captain Bligh. Although a rebel he certainly was, Lt. Christian Fletcher did have a motive and rationale for the risks he took too (Nordoff and Hall, 1948). I had almost forgotten about Jacques Cousteau as you said that was my most beloved show and family time as a kid."

Cop Doc Dan: "One of my mentors was the inestimable clinician and author – psychoanalyst's Dr. Professor Charles Brenner (Brenner, 2005) who pointed out to me more then once in my queries of the unconscious motivations that sometimes compel us to move towards, away from or leap into situation s where angels fear to leap is a truth that the drives underlying our behaviour both aggressive, sexual and we can add existential are ubiquitous and do not know time as bounds until they are discovered and remembered. Perhaps in reassessing your actions as keenly motivated to remember some wishes left deep inside your psyches unfulfilled wishes and repeated because your merger was incomplete until you took on the risk and mastered the wish behind the fear and anxiety. The shark while quite rare was also metaphor that was made real and one can say reified in reality awakening in you the need to conserve and cherish your life and not take such risks again without adequate support and instruction. The unconscious both psycho-dynamically and I will arguably posit existentially are quite prominent and lay under the rock much as the Rock of Hammond. Remember because one, meaning you and I or anyone does something once that is odd, out of the norm does not mean you and I are labelled as being that way or defined in that way unless you, I or anyone irrationally chooses to define himself that way! Does this make sense good commander Sgt. Matt Moloney to you in placing this almost tragic event in some new perspective to use in your future piloting your police career? I mean consciously and unconsciously as well?"

Sgt. Commander Matt M: "Yes, what you've said makes great sense to me and also places my own actions in perspective well. I am not a great risk taker although I did take great risk here. I felt being compelled now was not without reason and unconscious motivation that is sensible and, in a way, makes me understand my action may have been bold but not stupid, and motivated by darker forces but not all dark. I also understand in light of my actions I have learnt some important side of my own psychology in a cultural context shaped by the background of my life's history and me as Matt Moloney. Aye mate thanks."

Cop Doc Dan: "Well, I am not finished in looking at this multiple layered event you experienced, if it works for you would you mind viewing your rescue from a complimentary perspective? [Sgt. Matt nods assent again]."

"First, we've seen how this makes sense and if we can leave behind some labelling of your behaviour as true of judgment related to your behaviour. As you've seen yourself, 'It' makes sense to leave out the judgment of your action which in part emulates some of the very founders of the continent you live in. Although imports from England Captain Cook and Lieutenant Fletcher were in some ways not only quite the adventurer but took very bold risks even beyond your own, perhaps as a legendary copper Sgt Commander (Cook, 1773; Nordoff and Hall, 1948). Does that make sense to you?"

Sgt. Commander Matt M: "It does make sense to me. I get your point."

Cop Doc Dan: "Good, the complimentary perspective I would ask you to consider is you sought out mastery and competence in skill sets to use within the unit quite consciously but from an ethologically paradigm and with unconscious motivation as well – you stood to gain speciation in a new unit within an eco-ethological niche primed for survival: So in the shaping and context of skill sets and building becoming a diver who could forage among the Clift's and crevices of the Reef and find cray fish your dive also made superb sense within the eco-ethological niche your skills were shaped in."

Commander Sgt. Matt: "I like that understanding which sits well with me as I do at times get hyper-excited and can bite off a bit more at times then I can chew, as you like to say Doc, no pun intended and you can punt off now that I feel better about my unconscious ethological motivation which is cool in that yes as coppers we have to always get better at survival amongst predators."

Cop Doc Dan: "Would it have been acceptable if that shark would have reappeared and aggressively as a bull shark or oceanic white tipped shark is and known to be it could have tried to grab you above the surface if it sensed you close enough to the Rock ledge itself, (Cousteau & Cousteau, 1970). If you slipped and fell into the water and needed to swim back to the rock ledge who can guarantee you'd be successful? What if the current was counter to establishing a landing back on the rock? Could hyperthermia take place and due to the adrenalin surge spike body heat, and consequent exhaustion? Is it possible under shock your cardiovascular and neurological nervous system ANS/CNS could have broken down and triggered defibrillation state? Is it possible for extreme distress could cause lactic acid to increase, and also depletion of electrolytes and arrythmia to palpation's and even heart attack or stroke?"

The Thwarted Shark Attack

Commander Sgt. Matt: "Doc, I get your line of questioning and believe me the Torres Strait Officers and my Queensland Coppers were close by and could have swept me out of the water if need be."

Cop Doc Dan: "My point takes us back to a cultural dimension that on one hand makes sense of your peer's admonition and warning you to not try something out until you've gained sufficient skill. That said they also responded forthwith and was there in body and with action to assist. On the other hand, the fact you were left close to the boat but they continued pole fishing for the assorted indigenous fish for a half hour was without sense and sensibility. Any threat I shared just a moment earlier could have become reality and secondly other threats we can't fathom at present could have culminated your trauma experience. I suggest those present are able to own their mistakes and learn the lesson to not play with your life, your mental health and after care which is as crucial as your initial assistance for physical aid. In that regard they messed up in a way that could have been as life threatening as the Oceanic White Tipped Shark that sized you up for prey food."

Commander Sgt. Matt: "I do confess I felt so relieved and so much angst after the wait seemed like another eternity but I knew it was short lived. I also feel your analysis is helpful to me and put in context as you've shared it will be helpful to the Torres Strait Islander Support Police as well. As you said while no malice was meant it could have turned out very different if I had been weaker, ill or not in the good shape I was in after the almost fatal shark attack."

Cop Doc Dan: "Yes, we are on the same front page. Finally, the most crucial insight for this chapter is your own humanity shines throughout our narrative. Let me qualify what I am going to say as being my own thought and regardless this will remain unedited and unexpurgated when in print! I take full responsibility in disclosing I have so much respect and empathy with you and not sympathy for you Commander Sgt Matt Moloney for being a humane being and always looking for the humane in others regardless of behaviours. [Smiling genuinely in looking at Matt] I am unsure if the Almighty will look on those who have been rude, crude and callous regardless of culture which is sometimes descend by those who play gods with a small g when compassion and empathy is needed. Here I think we see an unintended and honest piece for history including your own unique experience. It was a moment of ignorance and a window for learning on a curve you may teach others in the land down under. I thank G-d you are not somewhere under the blue sea due to some mishaps that were taboos medically and psychiatrically/psychologically speaking in the initial follow up to an otherwise excellent intervention at first by both some Torres Strait Islander Support Police and some Queensland Police alike. While no conscious mal-intent was designed, nor conspiracy was weighed against you, nor the result for you, your immediate family including your Dad as an outstanding manager and loving you as a LEO and the international community of police that affectionately look to you as a legend in your own right could have been lost. Thankfully you did not succumb to: Shock; hyperthermia; hypothermia; or an aggressive shark with urine, uric acid and traces of blood which are all triggers for attraction and feeding. As you know the heat you give off is picked up by the hyper-sensitive specificity of a shark and the Ampulla of Lorenzo that tracks heat and distress from mammals as fear and sweat are dispersed into the ecology in which a shark feed. Leaving for even a moment, yes one unnecessary moment without jumping across to you is almost like leaving a fellow officer behind: My lecture consists of the admonition to this irresponsible moment in response to emergencies is it is not 'legit' – then; not 'legit' – now; and not 'legit' – ever! Semper Fidelis includes not pontificating as one drop of blood from your precious person can be risked. That is true even if you made a minor mistake or a major disaster in error, it is of no relevance to a first responder from my neck of the concrete jungle. Notwithstanding bureaucrats and that psychopathology of institutes and institutionalization ceilings I think you preferably can best receive an apology from that peer and any participant in this event toward healing and some change that incorporates this invaluable lesson."

The Thwarted Shark Attack

"Finally, Sgt Commander Matt Moloney this chapter again from the centre of your existence underscores a testament as to your own decency. While these officers are mostly decent and excellent mates as you've pointed out they too have a lesson of wisdom and emotional empathy to learn from you. Not villain's and with conscience this lesson in my opinion is for each officer to learn. As a Churchill fellow I say with you, "there go I, but for the grace of G-d, go I!"

Commander Sgt Matt: "I will say that again and I have really gained a lot from this experience which as you know Doc, I did not consider so significant but now I do and cherish including I am alive to talk about the shark trauma with you. I understand some dynamics psychologically I did not before our interview and ongoing dialogue."

Doc Dan R: "Moving forward Sgt Matt those blue glistening sea walls collide with the dark world of blue strands of silence that bridge both the cultures of Torres Strait Islanders and Queensland Non-Indigenous Officers. I did not premeditate an eco-ethological existential analysis but one that emerged in the secure bailiwick of being a cop doc who values and truly appreciates the gift of trust and passion of peer support. As a cop Sgt and Commander and cop doc bond we did this analysis as pilot and navigator together. We are bound via ropes of rescue and while much is left existentially left unsaid here, even more is to be done at a later time, perhaps together on point. Poignancy in bolstering the buoyancy of staying afloat and not aplomb when the blue dart of derivatives of unconscious aggression and competition emerge also were etched where fraternal teeth could potentially strike with shark like tenacity. Sometimes peers can be the harshest of critics and seemingly indifferent to their fellow's trauma under the guise of doing the job. I don't think this happened here but that too is illustrative when one's self-righteous stance can transform a really nice officer into a careless zealot on a quest that is undone when justice is not tempered by compassion and mercy."

"The surface is never as clear about motivations from the depths. It is through your harrowing experience that a learning curve still may in fact and in-deed hide some other unspoken levels of complex trauma in its full cast and hue and the resilience you've presented then and more so, now. Some casts of traumatic loss may be drawn only years later. Unspoken that aftermath is sought for in the light of day and in a place where what is forgotten is finally explored, not as a memory but as a memorial and testament. The all too human aspect of your own rescue and survival place an eco-ethological framework as the life preserver over the entire experience you've endured heroically. In the truest sense of stoic fortitude and emotional equanimity you've developed as you have."

"It appears to me some unknown, disenfranchised losses have been re-enfranchised and witnessed from me as a mirror reflecting back to you, Sgt. Commander and scholar-teacher Matt Moloney to internally witness for yourself. Thank you for that gift."

"Finally, some of the great sages of Judaism have emphasized to be a true teacher one ought to be able to learn from each of his/her students some new aspect of life and living. Matt you've taught me well in your humility, your humanity, and humane equanimity. I have hopefully learned much from you as your ability is something most of us are not born with. Many of us through the greatest of effort learn to appreciate and sometime integrate as their own gains too what you do almost naturally."

"If it works let's move on from the Sea danger and to a larger Sea-Island challenge shaped by an amorphous cyclone ready to beach in your Port. After all Cyclones do not see Queenslanders as Aborigine Clan citizens distinct from non-Indigenous citizens and any permutation of any mixture of cultures, religion or race: Save the race to take on the Cyclonic strike as 'It' slams into Queensland port striking without conscience."

"It seems to me the management of such natural crisis creates exits unblocked where the taming of the tempest unfurls as the flags of a united front must establish sane rational synergy to stave the storm: As we look at the cyclone, I am hoping we could sail the fierce winds as they whisper down to a lull as all Tempests do. As Tempests abate, the dim light of fires forcing agricultural sweeping where land needs rest and replenishing the cropping of excess grass is achieved by landowners, while cattle-owners must find food and refuge for the shepherded flock. As the shivering shrew to bellowing salt water crocodile endure the wind as do all human survivors as the fires stoke awe and fear."

"The hiding animals hanker down the front of their habitats in the land down under as conflict by feuding interest and parties are met by emergency management: Such challenge paradoxically lands the most humane solutions. It is in the centre of potential catastrophic collisions that conscience actually takes precedence at times over the bureaucratic tangles and solves catastrophic potency in solvable options as we port into Queensland as all are aboard and we sail into Chapter 5."

Chapter 5

Totem and Animism, Wind and Fire Catalysts - Different Solutions

Introduction

In this chapter totemic and hierarchal layouts become focused on differences, commonalities and conflicts in aboriginal clan culture as experienced in North Queensland. Insight into the subtle and explicit rules of the culture of indigenous Australians is explored through dialogue and experiences of Commander Sgt. Matthew Moloney, and me. The spontaneous flow of our dialogue is not done in a pedagogical manner, it is explored in subtle and at times quite direct ways. Understanding the formal rules that layout a secure living and knowledge of the culture is the groundwork and infrastructure in getting some understanding of the people under study (Durkheim, 1915).

The mores and customs are part of that first layer, and what happens when those mores and customs are broken by a member and his/her status within that community is a second more telling layer of knowledge.

What happens to a person who is an outsider trying to get in that society that is secured by its mores is yet another ledge on the first layer teetering on to the edge of the next layers crawlspace. That is portentous if a taboo is violated and whether punishment is one that is corporeal and vengeful, or more soulful and mystical.

The corporeal punishment is one that can be measured and understood within a paradigmatic framework as an operationally defined concept. This first layer of knowledge is also amenable to scientific analysis over time and repeated measurement. Getting a hold on the value and real wisdom one may learn as channelled in flux within the qualitative realm of process: That process can be tangibly fleshed out with content formed after pauses and definitions follow up from conjecture. Clarification follows conjecture and co-occurs as relationships further define and heuristically test the bounds of what education and exploration yield.

In moving to the second layer, knowledge becomes wisdom as it revolves, and slowly evolves. Evolution is not always beneficently progressive, in fact regardless of nomenclature change can be regressive and destructive. The first layer to second layer is also shaped by the existential glue. That existential glue is not reducible as the first layer is in part, but must be expanded to insights that are qualitatively culled from the field experiment of interactions that become defined in relationship's and the fleshing out of real emotions and feelings expressed behind the words of alliance or resistance to change.

It is here that the science becomes applied and therapeutic gains are made in the balance of power in the resistance to forceful evolutionary change.

Operational definitions are coordinates laying out the design of management. Management in this context to be effective and of service perforce need give way to the counter-intuitive design that is flexible, fallible and doable in the long walk. I avoid the word run with my colleague because walking allows time to pause, reflect and develop lessons worth the task of patience, perseverance and attention to the details. In a paradoxical way details do not bedevil us, as the sarcastic quip affirms that 'the devil is in the details' but perhaps we can oscillate that value to its opposite insight which is, "the details may bring more clarity to our lenses where other aspects of life and living become visible. With a forward vision potential is planted as possibility and even more so doable. Reality is not seated in perfect columns and rows in chemistry as static analogue; but in the fluid stability and combustion different elements can take when combined: Why do we believe with humans we are even more clear and pure then the elements we are made up of at the base level of life?

More so, why do we hold onto a purely elemental level of thinking as the only means of understanding how to get along as different peoples and cultures when life is so much more than just the base elements we are in part composed of: Being self-evident it may be time to move beyond this faulty paradigm and centre our existence as at least greater than the meaning of its elements, and yet at its base level it is never fixed and linear. So, why hold onto the impoverished myth that we all are linear, controllable and to be controlled by corrections made in texts that are more modelled on politics and can only model failure by pursuing total success as its only measure.

The distinct quality of a scientist practitioner is to use empathy in active listening and persuasive motivation rather than forceful directives, and speculative impositions and postulations to guide interventions without adequate assessment, (Kitaeff, 2007; Lillenfeld, Lynn, Ruscio & Beyerstein, 2010; Lilienfeld, S.O., Lynn, S.J. & Lohr, J.M., 2013). Discrimination between what is acceptable and what is not is crucial glue to use or discard in bridging gaps. Not every trainer, or well-meaning educator will achieve an alliance until their own assumptions are re-placed by acknowledging and learning from the community, they are given permission to enter into respectfully and acknowledging one can only know others in part, and not whole. In this chapter distilling wisdom honestly and with integrity includes not side-stepping the challenges, pitfalls and effective responses toward achieving service goals imperfectly: In walking nice and easily a rational and humane response is presented within an ongoing dialogue with Sgt. Matt Moloney, and me. The idea that success is not the supreme arbiter of reality especially when dealing with culture, personality and religion is Professor Albert Einstein, (Einstein, 2010) in his own timeless words not relative to the time of his own existence and space but to the farther reaches of our own imagination and beyond, put it well,

"It is high time that the ideal of success should be replaced by the ideal of service."

In a comparative and gentle suggestion of service experiences outside of Queensland, but comparatively within context, the reader is taken to the Big Apple. The Big Apple has many problems including one of reality, multiple minorities and cultures and the inevitable clashes that occur. The other-side of the political is the very real cultural life of the potlach sharing that constitutes the real living and life among all city dwellers. Yes, NYC is a giant manmade Asphalt city notwithstanding the fact scaffolding effective interventions and failures can be catalysts and cross-comparisons for and with Aborigine Clans in the land down-under. Staying afloat and atop of cross-winds and fires that threaten potential razing, hazing and rage within, and without walled and unwalled cities whether walls are visible or not is at the top of goals of co-existence: Life is so much more in the land down under and the land juxtaposed as cement, blue rock and asphalt.

Specifically, this chapter is thrust into a tripartite form where an equidistant triangle of three different challenges are all answered in some way by Sgt. Commander Matt. His challenges and service have many potential pitfalls which he sails through as the tempestuous waters churn havoc, and the air its turbulent fires. All these events impact on Sgt. Matt and that is also a challenge as all the folks that are non-indigenous and aborigine clan citizens; civilians and uniform members struggle with the reality of life and death. Sgt. Commander Matt Moloney's service style while incorporating rules and regulation's does not reduce his identity

Totem and Animism, Wind and Fire 119

toward strict enforcement. With savvy and diplomacy authoritatively, Sgt. Matt opens shared space of aborigine clans that live and work with non-indigenous police and other fellow citizens. In some ways the threats escalate while Sgt. Matt handles dilemmas with a balance well measured, better handled and understood.

The first side of the triangle is fires where a deep and primordial force is thrust into the laps and dens of its denizens. Fires taken out of control threaten major areas of life [human and animal]. The property of those who own much of this land under the billowing fire alarms is threatened as is their security they are heir too.

Fire strikes deep one can say in the airborne scents first responders encounter: Medics/emergency medical technician deal with cardiac and respiratory distress calls; Police Officers deal with traffic and evacuation calls from fleeing citizens; and Firefighters dare to tackle the gift Prometheus stole to capture our fascination with equal attraction and opposite repulsion. Flames consume life and livelihood without any conscience.

Another incredibly rewarding and devastating issue of matter and concern forms the second side of the triangle and is held most often in the winds of distress such as cyclones. In New York, and the east and west coast of America we call cyclones, Hurricanes. This second challenge in the tripartite marathon of police work is culled out of the empty conch shells to hear the lulling of the monster waves as they ready to hit the shore of Queensland. Finally, the last challenge will be organising, troubleshooting and ensuring safety is extant as Sgt. Matt Moloney runs the voluntary emergency management response in Coen and North Queensland.

In a comparative manner NYPD coppers deal with major urban fires. Equivalent in some manner with Queensland Coppers and firefighters doing rescue work such as dosing out major fires is explored: Accidentally, stoked, or with bad intention buildings are set on fire. Insurance fraud claims, and in some cases simple vengeance schemes are replete in sundry details. But seldom are NY Coppers asked to struggle with the power of conflict when with good intention for agricultural purposes large areas of land are set to inferno levels by some members of the community while impacting dismay onto others.

NY Coppers have dealt with the aftermath of Hurricanes such as Katrina and Andrew with good service and outcome. Hurricane Sandy with devastating effects on the city that never sleeps did not work out so well and many are still recovering.

But for NY Coppers and for Queensland Coppers much can me learnt via the problems and some solutions Sgt. Commander highlights. In part, insight and responsible learning remains the bailiwick of his approach. The does and don'ts for Aborigine clan folks and non-Indigenous folks emerge. Supporting the personal identity of the indigenous officer through gradual and protective methods learnt through the experience of police practitioners is more likely to be empathically integrated. Sgt. Matt goes against glass and crystal ceilings where growth is more likely to be halted.

Cop Doc Dan R: "Commander Sgt. Matt could you kindly begin with your experience of the cyclone warnings to flood the Queensland geographic and ecological homeland."

Commander Sgt Matt Moloney: "Well, Dr. Dan it is important to fill you in some facts as to the history of what is known as the Coen Emergency Response Committee (C.E.R.C). This group can be defined by the work and outcomes of police and fire response of which I am privileged to be part of. That is, the fact that two emergency service organizations are manned by volunteers: The State Emergency Service which is used as an investigative arm by coordinating and doing searches for missing and endangered citizens both/and providing necessary labour during disasters. The second emergency service organization is the Rural Fire Brigade. The Rural Fire Brigade perform fire officer duties which include road side rescue, and at times tragic recovery of civilians and uniform members trapped in vehicles."

Totem and Animism, Wind and Fire

Cop Doc Dan R: "In this voluntary and critical response team it sounds like some or many members are also full time sworn uniform police personnel. Let me ask you good Sgt. Commander what rank or appointment you held?"

Commander Sgt Matt Moloney: "I held the rank of President of C.E.R.C. The Coen Emergency Committee was a true community group and our members performed the duties of the local disaster emergency management team. In order to join our Emergency trained rescue and fire response unit you had to be a volunteer and live locally and commit to doing your job without payment. This position was distinct from my police officer duties and responsibilities."

Cop Doc Dan R: "So if I am getting this right and I may not be my good Sgt. Matt Moloney, outside of the complex, endurance test of being a Sgt. Commander, it seems you took on running the entire helm of what we would call an emergency voluntary fire department and police department: In my experience having been a Chief Psychologist for the MAP Program of the NYPD and for the DEA, US Dept of Justice nationwide under the Aegis of Health and Human Services I could hardly find time to defuse and enjoy the mundane beautiful dimensions of my own and my family life. I did but only at great burden. For me what's more than impressive, is your willingness to tackle such a huge obligation to manage, and quite a large onus to swallow as a police and fire rescue department. Your being President of C.E.R.C of Coen, Queensland Australia entails your accepting being unpaid, staying a local resident within the eco-ethological niche that you work and enduring all the responsibility and commitment as an emergency management coordinator where violence and much losses to be endured. Being President can put you in the cross hairs of fire and can provoke your own loss of life under the combined perfect storm if all goes wrong which in speaking frankly, at times can happen. I am taking pause because of the enormous additional stress and strain on your family and personal life as well as professional responsibilities as a sworn Police Commander. Standing at the helm as President of C.E.R.C. within your own ecological niche where an ethological surround of life and death permeates boundaries of survival and purpose – this outside of being a police sergeant and family man?!? It appears something may have motivated you deeper then your sense of adventure and ambition per se? I have you right when I say you are the Churchill Scholar with a soulful dimension! It is my read on your ability to connect with much success."

Commander Sgt Matt Moloney: "Well, the way I look at it and did when I got involved in the Coen Emergency Management Program was to realize that inspiration from the bible was from Noah. Noah not only knew of the impending doom of the great floods but also of the wayward nature of all folks to procrastinate and to allow disaster to almost come into their living space before they take real action. [Pausing and with serious focus]. That is way too late. I decided to take action and I guess to take my cues from Noah. Although ancient his approach uses the right style of intervention by prevention and good planning. Planning must include taking into the account the jealousies, the ego and swollen pride within men and women's bosom, and squabbles over territory between the aborigine clans and the non-indigenous citizens of Coen. It is no easy task but preparing to get almost the entire community on board is crucial. The blocks toward planning, putting differences aside and sharing a vision that unites others in the face of oncoming disasters is the apex of planning for emergencies. I know the human characteristics of the different characters who are major movers and shakers are important as is the indigenous community and as we established together includes differences that need not be merged but respected as practiced."

Cop Doc Dan R: "You've shared your deeply spiritual and powerful example of Noah who as legend dealt with the awesome power of transcendence against the forces let loose by nature and human being's failure to take heed of all the warnings given by the Almighty. Noah by proxy becomes the penultimate Emergency Management Commander who had to mediate between the ignorance and gross denial of his fellow

Totem and Animism, Wind and Fire

citizens and a change in wisdom exacted to change the course of events. While comparisons and differences abound between you and Noah, I am sure, the metaphor is worth living as modified and one that does inspire within your own example to other administrators, and clinicians in executive positions, including myself. In looking at it from another perspective, Professor Joseph Campbell offers enlightenment",

> "When we quit thinking primarily about ourselves and our own self-preservation, we undergo a truly heroic transformation of consciousness."

"It appears to me before we get into the heart of other matters it is worthwhile to reflect on your own internal witnessing. The fact you are truly a giver and educator who lives as he thinks is rare enough. What I mean is your ability to centre your own self, not on being less than self, as in self-less; but using your own ego and development in synch with helping and caring for others it is important to not neglect your own psychology: Caring for others is indubitably part of who you are, but not neglecting your-self and your own remarkable achievements is crucial to witness for yourself. Does that make sense to you?"

Commander Sgt Matt Moloney: "It makes sense to me that I do acknowledge my efforts to assist others and to try my best which I appreciate and do for a few moments until I get upset about the conditions in reality that are ignored in terms of getting the aborigine clans on board with a can-do attitude and not allowing each person to fall back into complacency rather then striving to serve one-self and their actual networks of family. Let me simply state a fact pattern, as an outgrowth of the laws of physics and an understanding of the limitations of government. The government often has responses to cyclones or as you say Hurricanes in North Queensland each year. In Coen although it is geologically situated inland it is spared the impact of such natural events as strong cyclones. Some cyclones have moved in North-easterly directions destroying numerous communities that are indigenous and non-indigenous alike. Planning rescue operations cannot hold weathered responses when they are not tempered with respecting the truth that the community itself needs to own its own recovery and not be given aid as if it is an incapable and feeble minded and bodied amalgam of people thrust together. What I mean is that the people impacted by such disasters when they are identified as indigenous are suddenly marked as if they are feeble and cannot take on tasks including manning and delegating and being part of the responding first responder cadre. The core of this issue is a dilemma in which victimization and patronage takes the position and place of real responsibility and recovery. At times when the government affords rescue teams being flown in to effect major disaster recovery effort although the terms qualify as community rehabilitation it is not!"

Cop Doc Dan R: "We did examine this issue of social problems and the psychological impact earlier. I think we are on to analysing this situation from an eco-ethological niche level of community. Existentially we are back to a decentring process where the actual participants are pushed aside although the intent in rescue is so well meant the result is so off centre as to the value of growth through challenge and conflict that can be tolerated and worked through to real developmental peaks for all involved. Specifically, what examples come to mind?"

Commander Sgt Matt Moloney: "For example, flying in disaster specialists such as helicopter first responder medics to rescue victims no stable unit trained as indigenous first responders are present in considerable numbers to meet these challenges. Some problems arise again and again. Such problems being the rescuers are outsiders, idealized and immortalized, but within the community a sense of being a victim and lack of competency is enhanced. Victimhood is not an automatic and rather than confronting such a label it is just accepted as fact. Further no one really has brought these issues to public awareness and within a sense of community responses to homeland safety, policing and service dynamics. The government is hardly trusted and takes on too many promises too soon and take action in trying to correct the politics underlying the essential tightknit communities of aborigine clans often

Totem and Animism, Wind and Fire

upsetting the balance and creating wars within and among clans. To create a community resiliency and recovery within as an infrastructure the forced interventions foster a sense of entitlement and create as you suggested earlier in our dialogues a sense of dependency. This all sums up my point that the way government run intervention does its patch up work does not assist recovery. It actively delays recovery".

Cop Doc Dan R: "It is interesting how you frame the way government on a large-scale agenda-based leadership stymies recovery at a real grass roots level: the fact that you see the forcing of interventions as not leading to growth but to dwarfing the actual process of struggle and innovation. It also halts real thinking and acting on one's behalf interrupting the process of survival motivation within ones ethological-ecological niche. I may be seeing your meaning of delaying recovery in a different way than you do. Could you elaborate on your thoughts?"

Commander Sgt Matt Moloney: "Recovery in my hands-on work with all parties involved focuses on 'how' the emergency management professionals can best ensure community resilience. What I mean by resilience is how the emergency management professionals ensures the community gets back to a state of self-governance. By self-governance I do not mean the idea of social services being flown in to assist. I mean a sense of independence for the community and self-sufficiency at best. The best possible scenario is not always possible, but as a goal that is workable it is something that can be achieved."

"Independence is not having government workers turning up in helicopters and wearing Superwoman capes and riding shotgun with Batman as the canopy drapes over into the horizon. Hero worship and rescue is especially relevant and poignant for Indigenous Aborigine clans. As you've intimated in many discussions Doc Dan, a temptation exists for rescue workers to treat each situation that threatens crisis as if all are the same and each is a total rescue operation."

Reality is different as you point out well, knowing the eco-ethological niches and the existential issues and challenges as well as major shakers and citizens needs is crucial. The fact that rescue operation as you put it, improves when you include in the management and decision process the participants and managers from the community itself. Letting members onto the board and into the saddle of innovation, risk, and bold measures who are selected from the community challenged is crucial in gaining respect and securing a real potential for change".

"The change you've worked for and battled for decades Dr. Dan is not to succumb to the unionization or homogenization of any people, tribe, clan or group who conserve their traditions and culture which is being swept away in storms of coercion: I can't agree more with your attitude. Your attitude is respectful and empathic as you highlight again and again – active listening, not simply appeasement and support without teaching responsibility and duty. To expect all the solutions and efforts of responsibility to come from non-indigenous citizens that impact on indigenous clans collectively make little sense to the citizens impacted and those who are doing the services as well. Those individual persons are the real-life citizens on board in the rescue effort. The division of indigenous and non-indigenous become artificial lines drawn in the relationships built when times are less rough riding. In major catastrophic events or the potential for such catastrophic events where resentments and adverse impact is spread and contagious to each employee's work, civilian status/uniform status and profession over time. In the mix indigenous and non-indigenous rescue and service professionals find they have conflicts over the formal rules prescribed for each event. That is to say in my opinion that expecting everything of support from the non-indigenous community and little from the indigenous community is perpetuating the dysfunctional myth that aborigine clan citizens can be little more than passive-receivers and is counter-productive in output. Didn't you write in your almost prophetic work on, "Complex Trauma and Grief: A Clinical Guide toward healing from Terrorism as Human Evil for military, police and public safety officers and their families" (2012) that an understanding of the ecological-ethological framework of the community is crucial. You followed by stating that reasonable and gradual changes preferably noted and supported in clearly identified ways lay out a clear trajectory as to achieving recovery and a state of resilience. All these are necessary coordinates to effect service changes that last the mettle of time in part as I recall you suggested?"

Cop Dr. Dan R: "I do believe, I wrote, as you observed - that goal setting that is modest in scope, humble and crafter interventions and moving nice and easy in part as your attributing to me help stoke resilience and recovery in communities as it does in different personalities. I also would add in our case here, Dr, Frankl can offer wisdom and solutions, (Frankl, 1973). In his experience of post holocaust survivors who lived auspiciously and in appellation what could be said to be the lowest moment in human history and inhumanity of man to man, attitude is crucial to survival. The existential dimension does not mean a transcendence of being human and more so a rare humane being: Paradoxically one's existential attitude is made on the premise one is truly human and being humane is the most important motivator toward resilience and recovery in tackling post traumatic events."

"The most controversial and yet honest response when asked about the collective responsibility that all Germans held in being admonished to pay back the victims and their families for the crimes of the Nazis, Dr. Frankl held back and paused. He said it would be egregious and inhumane to do so, because not all Germans were Nazis (Frankl, 1973). Although some would point the finger of complicity to appeasement, Dr. Professor Frankl was neither, he was in search of honesty and truth."

"The point here is that if one looks to balance the conflicts of two peoples the elixir is knowing none exists save the ability to recover is not to blame one's helpers. In not blaming those earnestly trying to assist a group historically undermined and disrespected it is crucial a genuine attitude of gratitude is cultivated. Equal to gratitude by those helped is those who are doing the helping avoiding that the helped community can't walk, can't talk, can't think, and can't speak on their own different levels of adaptation too the mal-adaptive."

"Applying this to the Aborigine Cults the word differences jump out and the fight against entitlement as well. One who is doing rescue now can and should not be held responsible for all the evils no matter how heinously perpetrated by the ancestors of the non-indigenous citizens. It is crucial not to hold one unrelated successor responsible for the sins of their fathers and mothers. This is highly relevant to the Queensland Police as is true of Police in the United States who are often put up to highly irrational and unachievable goals of perfection. Disturbing standards of being invincible and invulnerable subjects the police officer toward being objectified as if he/she is a reified Robocop as the movie by that name disturbingly portends."

"In counter-clockwise direction the reciprocal nadir is realizable as stereotypes such as the Aborigine Clans member are helpless victims crushed by elemental forces of which all humane beings must face and solve. It by proxy leaves the Aborigine clan member as inadequately and woefully incompetent to overcome the negative self-fulfilling labels affixed to their identity. If I have gotten your attitude realistically, clearly your insight is parallel to what Psychoanalysts call infantilization by which an adult is kept ill to satisfy some morbid way to keep another adult a childlike dependent: It is akin to a very severe disorder called Munchausen by proxy," (Levin & Sheridan, 1996; Feldman, D. M., Feldman, F & Smith, R. 2004)).

"Suggesting, actual real-life implicit ways and mores of doing rescue work is lighter and also more cooperative for the Aborigine clan members and indigenous members if and when agendas and forced compliance is not pushed too hard. When balance respectfully compliments evolutionary processes to occur organically as a style that strengthens dams of unity and cooperation against flooding halts the Tempest from flooding the gates of conservation, rather than overflooding the dams of chaos done in haste. In essence than I do believe that those impacted whether indigenous aborigine clan members or non-indigenous farmers are led to believe each person is entitled to perfect service and no participative

Totem and Animism, Wind and Fire 129

responsibility is requisite then although a reversal of a caste system is alleged, in reality tumultuous conflicts brew under the surface of each person's mal-content as each community leans toward its own convoluted and irrational skewed interest negating the real needs shared by both and the promise of compromise inhered in the process of becoming humane. The fires of passion and desire if left to burn without the sensible path ironed out in the parallel tracks of compassion and cautious optimism nice and easy – burn out as a flash fire and backdraft: Can you iron out the fires that burned in North Queensland as you were thrust in the Presidents identity mode?"

Commander Sgt Matt Moloney: "The fires that burned the bush had left substantial regions of land ravished in flames. A couple of land owners as farmers were devastated as a result of these fires. I mean not only physically but mentally as well. Think about the context of the fire from the farmers perspective as they make their livelihood and watched as all the grass quite literally go up in smoke. Their future livelihood depends on grass being lush and thick for the cattle they own as food items for the large populations needs for nutrition and health depends on well fed and healthy cattle for slaughter."

"The State Emergency Service did its job as good as it gets according to the citizens served. But the rural fire impacted in ways that were far from good, and certainly not good enough. The problem was funding allocated to do the service and the fact Rural Fire was undermanned with the minimum of 3 uniformed members of service but ideally 5 is needed to run smoothly. The crux of one problem here is in the area of recruitment, training and retention of fire officers to stay on board in doing the actual rescue and recovery operations. This problem was social and psychological as the influential board members of C.E.R.C. and S.E.S. had not trusted the larger government connections to SES and CERC. Cynicism and scepticism trickled from board members to the small staff at times. While Coen had many supporters of the voluntary emergency management groups in the general population the influence gravitated toward resistance of support by the larger Queensland government oversight."

"Spearheading a responsive intervention, I held a debriefing to gather the intelligence of my members and to affect a better service to the citizens of the area we served. The dilemma was the landowners who had invested a great deal in the hope and promise of Rural Fire and C.E.R.C. thwarting the rolling winds of fire from consuming their livelihood, livestock and promises to the other citizens including the Aborigine Clans to supply healthy and prime meat as supply demanded without a blockage. The culture of livestock cattle farming includes pride in the quality assured by specimens being free of rickets and other diseases. Fire plagues bovines through secondary and lasting depletion of water and grasses. The lack of oxygenation and nutrients when fire scourges the countryside is offset when the fields are allowed to breathe well and rest from being used as much as the biproducts of fires offer nutrients to the soil as it regrows. The dilemma is at times amongst those with huge investments in their day to day living as cattle owners which diverge from those who live in a pastoral and itinerant manner of lifestyle. Such divergence occurs with non-indigenous farm owners in distinction from Aborigine clans such as the Torres Strait Islanders, Kunju Aborigine Clan and Lama Lama Aborigine Clan members. Mind the fact some eminent members of the Aborigine clan's hold positions within their own internal structure as cattle and other livestock owners with or without portfolio."

Cop Doc Dan R: "It appears that the dilemma is more along dealing with the bureaucratic tangles rather then the issue of dealing with the cultural issues and conflict of disparate points of view?"

Commander Sgt Matt Moloney: "The composition of S.E.S. was improved by proportionately being made up of members who were indigenous in line with their representation in the community. The local S.E.S. controller had an in-depth knowledge of indigenous local culture and the subtle but critically important nuances of mores and taboos within the community. Notwithstanding all these facts, the actual recruitment of volunteers was down and many members felt defeated because the funding was not generated by the government and not assisting the real workers who were volunteers. Yet, a paid member from Rural Fire Service Queensland could not run it effectively from afar. The committee also proposed that having the centre of government at the hub of judgments that impact on communities and individuals would be oppressive and daft as the issues impacting on rural society is far removed from the bureaucratic files of government agencies which are located away from the centre of Aborigine clans and the rural farmers I've discussed."

"The rural fires offer a keen example. To keep it specific to indigenous occupational issues that overlap cultural adjustment conflicts lets look at the Firewarden who is appointed to oversee fire operations and control of these fires that get out of control. As you know fires are started at times to clear the land and ideally falls under the venue of the Firewarden. The Firewarden becomes the key person to authorize the issuances of fire permits to legitimately start fires for agricultural development."

"Becoming appointed a firewarden is truly a major acquisition of representative government. The firewarden impacts on both the Aborigine Clans and the cattle farmers in North Queensland. Let's return to the impact of the firewarden on cattle farmers in the Northern province of Queensland Australia. Here in major portions of Queensland, the soil is poor, vegetation is dry eucalypt and grasses that are not very nutritious for cattle. Still, dry eucalypt and withered grass remains a substantive source of nutrition for the Bovines. One cow or bull for every five hectares' is the average capacity the grassy soil offers for nutritive value. This interprets in plain English to the fact that larger cattle stations which interprets into grass and eucalypt lands that hold nutritional value for a few thousand cattle. In asking the Cattle and land owners as to what has primacy land or cattle; grassy lands dominate in value over cattle. Indeed I have almost been scolded with pointed jabs by an understandably irate cattle farmer with such pointed remarks, '

"Copper' you are not the keeper of cattle, but as a keeper of grassy lands and eucalypt I am and the fires consume our livelihood by destroying the cattle's food source."

"I was told in substance, that if you care for the grass by watering it well the cattle will look after their own well-being. Further intelligence sources from the non-indigenous farmers clarified the fact that if you destroy their source of grass, even if arid and not very nutritious you have just trampled over the cattle farmers livelihood for now, and the foreseeable future."

"This destruction of livelihood implicitly highlights the fact that even if the infrastructure of cattle herding could be maintained their cattle would fail to not only thrive but fail to survive without the paltry grass and eucalypt area to graze on. *For the cattle farmers the no-burn policy makes superb sense as their bovine are preserved.*

But for the general aboriginal citizenry a reciprocal position makes superb sense – fire starting is the way to gain back the fresh lands left unfettered by the indigenous peoples. To the Torres Strait Islanders, Lama Lama, and Kanju indigenous folks, the *no burn policy* is unintelligible as it stands. The fire-starting and control is the crux of some employment and livelihood resource that preserve a means of making a living when given the autonomy to ensure responsible treatment is exacted and cultivated. This makes for a healthier regenerative fertility of the land itself biologically speaking and eco-ethologically within the niches of farming principles in the long run. It is a sabbatical of sorts as the land gets to rest and rejuvenate from over usage of nutrients and in doing the controlled fires the elements of mineral resources are stimulated."

One other major interest group which does not help either the Aborigine Clan citizens or the cattle farmer citizens is the reality that much of the land is kept as national park niches – eco-ethologically un-interrupted essential lands that are left to natural processes for the most part and not controlled by any interest group save the supreme leadership of government and bureaucratic webs which can be run with *"superb-*

sensibility" as I've learnt to express and use in an eco-ethological sense of niches and when existentially I can provide the normalizing of some otherwise seemingly insensible process that is now made clearly and arguably sensible to all parties involved as you've been arguing Dr. Rudofossi since 1994.

Cop Doc Dan R: "Since you've given me so much information and provoking thoughts to mull over and richly graze on myself, mind you my Chinese birth sign is the Ox and I can be stubborn at times. Commander Moloney I think I can scratch out the ground of what you've shared and add yet other dimension to our dialogue of value here in identifying conflict and some resolutions that we can cull out together, if that makes sense? [Nodding and smile in assent] What is overarching both the cattle farmers and the aborigine clan members who we need to keep in mind as having both/and legitimate conflict here is an intra-clan conflict to not be pushed aside as to who and how members may get appointed due to cronyism, disparate treatment based on nepotism and other very human conflicts as mundane and earthy as jealousy and possession of power struggles which plague all group dynamics from a psychoanalytic and existential perspective. That is dynamically interfacing with one another personalities of each appointed leader will invariably collide in potent measure – at times. In fact, as the group expands the conflict may expand intra-culturally and as well inter-culturally without neglecting the economics of who is the landowners and who are the workers and their vested interests as being oppositional. Still notwithstanding the Fire warden issue, you so clearly weighted on as significant is the core problem psychologically speaking is assuaging the ego-conflicts that exist in all the representatives whether elected or appointed and the complexity of each difference in-deed and in-reality. Does this make sense to you good commander?"

Commander Sgt Matt Moloney: "It does make sense to me and adds perspective again as to the complexity Doc, but then what is the solution to this dilemma of multiple interests and the push and pull of personality and culture that creates an admixture of hostility and withdrawal at best and the passive-aggressive continuum of self and other sabotage we've discussed earlier?"

Doc Dan: "Well, if it makes sense lets tackle the situation with fires and hurricanes to see where two opposite strains of forces come down upon the Aborigine clans and the Cattle Farmers livelihood. If you can describe some of the actual experiences you've encountered with Aborigine clan members and farmers with capturing the interpersonal relationships on one hand that are expressed between members working toward rescue and emergency response and what has fallen under the equivalent of the Blue Line of silence to see what may be made verbal in your recall of recovery and resiliency in both groups as working toward solutions, rather than what did not work as defeating since we have reviewed this in large part to this point."

Commander Sgt Matt Moloney: "Let me start forward rather than backdraft in reverse as cyclones which are an ever-present threat do bounce back and forth over and through North Queensland. We get a number of cycles which destroy numerous communities as they are caught in the wake of a severe cyclone. Although North Queensland is inland and Coen particularly so, we have been struck on more than one occasion by mammoth cyclones."

"Again, success in this area of emergency management is evidenced when recovery of the community under siege returns back to normative living on its own initiative and some changes are established that are preventive. The most important aspect of training and for disaster management is organization, pre-planning, training, and the specificity of roles. The formation of real trust and comraderies of unit members. Not struggles for who is in charge only as the sole major criterion."

"To use the biblical analogy with Noah at the helm of the storm. The epitome of leadership is warnings are given as cooperation of getting all aboard and into the ark is the most critical key here. Shelter is the driving power behind the deluge as the basic source of security is the primary

Totem and Animism, Wind and Fire 135

goal here. Further along the route to resilience is preparing and building the ark before the flood cover's over the land and all inhabitants. The deluge took all inhabitants with equal veracity. The fact is the way things are run now, non-indigenous police service professionals which include some few who double up as volunteers manage fires and cyclones in Northern Queensland. We have learnt to hanker down towards complete survival as you well know having been a first responder Cop Doc. I think an important aspect of what we do so well is the fact we are all in it together. My survival includes ensuring that regardless of politics, religious, tribal and cultural strife that I stay being a leader by not backing down and out when the winds blow in. I and my team do the same with the exhausting and overwhelming fires."

Cop Doc Dan R: "You are right in realizing that cyclones and fires trigger very real crises. Engaging different techniques to deal with the fires or cyclones does not wash away your common goal towards tapping into the central spinal cord of life struggles where ethological motivation to survive is at the centre of what is to be done – survival of the community. Community as complex, different and even conflictual as it remains and has developed into is the bare nervous nexus of what we as humans have. The reality is that although different Aborigine clan representatives will clash with who is in charge and what to do – all members cooperate when it is down to the wire.

Remember the crux of the issues can be drawn to the bottom line of resistance to work with the Local Disaster Management Group [L.D.M.G.]. Many of the members of emergency networks who were aborigine clan members had felt the non-indigenous folks dominated even though they were the majority citizens. Remember for the first paid responder's as all sworn officers and in my case ranking officer as Sgt. our role was to ensure survival of all citizens and to stand aside of all conflicts. In reality I was the peace broker and had to ensure all members in spite of conflicts that were inter-tribal as would break out amongst Lama Lama and the Kanju Aborigine clan members would be put at a minimum during a state of emergency. My pitch although informal was to reach out and calm the different factions by actively listening to each leader and associate leaders and establishing that survival depended on unifying all resources against a natural disaster in the making. I also knew if the storm got that bad rescue would be extremely limited to the most serious and needy cases readied for triage and flown out. The cavalry could come in after only a few days. The crucial evidence is all of the different groups when challenged did not become divisive but actually forgot their differences when life was so challenged with uncertainty. The clans knew no booze, bets and domestic issues as these problems would only confuse the emergency and rescue efforts and somehow to a person almost no crimes and fighting among clan members occurred. The same is true of conflict with the cattle owners and aborigine clans and also within their insulated communities respectively. So, for me the funny and odd trajectory is the crisis at the level of real major catastrophe somehow created a road toward compromise and peaceful resolution to work together and cover each individual and group. My point is why wait till it is down to the wire to be real?!?"

Cop Doc Dan R: "It seems like you have discovered a very important process whereby existentially the tighter the ethological collar around the neck of survival the community as a whole faced the more the differences were not as important as the commonalities. The common centre of existence – existentially speaking was not the eco-ethological survival needs but the fact that life and living as all did and truly cherished was the fulcrum to drop the false presentation of self and selves as group membership divisiveness. Your suggestion Commander Matt is proven here as getting enough recovery professionals into the unit readied for the response to survive a real cyclonic or fire monster. It requires both indigenous and non-indigenous men and women reading their response locally. Because this incredible synergy was achieved under the radar – no one needed to acknowledge how well this worked and the reality of achieving service success. Sadly, but predictably internal quarrels and divisions after the survival was established continued at times with more zeal. This made superb sense when the issue of survival is at stake and keeping the score of who would win accolades and who would not did not really count. The critical question is who really knows and is willing to apply their knowledge as autonomous units without succouring the accolades as to who will make the best leaders. You again have illustrated leadership qualities that are bridges and have bridged the differences between what appears to be intransigent conflict while as when you said down to the wire tests all came together."

"The key is existentially framing the event is your own intervention which was to proscribe prescriptions directly while indirectly you did so fully and existentially confront directly with the major players. Each understood as in this dialogue we were able to establish the superb sensibility and normalize each different clan without also ignoring the plight of the just as human cattle farmer deserving and needing assistance of the emergency management team."

"So, when intra-tribal rivalry occurs a more objective testing that is culturally relevant is established to measure the potential of each future recruit and to establish a local coiffure to fund that unit an imperative may be to include the fact that cattle farmers are included as well as other community groups."

"Let me also share an antidote which is more than anecdotal in the history of the police department and some federal law enforcement agencies that will also add to the superb sensibility we are establishing as solutions from an eco-ethological existential perspective. I am unsure if you recall the once a year party established in some local high upended establishments where nice food and some spirits are served to patrons, Well one day a year in these bar (s) there is not only a truce between the patrons when the bar is shut to the general public but the patrons who under normal circumstances may be shooting it out at worse, and cordially waving a salutation at best as one is taken in cuffs into an unmarked car with police plaque and silent turret lights flashing with discrete pulses and no sound as they careen out of sight and into some prison or holding cell that is federal. Conversely and rarer a limousine may be escorting a number of very large men with dapper and impeccable taste in clothes and refined wine as they tag down an unmarked police vehicle and corner the officers likely in plainclothes for a whirling dervish of a time with fists flying and red carmine fluid colouring the streets. So, you get my poetic liberty in an otherwise serious chapter where the wise guys and the plain clothes agents and uniform detectives converge. Well the bar is lined with one side in blue blooded good guys and the other lined with wise guys in dapper threads and rhythm only members of this exclusive family could don without fan or fare save their image and reputation to open all doors.

"Well the lesson learned is although this may be made public as sensibility it is also a private sensitivity that has created a peaceful truce for one night in which the very real potlach includes respecting the differences of each family one in blue and one in red that co-exist under the umbrella held by a Hairy Monk which is the name of the establishment itself. The sociological and anthropological influence of each family is subtle and implicit agreements that the taboos of yesteryear will be respected that no uniform member will give their blood without a reciprocal bath and when collars are tightened around the wrists they will be done privately and discretely as not to offend the family members. Such totems as these dinners are met with the fact that taboo is not violated and all will go well and peacefully. I am unsure if you Queenslanders have such a pub and culture but perhaps a shindig on one of the cattle farmers offering a potlach to the different clan members of each aborigine family will work wonders as long as each clan member also brings his/her gift. The sharing of responsibility is the insights that portend not perfection in a script but service in a bottle of shared spirits."

"Finally, Sgt. Commander Matt next time you pick up a hose you've manned to dose another major brush fire I hope as the President of C.E.R.C. you are able to lead the rescue command as Commissioner for North Queensland. You did not request this I did as a Cop Doc. Your leadership moves the intuitive sensibility and existential awareness into a new level of adaptation. In dialogue with Sgt. Commander Matt I extend my concern and fear that without the sensitive and intuitive innovation he has presented – the survival of and integrity of the Aborigine Clans lay with the decimation of the holders of Ivory tusks: Last I heard, the Elephant hunters/poachers have almost extinguished the wisdom of the trusted Pachyderm's. Those who have the wisdom to conserve traditions and customs as mores understand each cultures totems exist for a lot more than just creating Ivory Beacons on Ivory Towers: Far removed from the heat of Infernos blown by Tempests natural made as much as man-made threaten both/and Indigenous and Aborigine Clan folks who cohabit one of the very tough regions in the land down under with soulfulness in the land – becoming won over – when leadership as Sgt. Commander Matt Moloney serves as his finest best! In the following chapter such long-term memory and cherished values as Pachyderm's trumpeting the herd, are no less sung when celebrations awaiting the honouring and sacred approbation of Queensland Police and all the fine citizens served so well for 150 Years offer a vision where a vista may open new doors: New doors can conserve traditions of an almost vanquished world against inhumane options - messy and necessary compromises again imperfectly planed offers unusually sensible solutions when proffered by those closest to conflict and compromises yet to be heard."

Chapter 6

Celebrating 150 Years of Queensland Policing and Aborigine Clan Unity

Introduction

Leaving behind the winds gathering dust where the North Queenslanders bonded together behind the table slated with formal rules and bureaucratic strictures - survival serviced by genuine community in which each group bridged differences for the common goal of ethological motivation as survival of the best leadership unity was dealt. The reality is this dealing of differences was done under the table but over the skew as balance played equivalent measures to each group as survival balances in the vast region of North Queensland was serviced - well. In chapter 5 exploration of this uncharted territory was given a living map with coordinates for tentative success in the heuristic definitions of what is possibility in analyzing the outcomes and operationalizing the successes.

Northern ecological niches of Australia remain harsh and unforgiving: Leaders push aside their own egotistical ballast of narcissistic overlay when reality deals harsh decked cards that can't win without some team cooperation: Narcissistic gilded cards that only allow membership for exclusive group self-interest and membership whether majority, minority, or sub-cultural underscores perpetual one person-upmanship. In a game which humans have played in which victimhood is always scored a subtle and unspoken systemic racially based accounting. The impact against those sworn to respond to the needs of the entire citizenry is always compromised in shame, sham and surreptitious caches when special interests become the focal point of justice and injustice reigns in the harvest. That systemic racism is a view where one group exclusively has the ears of others while others victimized are scapegoated as being worthy of bias because they may be the majority group members.

Bias is hatched when scientific catalysts to creative solutions are thwarted because of bureaucratic pathology to blocks in communications because stereotypes are reinforced in global ways —not about an individual or a preference in individuals but because of some persons race, religion or cultural affiliation from birth.

I have operationally defined briefly that bias against the blue culture of police and public safety as Centurioncide (Kitaeff, 2019). The credit of the Aborigine Clan members and the Queensland Farmers helped in creating a template toward ethological-ecological sensibility. This sensibility was aided by diplomacy and tactful interventions. The task of overcoming each groups tendency for bias which is almost always self-directed, other-directed, and globally directed is chaotic at first. The catalysts of Tempests a blow and fires struck aflame did not drown or conflagrate the citizens but did ensure leadership emergence was drawn from the decisive action that provoked leading others ensconced in such crisis and that was driven by Sgt. Commander Matt Moloney. The ingenuity of challenge and unity of the larger alliances against a common challenge was shaped within the eco-ethological affordances of each niche as interpreted by each clan and its members differences and responses synergistically. In part the catalyst was each crisis and catastrophic motivation from an ethological level of experience and motivation to survive as humane beings transcended their differences as blockades. By seeking the common ground differences were fully respected and biases that were inherent in human nature but not destructive by not being hoisted into a battlefield were dealt with on a local and benign level of all negative schema's and thoughts they were rendered sub-clinical aspects of human nature and not insurmountable impasses. This level of tolerance is paradoxical and existentially sound and sensible at its best.

Sgt. Matt unwittingly and without overt strategy created a novel dynamic particular to the challenges he faced as Commander. Sgt. Matt Moloney's heuristic approaches in the field of his hard-won innovation presents to me as a navigator his pilot studies where a new method of creating alliances beyond the measure of law and order and rules work as superb sensibility. The importance of each group working out dilemmas was not accidental, nor was it a grand plan. Further reflection is explanatory not claiming exclusivity in solution but insight to what responsibly worked in the field of crisis intervention which attends to the subtlety of elegance — effectiveness within the hold of service. Dr. Captain Alan Benner a colleague and friend of mine pushed the elasticity of this concept in some fine work we achieved together which he is credited with underscoring successes in crisis interventions are measured most of all by the effectiveness in the field of natural experimentation (Rudofossi, 2007). It is then more than intellectual interest but as a scientist to sift through effective solutions to find and identify the variables that make the difference in success of truly effective service changes. The ecological and general validity is clinically proven to work and ferreted out by dogged focus on the question of 'why?' And 'how?' working concepts saved the day rather than rued the future of these crises.

In this chapter dialogue once again is drawn from the process of Socratic questioning, reasoning and identifying the most crucial variables: These variables catalyze working hypotheses — tentatively offering solutions further fleshed out as problems not solvable with ease are offered towards gaining wisdom in attempting to define and offer solutions that may work in the future using the ones that worked in natural catastrophes but not with solvency in human made catastrophes.

The underlying ecological and ethological motivations are dimensionally explored as we move through a return to Tracker Barry Port and his confrontation with complex Centurioncide as a tracker and Commander Sgt. Matt Moloney's confrontation with systemic Centurioncide during a 150-year celebration dashed against police of Queensland.

Concluding this chapter, an exploration seeking cultural competence in how to identity and deal with intra-aborigine clans' struggles is one tier. The second tier is the inter-police and aborigine clans roughhewn building blocks woven together in compromise and real alliance built in friendship. The third tier are bifurcated into saboteurs who are racist and identified within their hidden hatred and self-righteous styled Centurioncide against police and public safety officers. The smaller other side of this bifurcation is the group of non-indigenous outsiders who style racial bias against aborigine clan members by forced compliance with political agendas hoisted upon the most vulnerable in order to destroy a sense of self and cultural pride without respecting the potential of each clan group and the members to solve their social and personal problems themselves slowly, and with gentle support not sudden and massive forced change.

All the issues wrap around the belly of the social beast emerging within a pandemic of Political Correctness undermining all parties invested in belied quick fix solutions. Such solutions stand no chance of actually working when pretense and coercion too conform to linear mindsets are legislated without slow and mindful different solutions. Expanding such gilded solutions to mindful growth can only happen when the pause of insight and accountability match the responsibility of interventions and are kept far from global solutions for the heart of each aborigine clan and community as different as individuals that compromise each - without needless and heedless conformity superimposed on what is super-ordinate into what is structurally and morally subordinate as a political agenda seeking to correct culture how trite and blight

Sesquicentennial Cape York Police Service - Honor and Celebration

Sgt. Commander Matt Moloney: "Cop Doc Dan this is a major area to be understood for it still brings me some of the worst gut-wrenching twists in my stomach and also challenging but worthwhile moments in being a police commander."

Cop Doc Dan R: "Isn't this the time when you shared with me the legendary tracker Barry Port as a respected and legendary law enforcement officer and Elder male who has venerated status within the Lama Lama Aborigine Clan was to be honored for having finally choosing to retire. Tracker Barry Port's retirement was from his prodigious and prolific contributions to Queensland police and citizenry - non-indigenous and Aborigine clan members?"

Sgt. Commander Matt Moloney: "Yes, that is one part of the planned celebration which was created in order to honor the founding of the Queensland Police Service for the Cape region. The year 2014 heralded in its 150th year of operation. The Cape York Peninsula is 288,800 kilometers which in conversion to United States measurement is 111,5000 square miles. I was given the privilege of organizing the event."

Cop Doc Dan R: "This sounds awesome as an event to honor the entire police service and the legendary tracker Barry Port who contributed his heart and soul to the police service he so generously and beneficently gave too."

Sgt. Commander Matt Moloney: "It was awesome, that is mid-year of 2014 Barry had come and seen me to have a chat. He wanted to retire from tracking and police service. We knew he was in his seventies but we were not sure of his exact year of birth. I had synchronized my feelings with his by confessing I was hoping Barry would continue serving and I being able to work with him for some more time before he retired due to age. It was simultaneous and unexpected but in synchrony as he would disclose to me. He said he felt after a year and half of elongated service he could retire and consequently the date of the 150th year anniversary would culminate in a major celebration. As we have discussed he truly was a dear friend and colleague and he said he discharged his duties to the service and working with me personally. He had as typical of his hyper-focused police style made an understatement of his service to police and to me personally as he helped break me in. Barry Port typically undermined his achievements to me as a way to remain humble and upswollen in his ego: In my mind he should get the Order of Australia."

Cop Doc Dan R: "The way you and Barry Port as a Tracker and legendary law enforcement officer connected here and also at other critical times is what Dr. Carl Gustav Jung called synchronicity (Jung, 2010). Synchronicity is an unconscious karma in which events and situations are catalytic and in harmony. Sometimes synchronicity also implies that dissonance co-occurs if the alignment is off. In the case of you and Barry Port it appears synchronicity was on a roll – rolling right off the stalwart rock of your friendship. You also hit the police style on the head with seeing Barry Port as hyper focused on doing the job perfectly and in his own lifestyle. Hardly changing his hat from tracker, to elder, to investigative team member before his next assignment — without enjoying any accolade brought for him to wear even for a moment is clearly an indicator of his ingenuity and drive. It suggests to me, that at times, Barry did not relish his shine and glean as much as he could: That is, if Barry could learn to pause long enough to notice his own ingenuity in-deed, he may have observed his own gifts. You noticing and giving him his due credit is what is reality helped him to embrace his actual potential as truly actualizing. Your contribution offered young potential trackers the motivation to seek and try to achieve the wonders and struggles Barry Port with Sandals and Hat plodded through and succeeded in doing."

Commander Sgt. Matt Moloney: "Dr. Dan it appears the resistance by all sides were the politicization of what could be summarized as those who instigate a conflict rather than a compromise to solve the problem of assimilation of Aborigine Clans into a different but consolidated overall culture and religion of Queensland. Let me explain exactly what is meant by this situation as illustrated by the many potential tragedies averted by the sensibility as identified in our former discussions. Wisdom culled from understanding the eco-ethological niches as they were shaped and developed. Your example of the motivation to create havoc and divide by sensationalism and drama is well taken. It is strikingly truthful when it comes toward understanding Barry Port. It is crucial to understand that the survival, ethologically speaking was not consciously pursued. I realize it was intuitively reached by getting the cooler headed citizens of each clan to sit down and talk with me first. I appealed to each clan member who represented each aborigine clan that his/her own survival and each family would need to be reliant on other clans for cooperation during crisis. Using humor as a slant into a skew that leaned against all compromise publicly admitted was done quietly and discretely. We did boldly go with that well-established maxim, "Don't ask and I will not tell to each member about the others involved. Save the exception that all would throw in their limbs and mind to save each other and not rue the day each insisted on being publicly made right or wrong. The humor all the tribal leaders truly resonated on was that all the intra-tribal and intra-clan feuds could continue after the natural threat would invariably abate. In reality you witnessed and helped me witness as a Cop Doc the success and the mending of broken links in our trellis kept lightly brushed with gains. Gains that were modest lasted more than expected, and blood shed has not returned post crisis, as before. That is a gain I have kept in my own as you call it, "Internal-Witnessing'. I am sure the readers of this guide understand the battle to conserve the Aborigine Clan integrity is pronounced and intense as those who are opportunists and outside saboteurs."

Cop Doc Dan R: "Meaning whom good Sgt. Commander Matt?"

Commander Sgt. Matt Moloney: "Meaning, specifically 'outsiders' firstly engender wars over politics and political correctness. More so the dividing of the real lives and clans with all the traditions and mores of each being threatened in the guise of modernity. Divisiveness makes sense in the eco-ethological existential perspective, because the intra-tribal and inter-tribal strife and stress is not accidental but provided by some of the leadership formally and informally developed. I know some truly terrible things like massacres, widespread dislocation and dispossession happened. I personally have seen real undeniable evidence. The fact that it is inaccurate to label the entire colonial experiment by these incidents or that some incidents were exaggerated is to some degree irrelevant to the suffering endured by the Aborigine citizens. There can be no denying the heartbreak and painful lumps of trauma. All police to some degree today are still cleaning up the bloody messes left. It's not as simplistic as some would have everyone believe. I also know of the settlers and the aborigine clans' citizens made deals, broke bread and shared heartfelt joy and pain as well as those who warred on one another and their own. Actual evidence and shared cooperation in doing service for one another is and was forgotten since the historical revisionists moved on and retold others stories via lenses of colonialism and oppression. As much as I know of real history of day to day working together as indigenous citizens and police unite for mutual benefit."

"This happened in the past and continues to this day. Many indigenous people continue to bravely battle against severe cases of domestic violence, wide spread abuse of kids, vulnerable adults for pornographic and other sordid purposes. A real history if taken by oral historians without agendas would yield an undiscovered world where police are openly and highly respected by regular folk who are the indigenous and non-indigenous. The non-politically motivated salt of the earth folks you mention who live in areas where police do interventions are truly involved with working together. Some, but not all of those police officers are far removed from thwarting bank robbers and kidnappers in doing service and are I would say highly valued in their communities. Still, there is a valiant service by both aboriginal officers and Queensland Police that is durable and long in tenure."

"Every country has an outlaw who was lionized. America had Jessie James. We had Ned Kelly. Ned Kelly murdered police officers and civilians alike, he was a horse thief and bank robber. Kelly and his gang caused no end of trouble in the colony of Victoria. It was Queensland Aboriginal police trackers who tracked, faced him and his gang in what you Yankees call a 'show down'. The Queensland Aboriginal police trackers were instrumental in bringing the Kelly Gang to justice. So, it wasn't just the day to day community police service. The skill and bravery of these men thwarted one of Australia's greatest villains in the siege of Glenrowan, a shoot-out that went considerably longer than the O.K. Corral."

"Again, this is not to minimize the fact that in earlier days of policing violence did occur by some police officers who were not screened well as candidates. Some of these officers who were ill trained and mentally ill law enforcement officers may have abused their power, use of force, and privilege. One such Constable was William Murray. Constable Murray was responsible for a terrible massacre in 1928."

"In 1928, at least seventeen but possibly seventy aboriginal people were murdered. But it's still not a simplistic story. Murray's acting out may have in part been due to his being traumatized by his service in World War I. I feel dread and pain for those victims of the past. Having said that it is true that most officer did their job well and with great care. In my own opinion and deepest thoughts, it is inaccurate and wrong to categorize Aboriginal citizens for example as murderers and cannibals as some Aussies do! Yes, cases of ruthless murderers and credible reports of cannibalism in the past occurred amongst the Aborigine. But, to say all are like that, is wrong. This is true in categorizing all police as murderers."

"Doc, do not confuse the fact, I feel dread and pain for those victims of the past and in being the law enforcement officer I am I would not hesitate to prosecute such an officer if he/she committed violence against an Aborigine citizen based on their race and culture. But this is the rare exception nowadays and to admonish the police over some bad apples within our rank and file is wrong too. To present the view of police and officers' families who suffer from a bias against all of us is a bias related incident too. It is egregious such current bias is not dealt with as well: I know in your chapter I read on Centurioncide such bias is dealt with but it ought to be an education throughout this particular region."

Cop Doc Dan R: "I can't agree more with you Sgt. Matt that stereotyping any group including police and public safety officers is Centurioncide which I am trying to get noticed and even legally dealt with on a large scale through possible legislation when crimes are instigated against members of our culture and vocation. The same ought to be true of all Aborigine clan members from the onslaught of bias crimes and also the instigation of hatred and the resulting damage to the victim and their family members: Usurping the voices of non-politically motivated inspirational and meaningful experiences that were existentially powerful antidotes coming from Queensland officers is egregious in and of itself. If you could pause, a moment good Commander Matt and tell me, what happened at the Sesquicentennial celebration you were appointed to handle with all the stress and strain I could gain a handle on the event itself as you can recount best. Including as guideposts the Eu-Stress as positive and Dis-stress as potentially painful if that works for you?"

Sgt. Commander Matt Moloney: "I hesitate to share with you how aggravating and nasty some of the people I tried to reach in creating peace and instead had to overcome bypassing their hatred. The premeditated and planned destruction of all we worked for in making the Sesquicentennial celebration a positive and meaningful event for all invited and I mean all was almost overwhelming. It became apparent that forces that triggered dissent were not peaceful and not intended to be solved with anyone's gain. Again, it was a very small but very vocal group of hateful people that clearly meant to cause and express hate and racism against police and public safety as you have coined it, Centurioncide. I believe your chapter in the forthcoming Handbook of Police Psychology ought to be part of training for all communities of police and public safety and obligatory training for community leaders aspiring to propose Community Policing initiatives that work (Kitaeff, 2019). It is Barry Port as the last tracker that comes to mind as a perfect living example as a man who because of ageism as being biased against due to his age, the fact he did not raise any banner abasing and demeaning the police community, the non-indigenous community and neither any of the Aborigine clans that he became the recipient of what is worse than direct hatred, and blind idealization — Apathy! This is true of the big party leaders involved after his quiet and non-egotistical performance but amongst the real world of documentaries and the salt of the earth citizens he remains the legend and as celebrated successfully during the Sesquicentennial he was fully bequeathed honor and respect."

Cop Doc Dan R: "Let me say that such legendary men and women who stood up to ensure peace and cooperation existed amongst different cultures and people. Tracker and Law Enforcement Professional Barry Port has gifted the readers of this book because he resolved his shyness to ensure others are educated by the contribution of the greatest of gifts, his life of service [s]. Again, forgive me if I am wrong but if I am getting it right Sgt. Commander Matt Moloney your success as a commander was not made easy but placed under stress and strain when some saboteurs attempted to sabotage the actual ceremonious celebration. A small group of the saboteurs were those from an Aborigine Clan that were jealous of the honor to be bestowed on Barry Port as one of the Queensland and Aborigine Clans favorites. Further the sabotage as many are were cached. Openness and teasing words proffer hiding the passive aggressive rub of indirect racism you experienced as a Police Officer-Sgt. Commander Matt. You were given the task to arrange this momentous and groundbreaking bridge from your heart of hearts and soulfulness it is very important you and I open this up to memory for us to truly commemorate if I am correct and you willing to share?"

Commander Sgt. Matt Moloney: "Dr Dan Rudofossi Sgt. NYPD I do agree. So here it goes as best as I can whittle down a huge drama into a few lines that cover it all. Let me give some more flesh to the bare bones of this event and my experience of it. I was told I was handed a poisoned Chalice. I was. Besides the other goals I've discussed it was an opportunity to overcome the intra-tribal groups in Coen and what is called the district as follows: The six tribal clans are the Kanju, the Lama Lama, Wik; Umpilla, Mungkan and Olkala. The inter-relationships of each tribe held much of the old tensions as peaceful interactions and niceties emerged in the initial set up of the celebration. Tension and conflict abruptly show up as territoriality disputes axe their way in to situations. Exchanging loggerheads usually cascade into heavy waterfalls and dams that hardly let light and communication flow well when territory is at stake. I however as a copper in North Queensland got some of the Tribal leaders and members to bury the proverbial hatchet. I had intended to bridge the axes of each tribe and clan by having them embrace the meaning of each of them in a major public event."

"In honoring our law enforcement including indigenous law enforcement professionals who served with merit I had invited historians, musicians, retired police officers, elders from each tribe and others involved in justice administration to join in what was an open forum to establish peace and pride in serving justice. I also mobilized a jumping castle for the children, traditional indigenous sports and games, screen documentary shorts sourced from the Australian Film and sound archive: The glory of the events were a trailer for a documentary being made on Australia's last indigenous tracker Barry Port. I had attempted to get the local indigenous dance teams, local artists and various ranger and wildlife groups that work in and around Coen to herald in the fanfare surrounding the celebration of culture and unity while respecting the differences of each clan and the non-indigenous police and public safety community as one front."

Cop Doc Dan R: "So as you've shared earlier with me your passion and excitement overcame your fear of potential catastrophic failure. Tell me how and why such catastrophic fears were overcome and in reality, what would you say provoked it?"

Commander Sgt. Matt Moloney: "I did fear catastrophe. It was the hatred of one leader of the Kanju which in particular stood out above the rest. He actually communicated to many of his fellow clan members that because of my being a police sergeant and different then him I was worthy of being less then who I was and very easily as I learnt was caricatured as a stereotype and not as a human being I am. What was so disturbing to me was not his hatred as an individual but the ability to engender hatred in a contagious manner which spread like the wild fires and cyclones we discussed earlier. This leader was particularly effective and inspired another leader. Combined, they spent their energy on tearing down the bridges I was working hard at building and creating by moving beyond racial finger pointing and imprinting falsehoods and non-sensibility about all police: As if all police were oppressive and hard-core hateful racists including the aboriginal police officials. I again will say the one solace Your operational definition of Centurioncide helped me put things in perspective. Prior to you revealing Centurioncide I was blaming myself. In reality I realize those who hate police officers because of our vocation instigate their own destructive impulses to separate truly caring and compassionate officers from the Aborigine Clans. He enflamed with fear and exclusion any one labeled as outsiders as malevolent. The fact he did influence so many folks negatively appalled my own sensibilities. But overall, he was not as effective in spreading hate and bias as he wished to do. Not everyone he spoke to were enflamed with fear and exclusion of outsiders as malevolent. In fact, a number of people came and spoke to me on the QT, as you NYPD coppers call it. They informed me of what was happening between the lines. The actual cause was a need to control his clan members from an open-minded collaboration in which joint ventures could be forged and worked on with the North Queensland Police and with other Aborigine Clan members. Those who would not do his bidding and he could not control were deemed less than human and therefore could be dis-enfranchised. This is of course not acceptable in a democratic society which is truly even marginally living up to its standards. By trying to confront a bias against one group creating walls of acceptable racism is not tenable when scrutinized by logic and rational approaches attempting to heal genuine wounds and decrease the likelihood of new wounds caused by newer and more virulent strains of hatred and global pre-judgment. In my desire to engage the Kanju and invite the local indigenous members including specialists such as dancers I approached two ladies. One a Kanju elder and the other a young woman who had ties to both Kanju and Ayapathu to enjoin my efforts. I approached them with respect and sensitivity to rituals, mores and avoiding any scent of taboo or overbearing suggestions."

Cop Doc Dan R: "Sgt. Commander Matt Moloney was your approach fully planned before hand?"

Commander Sgt. Matt Moloney: "No, it was impromptu. Doc, in fact it was grabbing hold of an opportunity to enhance rather than to track the Kanju for an opening. I moved within the eco-ethological niche where we were all swimming near a local water hole. I approached both ladies and mentioned I would truly like to showcase skills of the Allkumo Malkatri Dance group to a larger audience if that could work for them. I ensured them the dance team if larger would be an important component of art and ritual for the celebration and both ladies said it was a good idea and would have to run it by the other Dance group and clan leadership."

"There was agreement in principle. Buoyed by this support, I had started to advertise the dance troupe for the ceremony. I had put their names on fliers. Within an advertising blitz as you may call what I aspired to do by getting folks to come and see the rich dance troupe perform I was informed that a wrench was thrust into the picture ripping open my plans. While I was hastily and quite curtly informed that the group vote of all the dance group leadership and elders – some dance group members leaked intelligence to let me know sabotage was at play.

I was told that there was support for the invitation. Some members recognized the rich opportunity proffered by the celebration planed. I had a sit-down meeting of the Allkumo Malkatri dance group and Kanju leaders who were more open to frank communication. I turned up early and waited for members to come in. I had in my style of helping others, arranged the seating and assisted in a preemptive way to ease any burden. It was in this room that a Pinya (an influential young male who is transitioning into becoming an Elder in training) was hiding. That person despite having police officers in his own family had more than a touch of Centurioncide tendencies. Especially biased was his view of Officers who were Caucasian. It was unusual I seemingly serendipitously found him listening in, but ostensibly not participating."

"During the meeting a new agreement was forged and any equipment needed would be organized and paid for with the monies I had raised. It was agreed the dancers would honor the contract with many codicils added. The agreement was achieved in a tense eco-ethological niche. The hidden presence and behavior were underhanded as he remained unseen with intention. The meeting was successful, I still worried a lot in a way that was quite unsettling for me. I thought my not getting reactive and being gentle and persuasive would bridge the gap here and the contract would be honored. I was so wrong and disappointingly I received an email from the female leadership later that their agreement and decision was reversed. They said they would not be coming. I had tried really hard, extending my hand in friendship but I was treated as if I was not there. It was as if no one had heard anything I said, or saw anything I did."

Cop Doc Dan R: "How disheartening and painfully traumatic for you to be treated as an invisible man. As you know, Ralph Ellison the African American writer ironically called the plight of the African man and woman was invisible, when civil rights were being hard won (Ellison, 1952). It is ironic that now as a caring and compassionate humane being and police sergeant you are in turn being treated as if you were a caricature and made invisible by what feels like betrayal to you. The teasing of cooperation blighted by malevolence because you were a police officer and non-indigenous was aggression and egregious as it gets. You held your composure so well again as you and I witnessed in an early dialogue. Like your hero Barry Port, it appears you as he did were subjects of Centurioncide. Having shared with you my opinion from what you've shared with me, I would like to know, how did you respond after the contract was broken twice, once informally, and the second breach, formally?"

Commander Sgt. Matt Moloney: "I called her the senior female elder of the Kanju tribal leadership that I spoke to at the watering hole. A deep culturally aware lady who was very influential in Allkumo Dance Group decision making. When I called to question her changing abruptly in her commitment, I heard triumph in her voice when she told me, they are not coming Matt. Get it through your head!" I got it in my head this opportunity was to dismiss me and discredit the police and community celebration. I was personally and racially targeted as the police officer - out due to my professional and personal status as non-Aborigine. I was later told that after I left, the hidden Pinya came out of his hidden place and had lambasted the group for being so weak. Lambasting them for making an agreement with the hated police oppressors who he said we are still guilty for the massacres of the past. I engendered a real sense of both sadness and anger in me. It angered me because I knew this was a slight against me and the police and we weren't the one dimensional bad-guys spun in his paranoia. But it saddened me more for a number of additional reasons. One reason was I knew that the bullying bigots had won. Some others might come and sympathize with me, even patronize me but no one in the clan or Allkumo Malkatri Dance group was going to stand up against the haters. The bullies had been effective in painting the entire police department as the hated oppressors. This demonstrated to me hate is a surprisingly effective motivating force. Secondly, I thought that a rational mind would win over prejudice, bigotry and hate. I was hurt I was wrong. If reason can't win in this small scale for this event, what implication does this have for the Aborigine clans and the non-indigenous relations in Australia? What implications is there for tackling your concept Dr. Dan of Centurioncide on a global level? Thirdly, because I knew this event would get a high media profile, the Dance group would as well. The opportunity was there to benefit all involved and to bury the hatchet of hate and bias in all directions. No losers, only winners. Yet, hate got in the way once again. These dynamics of bias and hatred genuinely saddened me. Situations like these make provoke questions in me such as, is reconciliation really possible? I think it is and I am able to keep things in perspective. Your chapter on Centurioncide and your own explanation of what it means in real down to earth terms has also gifted me with being able to turn around my skepticism and doubt which has not fully abated. The pain and suffering by a perp who had knocked my teeth out who was a member of this Aborigine clan while performing my duties and responsibilities as a police officer for example was real and personal and not abstract. I do know about rising above, and the power within to use my own compassion, understanding, tolerance and forgiveness. I am asking those who have been intolerant to have understanding and tolerance. I don't think that is unreasonable."

Cop Doc Dan R: "It is not unreasonable to ask for others and wish for them to Stop. Pause and reclaim their own responsibility. You maturely and genuinely expressed your feelings and how and why you are upset and with reason. I can again only imagine how angry and pained with shock and trauma you endured when you planned and genuinely loved to work with the Kanju citizens and were burdened with guilt that was not yours to own. It is sad but also true that the Kanju leadership also tragically held on to the traumatic losses of their past and could not let go. I would reframe your being humane and raising your voice of dissent as not doing any breach in etiquette, or gentility. The poisonous harvest you alluded to earlier again makes superb sense to you and I: Perhaps if we look at the Chalice offered to you as given in poor taste and with dour results. The Chalice was stolen from you and good wine replaced with bad wine because of your profession and race which is racism and adverse treatment as well. But more so the poison is the radical and extremely abusive nature of not letting the clan members decide for themselves based on their own conscience. To advocate and try to persuade the other members of the ill-intentioned and even racist beliefs as the senior leadership had done and no matter how distasteful Sgt. Commander Matt it is not as noxious and toxic as the fact coercion was used to gain conformity. The use of coercion may be legally challenged for example if the law is judicially balanced as bias applying to any group, or individual. Oppression does not rescue one from responsibility or abjure such actions as dismissing you as a fellow human being or those who stood by you by coercion of removing support and funding: That is blatant misuse of authority. How did you resolve this dilemma and go on with the celebration?"

Commander Sgt. Matt Moloney: "I was blessed with the fact that other dance groups including the Ayapathu group in Lockhart River agreed. Again, one Elder admonished other clans for agreeing to join in reconciliation with Queensland police. That one Elder actually called the Mayor of Lockhart and the leadership of the dancers and informed them they would breach traditional lore if they participated with the Celebration. This was not simple information shared but hardly veiled as a serious threat if any one breached this traditional lore! They succeeded in breaking down the wish of many for the sake of victory against dancers being honored along with the celebrators of the Sesquicentennial. The most pressing point is that the celebration while devoid of the authentic dancers who could really shake a leg as the expression goes. I've seen Allkumo Malkatri dance with passion and many times I was doused with inspiration from what I know is one of the best dance teams of the Cape. The irony of it all for me was that the haters took the stance they were the heroes taking up the torch for the little men and women, and with audacity declared it. But they were truly little people for stopping an opportunity for peace and repair. At least in my mind this is true. It is also true in the eyes of some of their own people."

Celebrating 150 Years

Cop Doc Dan R: "In my own perspective, I think the success of the Sesquicentennial is awesome: Awesome, not in spite of those who attempted to sabotage the event but the onward service you provided. Further, those who served during this event as I recall good Sgt were as you informed me, did garner local, international and BBC coverage for the event. It was subsequently mentioned in your State Parliament. It also drew a lot of funding from tourists and other Aussies into North Queensland and so you promoted and provoked real growth for the real salt of the earth citizenry of all backgrounds including the Aborigine clan and tribal members and the non-indigenous cattle farmers and others who live and work in North Queensland. The unsavory and racist diatribes of some tribal leadership did not rue the day or event. Unless you and I let the hatred and ignorance of a few forceful ill-informed lackluster leaders dominate our thoughts and plans to move forward. I choose to not look and frame your awe-inspiring service that way will you reframe your achievement as a gift of service that in the face of adversity still acclaim's a real deference to the ability of healing and solutions to be harvested and drunk from a Chalice of tragic optimism?!?"

Commander Sgt. Matt Moloney: "Yes, I have already found agreement with you and have reframed the Sesquicentennial as service with heart and soul and feel as a NYPD Cop Doc you have joined me in the spiritual celebration with Barry Port, himself a great respecter of religion and elders. You as a Cop Doc and Rabbi, I can say along with Barry and myself are seen as an elder of sorts. You are one who balances the well of peace with a Chalice well filled!"

Cop Doc Dan R: "Your comment is a gift of kind thoughts, thank you. 'Rabbi' in my own faith as a Jewish man and with faith in G-d to me means the Almighty is paradoxically ever present and involved in our day to day lives, our includes all peoples and at all times – G-d is not seen, but felt by all mortal's. Making peace as a goal is one of the most admirable in my faith, I hope to live up to as is being a decent humane being. So, with that said in all my fallibility and under my own humane foible's I think we can also perhaps before closing this dialogue move to another case you said had bothered you with that very stubborn and hate rider Pinya in a vehicle accident you encountered involving a senior Kanju man?"

Commander Sgt. Matt Moloney: "That case happened months after the Sesquicentennial event. There was a man who had a minor traffic accident who was working for the Kalan rangers and on duty at the time. He was related to the culture via marriage. This man had a license that was valid and was not drunk and didn't make any admissions other than he was driving the car. He was at work and had an accident. I suspect but can't conclusively that he fell asleep at the wheel. I attended to the accident investigation fully and thoroughly. I ascertained he was not intoxicated with drugs or alcohol and not charged with any crime, nor did I give him a citation. The Pinya who had been hiding was called to the scene of the accident at my request. I tried to talk to him and he related to me as if I was invisible. I had taken a move to let him know I was present and the law was not in his hand this time, in fact, the investigation of the accident was my authority. I told him the light pole damage had to be sorted through and that he would be given the input to follow up with some damage to the pole. He said he would do his part and we parted ways. Immediately following this police call I had to go the next call at the hospital. As I was in the hospital setting, the Pinya burst into the room and started screaming at me. He projected his hate onto me blaming me for the ills against 'his people and my hate.' Considering, I had let some of his family members off despite being a recipient of some poor behavior and real damage I still tried to appeal and appease this man's situation. I did remain calm and professional as well. The fact I trusted him to follow up, took his word as truthful, and consequentially gave him the benefit of the doubt in my own discretionary use of lawful authority – meant nothing to him. I concluded that little can change with those who have dyed their own attitude with prejudice."

Cop Doc Dan R: "Prejudice against you is no less than, or more than prejudice against any person who receives the painful casting of being placed in a slide show. That view reduces another person into a caricature: Oft times that snapshot is hardly recognizable in exaggeration of what is ill formed sketches of another human being. I have taught forensic psychology and other undergraduate and graduate police and forensic courses for many years. Having been an expert witness at times and having amassed a few hundred arrests and investigations as a uniformed police professional I have dealt with murder, assaults and other heinous crimes. I have learnt to value most an individual differences perspective. My perspective embraces the idiographic. That is who is this individual we are looking at closely."

"Getting to know the individual behind his/her mask of fear and projection helps you as a clinician and investigator learn — the unexplainable becomes very understood and no longer a mystery far removed from insight and responsible accounting. Through this interview you strongly brought insight to an enemy of the free thinking and responsible sobriety of a civically minded society which is racism is not solved by legislating morality as in political correcting agendas. That is no less or more then what one of my clinical supervisors' years ago envisioned as intellectual fascism (Ellis, 1973). Remember Plato gave a very firm and serious caveat for all adherents of his ideal Republic (Bloom, Kirsch & Plato, 2016)."

"The Republic was the uncrossed Rubicon of the cradle of civilization in our Western world that benefits the Aussies, the Americans and the native Americans and the Indigenous Clans and Tribes of Queensland included. Plato's Republic in spite of Professor Karl Poppers critique a few millennia later has not watershed its genius that has lasted the test of timeless value, (Popper, 2002). The Republic preceded even the United States Constitution and for that matter even the Nicomethian Ethics and Democracy his student Aristotle presented in practice and surpassed idealistically speaking (Aristotle, 2014). Plato's caveat is the most relevant to what you present now and with relevance to your brave and courageous stand worth taking Sgt. Matt as a commander with potential to expand way beyond the venue you now serve, *his warning was that the worst tyranny of all to be feared was the unrelenting lack of boundaries in a society run as putatively democratic by the masses,* (Bloom, Kirsch & Plato, 2016).*"*

"The politically forced correction of all cultures and discarding of the age-old traditions of differences I culture is as chilling dystopia as is the forced washing away of differences as cultural incompetence at its worst. Further in adding context to your struggle and success in service in dealing with Centurioncide is in an interview with my colleague and friend Dr. Stanton Samenow points out, "the last refuge of the scoundrel is attacking a person for their race, religion and gender", (Rudofossi, 2017).

"Racism and how antisocial personality disordered individuals search for cults and movements to join which legitimize their criminal behavior at worst and at best their anti-social drama and divisiveness is illustrative in many cases I teach to my students. Jim Jones is one sterling example of an anti-social personality disordered individual who set up others to join his cult in order to provoke the harm he did by slaying other children's animals, such as cats and dogs and then performing the ceremony over them after he slaughtered them as a savior."

"This schizotypal personality disordered person with severe anti-social traits loves to create drama of tragedy and rescue with narcissistic relish. It is their own illness in which they recreate what cannot be remembered often remnants of some earlier repressed traumatic loss. Nonetheless it is not to be ignored."

"It is you who Sgt. Matt that brilliantly and boldly discloses this lack of history by attempting to revise fact and reality over fiction presented as truth: An impoverished pseudo-reality created as Chimeras made public and contagious. Such Chimeras need to be exposed to the light of services day and your celebration of the Sesquicentennial which crossed the Rubicon of separation by shades of darkness with the fulgence of your light-shared. It is complimentary colors and faiths that are well-kept as distinct and valued for each of their own competencies with you at the helm that is in my judgment the most sensible of solutions. As chapter 7 opens, convergence facilitates you as pilot and I as navigator. Moving into a medium lighter than air and granular as sand — storms of a physical turbulence settle into the twilight. A twilight where faith and ritual, unveiling of covers and imagination traverse crime and detection. In this unique space taken in time without defection, protagonists boldly face insight and freedom matched by our responsibleness. Dr. Viktor Frankl the founder of Logotherapy and Existential Analysis posited the West Coast of Freedom is balanced by the East Coast of Responsibility (Frankl, 1978).

"This medium of balance is as keen as the template of justice anointed by the wine of mercy's libation. Let's move ahead into Chapter 7 as we drink a drop of wine and lift the pen to draw justice in the light of the lunar eclipse."

CHAPTER 7

UNVEILING PEAKS: TWILIGHT DIMENSIONS THE UNDULATING WAVES

INTRODUCTION

This chapter rises to grasp the peak of the Sesquicentennial celebrations nadir as it rises to the Zenith of what is existentially the center of life and living. That center holds a promise of transcending duality: Duality of the eco-ethological niche is not neglectful of what is the earthy and mundane moving into the realm of imagination as responsibility matched by inner-sight.

My colleague Commander Sgt. Matt Moloney illustrates the metal of his Scholarly mettle by giving a proposed concept a title, the Inservational man/woman. It is a working and potentially meaningful concept in our motivation to the study what was called up to very recently para-psychology and para-psychiatry.

What has been learned is that the unobservable in the physical realm that was conceptualized as being beyond empirical measurement -

is not! If one limits perception to the haptic tactual, and even what is observable within the primary senses - the aspect of intelligence which is a cornerstone of memory and most critically communication is misconceived as thwarted and delimited as un-researchable and further beyond clinical reach.

For example, emotional intelligence and strategy in hunting, procreation, food storage and territoriality are observable within ethograms. Ethograms are sequential frames of behavior recorded and analyzed painstakingly. Animal intelligence and behavioral patterns also have broadened our understanding of human intelligence and behavioral strategies. An example of compensatory learning such as fishing for termites and warfare strategy among primates to the degree it is observable behavior patterns did not immediately lead to the reality that the overall strategic and intra-cultural learning in primate communities was communicated in eco-ethological niches (Buckhardt, 2005; Berkoff & Goodall, 2002; Goodall, 1971; Lorenz, 1969 & 1997; Morris, 1971 & 1999).

Strategic thinking and novel means of escaping predators as well as predation by predators are all the invisible non-tactic haptic perceptions that clearly become visible via behavioral patterns reinforced and supported and shaped as viable while others are extinguished. Theory informs all research and the questions we ask, modify and revisit often heuristically modifying our insights and sometimes abandoning them for better models and applications. For example, the maternal warmth of some reptilians that are otherwise believed to be eating machines and visceral killers was a bite without teeth when the reality evidenced by painstaking research revealed a covert strategy in Crocodilian eco-ethological niches. That strategy was the finding that juvenile crocodiles in the mouth of the Nile crocodile were being protected from many predators by laying in the protective gulf of jaws with a threatening crushing bite of its mother – communication to other predators were clearly strategic (Griffin, 1981). That larger perspective disabused researchers who were misinformed. Misjudgment which was not based on narrowness of mind via hate, but contraction of the psychological and biological imagination by holding with tenacity to the belief cold blooded reptile means cold blooded killing machine with no parenting skills and innate propensities. Such impoverished beliefs take a while to dismantle and of course relate to cultural mis-attributions and misinformed beliefs as well (Buckhardt, 2005; Lorenz, 1969 & 1997; Morris, 1971 & 1999).

Another close example to the human family is in the greater realm of intelligence as being mainly concrete and based on intellect solely. Emotional intelligence was not developed by Daniel Goleman, but discovered through painstaking research (Goleman, 1995). Emotional intelligence added a new dimension to a very important dynamic in human relations and created a jump in the way humans would view intelligence to incorporate a world hither too unknown, and unseen.

In understanding culture and the sacred nature of different means in which each eco-ethological niche shapes human behavior and beliefs. Mysticism can be framed within a larger context of a need for some meaning and purpose in life. The aspects of human sexual and aggressive drives and their derivatives add a dimension of insight to our observations when human beings are analyzed collectively and of course as individuals (Brenner, 1957): At the NY Psychoanalytic Institute and Society my psychoanalytic cases as supervised individually with Dr. Charles Brenner yielded many deep insights.

In practice the iteration of these unconscious conflicts of ego and libidinal and Destrudo derivatives were ubiquitous and interminable in some patients as the key is not only enlightening a patient of an unconscious conflict but that patient remembering and believing deeply enough in the interpretation of some solution they find in their own narrative as the dynamic of psychoanalysis continues.

So as with emotional intelligence which is still in its nascent stages towards becoming relatively new to science, and our endeavors as scientists we are on a precipice in the region of myths and rituals, fears and repression, and the efficacy of some mores and folkways towards communicating between species and beyond the realm of death (Frankl, 1978 & 2000; Kubler Ross, 1970, 1997, & 2008). The regions of the brain we do know contain vast discrete areas that are well articulated and known to scientists and even to educated lay people that are interested. Yet, the most exciting vistas of the brain is the gestalt of the largely indiscrete experiences of the brain collectively and individually unknown and yet to be explored and investigated.

The indiscreet aspects of the human brain do not counter the discrete facts. For example, the fact that although long term memory can be located in the hippocampus region of the brain does not exclude the fact that the mind which uses the hippocampus is much more expansive then just long stored memories accessible to conscious awareness. In fact, it is non-sensible to speak of the brain being the location of memory alone in any discrete area and localized in the brain for the brain is impacted by and impacts all the body systems (Van Der Kolk, 1987 & 2015). Each branch connects with another such as the neurological to the cardiovascular and digestive system with the endocrine system and so on. The brief aspect of sharing with you the biology of the brains complexity which is quite observable directly and with microbiological precision and histology in enormous and encyclopedic detail is important to keep in the back of our mind. Yet, the biology of the brain includes the psychological and psychiatric sequela which is far beyond the reach of this chapter: For our purposes the point that you can't localize the humane components of memory into discrete anatomical regions of the brain and psychophysiological behaviors is crucial. More pressing is the fine point that mysticism and religious faith will find many connections that can be correlated with stimulation of discrete regions of the brain but that is not the full picture or gestalt. We are much broader and dynamic then one reductive model whatever model is and no matter how much investment put into that model – in reality and honestly speaking.

Let's return for a moment to the region of experience which encompasses reality. Reality is what we are aware of in our conscious thinking

Unveiling Peaks 169

and also what is below the surface of our awareness, that of the unconscious dimension of our knowledge: Within a psychoanalytic perspective wishes that are unfulfilled re-emerge. This re-emergence is presented through conflict and often symptoms that emerge in a veiled tapestry. This motif where unconscious wishes provoke fulfillment are usually of a sexual and aggressive derivative and rooted in such drives that are called Destrudo and Eros. Some are manifest and can be understood without much fanfare and others are symbolically presented in motifs that appear bizarre to the dreamer. Such bizarre and episodic segments we barely remember and without psychodynamic and/or existential analysis we may never make full sense of irk the dreamer, the thinker, and the realm of those who are more spiritually inclined.

Remember that dream like states can at times co-exist in wakefulness and also sleepfulness. The rich motifs of the Aborigine clans and tribal mores are filled with spirits and as described animism where differing animals and forces converge with and pronounce omens and also portend reality. For a psychoanalyst this is not disturbing and not jarring for the reality and values conserved by each participant within any culture as lived and valued collectively (Jung, 1961) is hidden and yet open to analysts who can decipher the cues, codes and condensed presentations. This is also true of the psychodynamic and existential analysis of the individual patient who participates in the journey and hard trail of therapy as treatment. As is true in scientific observation, and in clinical applications of science - correcting an individual's journey is not the venue of the scientists including psychoanalysts and existential analysts — it is anathema to both paths.

The latticework of culture is implacably intertwined with the drives of sexuality and aggression and their byproducts of sublimation, as Freud pointed out a century ago (Brenner, 1957). The rich and beautiful design of each Aborigine clan: Clan is used here in the context of a tight knit extended community with sharing of culture and values in an estimate of what can be thought of as an extended family. Clan establishes respect and support of a standard of certitude notwithstanding pressures to modernize, and transform to standards which breach the sacred values of the Aurukun, a small indigenous community – it is their strength to survive as a culture that lives. Antipathy experienced by each individual clan, and many members result in the energy that transcends forced changes and motivates creative etching of their artists and healers who dance, draw and teach the values of each.

As with all cultures that survive and have thwarted the process of becoming extinct, the conflict with unconscious wishes within totems and taboos emerges in the art work and defenses against outsiders. This is witnessed in this chapter too. In trying to connect to the travails of the Aborigine Clans the dark side always is an occlusion of light entering in to shadow the movement and dance of each member.

The shadow needs to be respected. If the shadow is not respected and valued the taboos become the first warning signs given which are usually benign. If the shadows in the culture that is threatened are still trampled on, violations may be answered with inane, fatalistic and intractable consequences.

In this chapter Commander and Churchill Scholar Sgt. Matt Moloney and I will try to shed light into the shadow and not lose our own shadows while we journey toward redeeming the sanguine texture illuminating the Aborigine clan sorrows. Sorrow where the vanquished and those who in effigy will never hear the sundry sounds and experiences of life's future inexorable march as their paths move forward. A case is presented where the missing person saunters into the ineffable and inimitable area in each of us which remains hidden beyond language and interred in what we can call with caution the twilight dimensions - where undulating waves of passion seeking equipoise of calm reside tensely and in flux.

Commander Sgt. Matt Moloney: "Doc, I will share with you a story, 'nay', better call it a fable, (pausing) a myth in which the Aurukun Clan which is a small indigenous community live by."

"My introduction to Aurukun Station was when I was a constable which is the same as police patrol officer in the late 1990's to early 2000's. During my tours of duty there was little public interest and even less media interest than there is now in Aurukun. Today there are up to fifteen police per platoon that patrol and investigate crimes in what is nowadays known as Aurukun township. Keeping it real, remember Aurukun is swallowed by the larger Cape York region, which in my days on patrol in total called for four police officers to handle. When I was stationed there the Sergeant had a house and family. All three constables including myself were single. We all lived and stayed in the barracks. The barracks were converted from an old police station, and a rat filled hovel it was. Each constable officer had his/her separate room. One day when all of us constables were off duty we were sitting in the back of the barracks and felt a nice wind breeze through the bushes and trees. If we heard a phone ring it would echo and reverberate into the backyard of the barracks. In the backyard, we all could hear and immediately respond. One afternoon, we suddenly heard a howl coming from around us. That howl jarred us all and it felt as if a pack of dogs were coming on top of us. The movement was fast and direct. It was if a command from some source directed the pack to howl at once."

"I felt chills that were as undefinable as my chest hairs lifting up, and tense. Mind you, I am not talking about a dog barking loud and others following suit. What happened is maddening because the noise was beyond ambient - I and my peers heard the howls from three hundred and sixty-degree angles. It had seemed that Aurukun was dominated by canines and not human beings. In fact, due to inter-breeding many dogs appear to be hybrids of Dingo and local breeds. As you know Dingo's don't bark, but they can howl like haunted soldiers. The howl of the Dingo hybrid can cause the Spartan in a North Queensland cop to freeze while standing his/her ground."

Cop Doc Dan R: "With your eidetic memory still strong it appears that eco-ethological event triggered a photo-auditory graphic memory still fully intact in you. I imagine from your description that your own trembling began when you heard the howls all converge in a chilling blast that permeated your very hearts rhythm and the bowels of your warrior soul! Correct me if I am wrong?"

Commander Sgt Matt M: "Hey Doc, Mate, your right on target because every skinny, mangy, hairless part dingo camp dog howled from every direction. I don't mind telling you Doc, I felt the howls more than somewhat disconcerting. I also remember another copper who didn't hide his upset at all. He suddenly shook his head like a bulldog needing as if letting go of some tense spring in his neck. I said, "Hey, what the heck is going on?" He said as true as you and I are real human beings Doc, "Someone just died. It's probably a murder or perhaps a suicide because no one I know in town is seriously sick or dying. I would suggest Constable-mate that you and me get ourselves ready to respond."

"As if on que, the phone rang. He answered it. I heard him say in a smooth soothing way, "mmm-hmmm, right oh, don't worry. The purple house, eh?" He paused after speaking on the phone, and he looked directly at me. Pausing he now told me, "I told you Matt, get your gear on and let's take a look at the murder scene. There has been another murder." Doc, we got there and confirmed that some poor soul had their life taken prematurely. A life stolen by violence, it was murder. The offender admitted and fully confessed to the murder he committed. This sensibility from an eco-ethological niche is understood as preventing his own murder by vengeful relatives and friends by ensuring he is charged and locked up first. So, we locked this sad fellow up and proceeded on getting charges filed and the prosecution going. The entire procedure was expedited quite smoothly. The next day although the prosecution was already underway, I had not forgotten the unsettling experience the previous afternoon and spoke to the community police officer who was a full-blooded initiated officer who knew the mores and traditions of the Aurukun people very well."

"The officer said to me, "Hey, newbie don't you know that the dogs howling meant someone died?" I had been a bit shocked at the idea that he was so certain that these dogs were the soothsayers of death and foreboding to officers that their howls meant death occurred usually by violent means."

Cop Doc Dan R: "I can imagine it was disconcerting for you to hear the hybrid dingo canines would synchronize communicating with each other and howl with such power. Also, what seems to be forewarning you is that the constables were aware and fully in synch with the Aurukun clan wisdom that howls portending such malevolent forces was extant. This included the murderer at lodge, if I got it right which for you Sgt. Matt would understandably be doubly perplexing?"

Commander Sgt. Matt M: "That is correct Doc! Yes, when the community police officer who was tenured and fully informed by experience with the Aurukun clan and their beliefs shook his head at me again and subtly let me know he felt that I, having experience in indigenous communities ought to know that the dogs were special I felt foolish. I somehow was expected to know the howling hybrid dogs had given warnings and cries of foul play to us as local coppers. The community police officer said to me,

"Constable Matt Moloney don't you know when someone is killed, the dogs can see the spirit – strait way (meaning in Aurukun culture straight away, or immediately). That is why they howled because they knew. They had seen the spirit."

Cop Doc Dan R: "Seeing the murdered victim's spirit is a powerful 'myth to live to live by" to quote Joseph Campbell. The dingo canine hybrids howled. A howl which was a hoot and a signal of communion with the victim as an Aurukun member spirit. The motif of the guardian dog is one of the collective unconscious that dates the Jewish commentary Rashi who said the sign the Almighty gave Cain after murdering Able that he was to follow to the cities of refuge from vengeance and retribution was no less than a dog. In the song of the Universe of King Solomon it is clearly a dog that ends the entire parable of eloquence and rhythm where all is metaphor and portrayed by each animal soul as he/she individually and collectively is associated with soulful qualities (Scherman, 2004). I imagine as the departing soul was flying up to heavenly spheres the Aurukun wisdom held on to that type of myth as wisdom to live by. Note Cerberus who guarded the netherworld or the doors to perdition or salvation and only tackled by no less than the mythical superman of Ancient Greece known as Hercules. It seems from your fellow community officer's wisdom having learned the Aurukun myths, not so different than the myth spun in the master sleuths, The Hound of the Baskervilles notoriety, was quite sanguine They knew the reality of the murder it seems good Sgt. Commander Matt Moloney, and that is no Baloney!"

Commander Sgt. Matt M: [Grin shown with some legitimate restraint] "What he meant was that the dingo's, dogs and half breeds howled at as they saw the departing soul walking around. They knew as canines that it was a violent death this person suffered. The person's life was taken before his time. Having giving me his lecture on what he felt all coppers should know, he simply turned on his heels, looked at me with what I felt was pity for my naïve lack of knowledge sacred to the Aurukun people, and continued with his duties. I can't say I had any rational answer as to why he as much as the Aurukun clan members believe this as reality and common sense. I do believe him and the members of the clan who reassured me it was true. What I did witness and can remember even now as I repeat the event and recall my senses when it happened many years ago was the howling all converging. I also remember the crime scene as being beyond doubt. It was seriously weird Doc Dan R! I hope you can shed light on this legendary howling of the dogs when foul play such as murder is committed in Aurukun? I mean is this myth I admit I experienced and cannot forget what the Aurukun folks believe as hybrid Dingo dogs being able to truly sense reality such as murder? Do they and the Aurukun people have such a bond? Is it really possible scientifically to have such uncanny ability to forewarn us coppers as to murder, suicide and even death?"

Cop Doc Dan R: "Well that myth may be one the Aurukun people live by as did the Community Police Officer who experienced these other times and has given it the credibility of being true. I can't answer as to your own beliefs and faith or lack of it that these hybrid dingo canines can actually pick up on murder and then disclose in their own grief and communion with humans. But it does appear that a reversal of the so-called stream of conscious awareness that denies what is mystical and spiritually possible for the Aurukun people and the officer who is a community police officer hold as sacred. It holds an inverse reciprocity by not defying but holding on to the reality which is humane experience that a power greater than one's own limited senses exists. The power of faith against forces that are brutal and senseless such as murder and the murderer who commits such a heinous act against another human being."

"This power is not other worldly but quite of this world and meaningful within the world of the Aborigine Clan Aurukun citizen and community police officer on the other hand. Meaning the choice to believe goes beyond the language and stricture of a macrocosm made dictum and dogma — no pun intended – such as non-Aborigine society that blindly and dogmatically rejects the inter-communication between these hybrid canines and the humans who cohabit the eco-ethological niches with them."

"Creative generativity reverses the 'so called pattern of progress' by illustrating skepticism is sometimes no more than hardly veiled arrogance in denial of what is alternative perception and paradigms to mundane vistas of reality, (Jasper, 1959). Symbols and myths give motivation and fuel to life and living. Modern thinking whatever that appellation truly aims at may be an outgrowth of what Lasch called the age of Narcissism which only allows the droll and drowning of essence by a homogenous view of life and who one is like in the mirror of their own image (Lasch, 1978). How boring and trite my dear Sgt. Matt Moloney. You are not and you have the ability to question and come to your own solutions. The hubris and narcissistic overlay of thinking one can correct a culture to accommodate one's own tradition of demanding so-called modern ideas for change as better, and in fact superior to a more sanguine sobriety."

"Sobriety of traditions is what staves off the rush to discard what for generation to generation has held sensible. Change forced is dangerous at best, and the true fascism of our times. It is power not of stubbornness but of sensibility from a deep rooted ethological-ethnological ecological wisdom that allows you and your community police officer to query and trust your own intuitive senses and reflections to understand a reality that now can make sense as to your experience with the case of the murdered Aurukun victim and his howling Dingo canine community members."

"In your query and open mindedness as a pilot you are exploring and I with you, that any plans to correct the Aborigine Aurukun clan's custom was balder-dashed by those of the Aurukun clan consciously provoking growth in the non-indigenous community. This counter-intuitive wisdom works and the most open-minded educators and learners, the police and public safety officers of Queensland Police Service, such as you and the community police officer learnt well."

"Your growth here lay in the fact that the community police officer from Aurukun himself was truly an observer who intuited and participated in his own growth. His development within the eco-ethological niche he worked and lived in was the powerful shaping influence and motivational force in his center of existence. If you think about the time an officer spends daily in his work environment, he/she truly lives in the community he/she polices for at least one third of his life as lived in his precinct or police service area. By understanding the culturally rich motifs and picking up on what has offered by the traditions of the people he lived among if you prefer to look at his service experience that way he was taught by experience, and no doubt the Aurukun elders. This is no less than your learning in your eco-ethological niche of living and service among the Aurukun people. For example, if you prefer to view your experience of the howling dogs associated with an alert of death in the air so to speak – then when you hear the synchrony of a cacophonous howling of dingo canines you too will know this signals death and likely murder. The qualifying wisdom is if you are willing to understand that you gained very useful knowledge by another community that you lived and experienced life within the scope of your life. How rich and interesting this experience is for you, for me and by extension of opening their minds the reader as well. The pause in learning about the community police officer's gainful knowledge, remembering that he too, and of course myself did not know this important piece of folklore and myths within the Aurukun clan. The community police officer learnt by accepting the local wisdom and folklore and using it to his best application by gaining ground and insight for himself too. He did not fight their wisdom but like you, took their knowledge and gained for himself unique and prized wisdom. It is telling too, that community officer forgot one key factor you did not, humility. Your humility serves well as a scholar for he too learnt as you did and was once uninformed about this rich myth among the Aurukun. Finally, for the skeptical and for your purpose and his regardless of the real cause of the canine dingo hybrids howling they do howl when they sense of pick up on dead or dying human beings. Since you asked, I will tell and add a very real and tragic peace to our dialogue in which I have responsively answered your query about this perplexing issue of dogs howling. If that makes sense to you Sgt. Matt?"

Sgt. Commander Matt Moloney: "It does make a lot of sense and I am absorbing what appears to me as an overall arching Eco-Ethological Existential Analysis if I am correct?"

Cop Doc Dan R: "You are correct and quite adeptly caught on to what I am doing here which is lay out the existential analysis as the overarching umbrella of the Eco-Ethological Existential Analytic Approach. The key here is that tragedy is a dear friend and colleague who died suddenly at 51 years of age, Rabbi Moshe Hillel Sperber who shared his thoughts about our query into the howling of dogs and clearly told me in the Talmud which is the deepest commentaries of the Torah with many aspects of an oral traditions wisdom over five millennia alive. Part of the living history of my own faith clearly speaks about the dogs howling as portending death. I asked Rabbi Moshe Hillel Sperber who as me received Semicha or Rabbinical Ordination by the Biala Rebbe (Biala, Rudofossi & Sperber, 2017) as to why this is believed as so? We discussed the eco-ethological interpretation earlier but we moved into the fact that animals as we have been finding out have communication with us and none is closer then the dog as domestic. As a rooster tells us it is the dawning of the morning the dog tells us to be-aware so that their vested interest in us as the leader of their pack is well guarded and we don't fall into the trap of the Angel of death. If we listen to our dogs, we are given the heads up so we don't lose our head that is metaphor and is-real! Although Jews are quite different in religious belief few would argue the Torah is not a sacred text. My point is that for whatever reason we actually reach together we have already plummeted many possibilities for the answer as to why the dogs howl, with no supernal one yet, the how of this soulful bridge created between human and dog is unbreakable."

"Using knowledge of folklore, myths and mores seems to me a lot wiser than downgrading and marginalizing such wisdom. It also serves you and other public service officers to full advantage in the domain of public service and safety. Finally, as your wisdom grows in this area of mythology among the Aurukun people the wisdom you offer in tutelage and gaining ground among the Aurukun is almost guaranteed by imitating and then incorporating their wisdom. More so, I suggest not apologetically or correcting your new gained wisdom."

"On a cultural level if we consider your unconscious level of growth it remains somewhat mysterious but not completely as we explore what is known and has been studied at length as emotional contagion. From a social psychological perspective suggestibility, and mass hysteria becomes reified or made tangible and concrete to each member as a reinforcement roughly occurs and co-occurs making certain behavioral patterns more durable by a model of reinforcement."

"From an existential perspective which centers the eco-ethological biopsychosocial including psychodynamic influence on learning certain behaviors as effective and others as not so worthy: Combine the noetic dimension that is not impacted and influenced by all these other factors preferably viewed as empirically connected, the observing participant transcends the eco-ethological influences and the faith one has is super-ordinate to such influences cognitively and spiritually. In other words, your ability to transcend your own training and learning modules to learn new ones transmitted within your own cultural sphere is a core element in your own abilities."

"Your ability to specifically discard what you've been taught from grade school which would label such associations that the Aurukun people made and even your own witnessing such associations as absurd. The superstitious peer police officer is perhaps what you can view the community police officer and even yourself if you accept and foreclose on this paradigm: His teaching you the introduction of this cultural sphere was intra-eco-ethological and ethnological. Remembering again, the community police officers learning this insight was observed by his own observation as an extended participant associate of the Aurukun clan."

"He courageously transcended his own sphere inter-eco-ethologically and ethnographically experiencing and introjecting the animistic aspect of his adapted culture. This Aurukun culture values and prizes the communication of yet another human to animal, and animal to human communication. This level of communication while complex adds to the insight of education and field observations use to spur research. It appears the lattice developed between the officer and the Clan members here is inter-dependent and intra-dependent via specialized behavior and emotion from an eco-ethnological sphere that is deemed useful in both communities. Both communities meaning the Aurukun people and the Queensland Officers. It also gives a sense of the roots of religion and spiritual vitality that moves in ebbs and flows in what we loosely call and identify as the richness of faith."

"In my view it again circles around as you put it the combined howls of "three hundred and sixty degrees" which is inestimable and infinite. What I mean is in your experience as time halts space with intra and inter-personal communication and relations to not only be respected but used is an act of faith. Faith transcending our obsession with empirical reality as what is only concrete and hardly abstract."

"My suggestion is that is the power within you as a police commander and Sgt embracing your own values and traditions without losing touch for example with the wisdom of the Aurukun is invaluable and rich as a leader in policing."

"Speaking of leadership, much is learned from tracking by LEO Barry Port an elder himself and much is learned in his methods which as I shared with you. It reminds me of the value of listening actively for King Solomon's Ring to reverberate as Konrad Lorenz took a bold move in educating himself and then the world about the power of observation and measuring behavior as it naturally unfolded, (Buckhardt, 2005; Lorenz, 1969 & 1997; Morris, 1971 & 1999). In fact, these canines may be responding to the learnt ethological mechanism of not eating human beings as prey food and alerting humans to remove such carcasses by their own learning within human-feral canine dingo dog interactions. Reverberating as the howls of mixed canine dingoes at their full circle informs us as much as them a response, they have conditioned humans to do is at least another plausible explanation to be explored. As a full circle it may be worthwhile to say we can leave causality to future research or to simply take a leap of faith in the wisdom of a guidance and power beyond our own. Let's now return to the legend of the missing girl you hinted at when we began this dialogue."

Sgt. Commander Matt Moloney: "As you like Doc. First, I want to pause as your interpretation does help me place that experience clearly in perspective. I can think with a reflection on my wisdom to accept I was able to learn not to feel naïve about the fact I could not have known what

I did not learn before I had learnt it. It is actually a nice addition for my other grown insight that I have a more open mind I credited myself for."

"Now to return to the missing person case it is crucial to understanding a challenge to what is known as Murri-Justice' when this missing Person of Interest [POI] was promulgated. 'Murri-Justice' in reality translates into a Toyota troop carrier with strong young men showing up at the POI's residence and kicking seven shades of shit out of him and perhaps killing him. If someone begins to embrace Murri rules and living in the Murri framework and abiding by their customs and eco-ethological niche they are subject as any member to their sense of real justice. It is a harsh and unparallel justice exacted at violating their taboo of decency and civil rules of their own societal structure."

Cop Doc Dan R: "However, like your Murri clan the American mafia operates in a commonality across cultures and has a similar sense of justice. When Mafia-Justice rituals are broken by an associate of that mafia family which is similar to an associate in the Murri clan vengeance is often exacted. The 'Murri-Justice' for violating rules sounds just like what happens for violating Mafia family rules. Violating mafia rules mean that you take a beating for disobedience. Special Agent Joseph Pistone aka Donnie Branco who infiltrated the Mafia explained this best to me (Pistone, 2017): For an associate within a crime family is never a family member, but is a cautiously trusted outsider who is allowed to be privy and assist the family's needs."

"The punishment for the Murri associate is parallel with the Mafia associate who violates the rules of the family. Taking a beating is a gentle slap on the face of shame and accepted as a warning. Further if the violation is deemed beyond instruction, the violating associate may pay with his/her life. If the associate's life is to be taken because he has gone beyond the rules of tolerance and mafia boundaries, he is informed, 'it is nothing personal'."

"How one's own life being whacked away by a group of Murri soldiers or mafioso foot soldiers being nothing to take personally is hard to figure out? But it suffices to understand this is acceptable within the walls that hold that culture intact. It is within the ecological niches that have shaped this protective defense that ethological sensibility the profane taking of a violator's life is purportedly to be better understood. No matter how unsavory and sanguine in a bloody mess type of way, this way of life is nonetheless sensible for the members of that culture. It is not judgment of that culture I can do or perhaps you good Sgt. Matt M., but you and I can witness stalking and take down as a result also not judging ourselves too harshly too when police try to gain custody of such perpetrators of our own cultural boundaries. I think a key to gaining respect and more intelligence within this community is to own we cannot change that culture from without, and perhaps even within, for those who abide by its rules and its prohibitions – are not likely to change because outsiders deem it wrong."

Sgt. Commander Matt Moloney: "I see that point well and in fact, what had saved the snuffing out of this POI by Coen Murries was the fact that he was with a Kowanyama girl who had Kowanyama people. The clan was not Coen clan warrior-based folks. When it came to threats within the family or extended family structure the Coen network of soldiers did not care as much for a Kowanyama family, or the missing girl as they would one of their own clan members child."

"I had received an email from a police officer in Kowanyama informing me she had two indigenous ladies come to the front counter of their police station informing her that a Kowanyama elder was on the way to Coen. The case was not one you may receive in NYPD Precincts or your Det. Squads. The case we received was of an elder who received a vision that the missing girl had traveled on sacred ground. She was seen in this vision to be in a cave. The actual email content of this astute officer sent to me was as follows,

> "I mention this because the 'vision' has gained some traction in the Kowanyama Community. There is a strong belief that she has been 'found' because of this vision. If this elder attends the Coen Station

Unveiling Peaks 183

please just be aware that the vision is being taken very seriously by the missing persons family and the broader community here."

Cop Doc Dan R: "So if I am getting it right this twilight dimension is eerily leaking in from intelligence garnered by this officer in the Kowanyama Station. Her medium of communication, intelligence gathering and operations are at the level of impasse due to the mystical beliefs underlying a missing girl being seen in a vision which is sacred by the Kowanyama clan members. As disclosed on what we call in the NYPD policing as the QT, or on the cuff of informants the vision within the community was shared as some secret surreptitiously with this officer and by extension again to you as the commander and in charge of the overall search to find this missing girl and we were told the family refused to allow the missing girls image to be used. If so a true cuff on your ability to investigate when the members of the clan clam up on all leads must have been stifling I imagine good Sgt. Commander Matt Moloney?"

Sgt. Commander Matt Moloney: "Exactly without missing a heartbeat Doc, I forgot you made a few hundred collars saddled in your street crime days in Bed Stuy and Fort Green mid 1980's and early 1990's on the midnight express with no civilian complaints to boot. [I nod in assent silently and actively listening to my colleague Sgt: Sgt] In fact even this girls' relatives clamed up to use your metaphor. Her family members held back giving us the photos to post of this girl. The lack of photos hindered us. We needed photos so we could get public assistance to find and locate her alive, or tragically recover her body. As we both know the timing of press releases is more than moderately significant, time used well is usually the measure between life and death by mobilizing all the eyes and ears outside of the Police world to inform us. Informing us as to a citizen in trouble and potential whereabouts is on a timer where nothing is more pressing then a missing girl who disappears in a flash. Traditional minded indigenous clan members have taboos against using photographs of dead people and even images of living people especially of their families. In my need to get out missing persons fliers I didn't expect any impasse. I was mistaken in this easy pass from my police colleagues. My colleagues from the Kow police ran it past the relatives of this missing girl and were told the family refused to allow the missing girls image used. This copper in Kow took on the role of victim liaison officer closest to the family and while I thought this refusal unusual, I initially held back from applying more pressure. I decided the greater wisdom was to leave the next move up to and the ownership of my colleague in the Kow Police."

"I was bothered and did not piece together the whole picture at first. The picture that emerged was that the family may create a disruption if we used an image of the missing girl. If we used such a picture that would breach a traditional taboo. From what I know, the family *were not actively anti-police.* They knew that if anyone used home style vigilante 'justice' that most citizens would call a beating, that this would divert police resources away from the missing girl. It would also cause them to become the focus of an investigation that could very well result in a prosecution. It was also clear that they were concentrating on finding their girl through their own methods. They didn't think the police were on the right track. They believed our actions were ineffective and pointless. In turn they went to their default setting to use an analogy and consulted whom they believed to be their real ultimate authority which was what they call, the Dreamtime: The ancestors. Those insightful individuals who can commune with the spirits who live in the Dreamtime. The message communicated to me was that while the family did not intend to actively hinder my investigative work, they believed that cooperation with me was not worth breaching taboos. In other words, in their minds I was unlikely to get results, so taking the risk would be less than optimal for them within their cultural eco-ethological niche."

"The metaphysical link to the missing girl and the area Coen centered on a hub which included a unique and special man whose nickname is 'Dundee'. He is a deeply spiritual Murri Man and his nickname 'Dundee' was given to him long before the famous Australian movie came out.

There was also a traditional and spiritual woman associated to Dundee who had contact with the family of the missing girl and part of the Kowanyama clan, Marilyn. Marilyn became the liaison between Dundee, the police in Coen, and informally the missing girl's family. Dundee is the traditional owner of that land, which for the purposes of ritual and tradition makes him the custodian of that place. Eco-ethologically speaking because of their status in the Aboriginal hierarchy, they had special customary duties and responsibilities to assist work through the spiritual quagmire the girl was in existentially. The need for Queensland Police to assist in ways that were different was pressing us and specifically me as the commander to assist with finding this missing girl. Are you with me so far Dr. Dan as cop doc and Det. Sgt?"

Cop Doc Dan R: "Well I haven't been in the saddle for a long time but I am with you Sgt. Commander Matt. If you can educate me about the interplay between this cross-cultural and inter-eco-ethological speciation or specialization that shadows the indigenous ways and means of communication it would help me. If you can focus on how Dundee and Marilyn managed to find and rescue this missing girl, or assist in the recovery effort I think we all would gain tremendously in understanding the interplay of power and existential dynamics. I mean in a way that can assist police and community relations in preliminary investigations, especially as we explored earlier when looking at the meaning of the howling dogs. Search and rescue could be assisted as you and I know. Especially, if kidnapping or even homicide occurs and recovery of the body is the best achieved and certainly that recovery of the body is very important to give peace to the survivors. Does this work for you good Commander Matt?"

Sgt. Commander Matt Moloney: "It does and let me give you an overall view of indigenous power structures. Indigenous clan power dynamics are embedded in the world of mysticism. Such dynamics exist and operate in what is called the Dreamtime which includes the invisible spirit country which covers the world like a vast magnetic field and in which each spirit has its own identity so to speak. In the English-speaking world, the word role does not really cover the vast background of what they mean in the aboriginal eco-ethological framework. I'll have to give you the briefest of insights into the complicated and yet fluid world of aboriginal spirituality, related customs, traditional structures and roles. The Dreamtime, often called the Dreaming is central to the Aboriginal world view. It is the creation time, but that time has never ended and therefore Aboriginal people do not see time as linear. It is a place where dead people go. But it is not like heaven or hell, because while there is consequences and some aspect of afterlife like karma there is no punishment and people retain much of their human soul. In that sense it's more like the Ancient Greek Underworld. It is the place where spirits including non-human ones live but is not really a netherworld because it is not lost to this world. The Dreamtime is with us and surrounds us and affects us all the time. It in my own viewpoint is somewhat like Alice's Wonderland and Rod Serling's Twilight Zone: It can be understood as a parallel universe within a paradigm of Quantum Physics", (Bettelheim, 1976; Parisi, 2018; Serling, 1990).

"It is all around us and impacts on each one of us, and we in turn effect it purely by perceiving it and the basis of the material world. To some degree it is recognizable, and in the same way that something upside down is a distorted sense of what we mostly would call reality. That distorted reality is recognizable in a dream or nightmare. It is so chaotic and surreal in placement where the unreal is normal, where down could be up and one can really talk only about probability and not certainty. In every community there is someone who is recognized as having a link with the Dreaming and associated Spirit world. The man who had the vision was one of those people. While not completely correct titles and descriptions, a person who performs the role of linking the Dreaming with the material world has a mix of some of the power of a witchdoctor, sorcerer and a shaman. A person who has that link with the 'Dreaming' is someone who can observe and perceive things that others don't and therefore has insight."

"They see and consequently can interpret, put in context and understand things that others cannot. There are so many concepts that are crammed together that to use a mash of English word titles is the only way to grip the concept. I'll combine the two concepts of insight and observation and suggest the title of Inservational person. The sequence of events follows a pattern. That pattern for example is as follows: An Inservational person has a vision and that vision passes information to the Kowanyama police and also Marilyn. An Inservational person cannot just come onto land that they do not have a connection with. Only and unless they are granted permission of the traditional owner of that land that he/she may, or may not actually own the land in the Australian legal sense of what that land ownership means. Dundee was not an Inservational man. But as the traditional owner and custodian of the spirits of that place had a duty to introduce any visiting Inservational person to the spirits of his country area. Those spirits include human spirits of dead heroes and human ancestors, totemic part-animal like ancestors who are like werewolves. It could be were-Kangaroo's for example. Also shape changers and other non-human spirits live in the Dreaming. *It's dangerous going into the Dreaming*! Few Inservational people do so, choosing to get spirits to act for them in his parallel spiritual dimensional world. Spirits that at time seem to be malevolent are actually good in nature and purpose."

"At other times spirits may visit and appear to be beneficent but are malevolent in their true character. Pretense and saboteurs abound in the Dreaming. Some situations can be growth provoking and add to insight and observational skills related to the spirit world. The Inservational person was entrusted with performing a spiritual search for the missing girl. He did so via communicating with his spirits who act for him in the dreaming. Dundee was given the duty to facilitate that communication by introducing the Inservational person and the spirits he brings with him to help with the search for the missing girl. The search is brought specifically to the guardian spirits of the country he is the traditional custodian of."

Cop Doc Dan R: "In the duality of the identity of Dundee where he became the traditional custodian of the guardian spirits as custodian his visits are by spirits that at times seem to be malevolent and are actually good: At other times spirits that may visit and appear to be beneficent, are malevolent in true character. Dundee is entrusted with facilitating communication with the spirits of the dead world and of ancestors to seek the whereabouts of missing people. *Situations are ambiguous as he is subject to attacks ranging from benign to violent.* Dundee's identity mode was nestled and shaped by his tasks of tracking through another level of the spirit world the were-animals. The were-animals to me sound like were-wolves and forgive me but vampiric creatures not of the material world: Not all are malevolent in the mythology of the Indo-European cultural motifs. Were-animals are not of the purely spiritual world as well. Were animals being close to the deceased spirits and come from a place in which the guides and mediums such as Dundee cannot enter fully. Neither can he perform treatments such as dream analysis. Dundee is not an analyst, certainly not a psychoanalyst or existential analyst. The spirits and were-animals can inform him of the mysteries he is readied to be privy to. Being privy to the underworld or netherworld is not without cost. It is quite costly if the wrong spirit or guardian of a story known as Spirit Stories are malevolent. If the Spirit Story is malevolent it can sabotage or terrorize the guide. Is this correct teacher and guide Commander Sgt. Matt Moloney?"

Sgt. Commander Matt Moloney: "Yes, it is also true in this world of spirits that the rite ritual, incantations and most important songs used well and with good intention will bring the right formula to fruition. If the formula proposed and delivered is not used right it can backfire and the Spirit Stories endangering the participant of that specific Spirit Story. The missing girl has her own Spirit Story journey she can become lost in. Remember that the Spirit Story actually fits as does identity modes as you presented in the world of trauma and loss you are a guide as cop doc in."

"As you've shared with me, the personality differences of each officer are shaped and molded within eco-ethological niches as you've taught me in my becoming a trained and professional peer support officer. Doc, using your own eco-ethological existential analytic method it makes a lot of sense in understanding this Spirit Story. It especially makes sense for the Aborigine Clan: The reason that made sense is because the Spirit Story is exactly where the missing girl was lost. It is given context with the Inservational person, having an impact and understanding as a unique and accepted guide. The critical factor in finding this missing girl and having the POI assist us is that spirit and story intermingle within an ecological niche. It is also shaped by survival motivation that is unique to each region, clan and community which your method is the only one I know that respectfully and socratically seeks insight and observation for the guide who tracks the Spirit Story of that missing person. It adds an understanding that can be missed. It also helps Queensland police understand this is sensible and can be learnt without undermining the culture and community we are working with. You read me Doc?"

Cop Doc Dan R: "I do read you and really resonate on your description of a Spirit Story and the guide who is akin to a Priest, Minister, Sufi Imam and in some ways, I can glean insight comparatively with the frame work of a Kabbalistic or Hasidic Rabbi. The essence of the spirit world is universal and perhaps as Dr. Carl Gustav Jung went beyond Freud into the world of different typologies and dreams with vistas that are spiritual and transcendent, ((Jung, 1961, 1991, & Stein, 1998). A world within this world and yet transcending our eco-ethological and cultural reality in a linear frame. Reaching beyond our boundaries is crucial to remain intact in the world of sanity. Sanity as a legal term and sanity in the realm of what is meaningful and grounded in the area of experience as real to our own unique private sense of what sanity means."

"Sanity meaning a world in which one will not lose his/her mind as a doctor of this soul is very telling as entering madness one can become mad without the proper safeguards. I recall Dr. Professor Viktor Frankl called himself a Doctor of the soul (Frankl, 1978 & 2000). It is an interesting title for a psychiatrist and for an existential analyst that is quite truthful. The great Rabbi and Philosopher Dr. Joseph Solevetchik called the realm where sinfulness becomes so entrenched in someone's life that one suffers from a soul sickness which parallels in some way the schizophrenic world in which reality and fantasy becomes hazy and blurred in translation (Solevetchik, 1984 & 2018). In grounding the officers, I have worked with as you know by having read my clinical texts and articles in the area of complex trauma and grief, I have attempted to aim for a sensibility always when traversing through worlds where the dirt stops, pitch dark tar, and asphalt of the concrete jungle is overwhelming. When ones return to sanity is done gradually and patiently over time, the frozen tundra of space frozen in moments opens to melting into fresh streams of water. Rather than being hit with a glacier adrift as the Titanic of trauma and loss hit to hard will blow over any survivor, no matter how tough, she/he is. Where no mental and spiritual map exists, one needs to explore creatively within each individuals' beliefs a road to sanity."

"In using words like 'roles' and 'role-plays' in dealing with the paradox of one's identity mode as sleuth in which you are provoked to enjoin as a Sgt doing a missing person search, you became connected to Dundee and to Marilyn. I am aware you've called Dundee as an aide to an Inservational man to coalesce the concepts of keen observation, and also insight into a world of the Aborigines. In the beating the Inservational person risks enduring as going into the Spirit Story in search of this missing girl. That risk is also existential, soulful and perhaps quantifiably the risk is soulful and existential insanity."

"The fear is they will not return to sanity if caught in a dream with were-animals that engulf him as invagination. This is not crazy or simplistic but is beautifully narrated to understand the religious and spiritual implications, to say nothing of the female psyche and the male psyche in the anum and animus of yin and yang. His insertion means he may risk being castrated and swallowed whole which is as a primary fear and unconsciously is also stimulating and tempting for him and you and Marilyn looking on as witnesses. The gatekeepers have their wisdom in closing the doors to further aid and investigation, perhaps in this interpretive context! Good Sgt and Sleuth how did the Spirit Story close or open too?"

Commander Sgt Matt Moloney: "We did not find the girl but the belief is her spirit became absorbed into the story which was, is, and will forever be part of the greater Dreaming story related to that place. Think of the dreaming as a story that was, is and will be told. She is now part of that Dreaming story."

Cop Doc Dan R: "It is well expressed good teacher and Commander Sgt Matt Moloney, as she was left missing and the assumption in essence was her spirit returned to a place she had wandered into. It was meant in a unique way for her to fall into and away from her way back. In her journey with her ancestors she was compelled to go back to the ancient predecessors and surrounded by Spirit Stories. In this eco-ethological niche in the spirit world she would merge into and vanquish in her-Spirit Story without any further open conversation. To the family she rejoined her ancestors and became a fabric of her own Dream Story. I will add that Complicated Grief and Complex Traumatic Loss (Rudofossi, 1997 & 2007) to a degree as you've been educated in part by my method as a peer support officer is now also found in the wonderful way you've educated me and many others in your narrative and creative use of Inservational person. As Teacher and Sgt. Commander Matt Moloney in this context of the Spiritual and Dream Story I've gained much knowledge and hopefully wisdom to put into use!"

Commander Sgt Matt Moloney: "Thanks Dr. Dan R! The Inservational person is the guide tracker who acts as the buffer, a go between to mediate the dreamlike existence for the person in need. For the police the case is now a cold one, where only the material facts matter. To clan members she disappeared but was reborn in a spirit world in which their medium and conduit guides couldn't rescue but must accept passively if not in faint inaudible protests. For me it was frustrating we didn't find the missing girl and I was unsuccessful. Like all jobs, going over it in my head there are some things I have learnt. In an earlier intervention utilizing Dundee's unique skills, cultural knowledge and insights including his practical knowledge of the country would have helped. Continuing the sum of the dilemma was Dundee isn't in the best physical shape and although as the traditional custodian of the land he was involved and a keeper of the Spirit Stories, he could not help as he wished he could have."

"The Inservational man who was brought from Kow needed Dundee's help as he was the wise associate who held the sensitive intelligence to answer questions related to Dundee's country region and also to support the Inservational spirit tracker. To complicate matters the Kirditcha man is tasked with ensuring associates like Dundee and Marilyn are on track and supporting the Inservational man. Legitimating permission, authority and support is crucial to make it all work together with Dundee again at the cornerstone of this investigative and tracking odyssey. The Kirditcha man known as the Pama like the spirits and were animals can also be the hand of punishment and vengeance if violations are noted. In the actual ritual which did take place and with Dundee's help the communication was lost and the repeated attempts to connect with the lost girl was eventually lost. The legend for her loss was redeemed in an interesting legend of immortality and the myth her folk and folklore developed around her as an Arwoo where she transformed into an ancestor. She is now a guardian spirit in this Spirit Story who is now and forever more 'part of the never-ending Dreamtime story'."

"Myee is the aboriginal word for food, and 'Taboo-Myee' for our purposes here means the food she is forbidden to eat. It is the belief she would have just eaten 'Taboo-Myee' due to hunger, or perhaps may have been given 'Taboo Myee' by Dreamtime spirits while she was missing. This ingestion of 'Taboo-Myee' would have a hallucinogenic impact which would place her into a deeper dreamlike state. By ingesting this food, she would be sucked into a dream and further into the Dreamtime without any awakening. Soon the surreal would be normalized. The more time she was dreaming the less she would be able to know the difference between dream, deception and reality. The surreal dreaming place becomes her country and she becomes more and more part of that Spirit Story."

"As she becomes more and more Arwoo she loses her identity as her physical characteristics metamorphize and she becomes unrecognizable even to her relatives. The missing girls sleep is one without any return path and inability to awake from this dream. A nightmare you cannot wake up from, and surreal — becomes reality. It is also a resolution for the family as the myth associated with her is told to embrace the fact, she a sacred part of the land and story. She has her own Spirit story. It is not as relevant to her family in their religious beliefs and conciliation with the possibility of another closure to her loss even if found and if anyone else is arrested, or not. Even if her body is never found she has become subsumed and engulfed by the great reality of the Dreaming becoming a Spirit that is entwined with her story and her essential tribe. In the end this solves the family's pain as she is no longer alone and missing but has become incorporated with the ancestors of her past in the present and the road to and within the future. Does that make sense to you as a Rabbi from a spiritual sense Cop Doc Dan?"

Cop Doc Dan R: "It is superbly sensible, and I would like to add two pathways perhaps to ease some pain and sensibility to this Spirit Story hopefully with the respect due someone within their own religious sensibility, and your own as well."

"Sgt. Matt you always suggest my adding in my own faith as an observant Jew and ordained Rabbi having achieved Semicha. Semicha on one hand means receiving and blessing, it also is related to the word happiness in a non-frivolous, but humor filled way (Rabinowitz, 2017). It also means laying one's hand upon the sacrifice in the Holy Temple in Jerusalem when rebuilt during the days of the messianic era we await for in my faith. It too requires a serious stance in life but one peppered with humor at times and at times with alacrity in transitioning an animal from life to death and beyond as well. A sacrificial animal is not a paltry offering but one that is without blemish and one that is given blessings in its animus if one wants to describe the animal's soul."

"In Tao Te Ching, storytelling by Lao Tzu speaks in substance of the wise sage who falls asleep and awakens to find he is a butterfly on a long journey: A journey to insight and awakening in which the sonorous tunes of ethereal existence are experienced (Lao Tzu,1989). It is when he awakes to find to in his daymare he is no longer a butterfly, but a man. Awakening to the reality he is a man qua man is tragic to him. and all of his identity becomes a metaphor of an open landscape. Like the missing girl wanted by the police who also is in a dream-scape the end point is not vanquished but ongoing and never ending as in infinity point. The denial of death is a theme not only relegated to western society and modernity but as old as civilization itself. I think in the Spirit Story of the missing girl we can say she is not an escape in the retelling of her loss, nor denial of death via reductionist thinking."

"The missing girl symbolizes an aspect of the forgotten language that sociologist and psychoanalyst Dr. Erich Fromm tried to capture in our collective unconscious when death heralds fear and trembling, (Fromm, 1957 & 1981). Fear of the unknown and even the best of trackers cannot fully account for the missing. A missing girl mourned in effigy. But in that effigy becomes an oblation that is held in our ability as humane beings to heal in each faith through a different door and window to peer out of."

"Vistas are visions as the Inservational person had. The allegory of the cave in Plato is the truth of the myth of survival and the surreal you hint at. In my lectures in identifying traumatic loss and the horror imprint of a missing young girl perhaps kidnapped and brutally murdered or devoured by natural predators is almost always described as being surreal. It is as if to say the reality is too hard to embrace without the spiritual lattice to help us come to terms with our own mortality and our own quest for immortality. Again, unless we are completely dogmatic and closed in mind the spiritual is a way of looking at the universe and all that lay within including the endless return of souls and life as generative."

"Let's for a moment shift the word and concepts of roles and role plays to identity modes and quantum moments of traumatic loss such as the eco-ethnological niche of Dundee's country as a traditional owner and custodian where a missing young girl was lost and his assisting the Inservational Spirit Tracker. We may obfuscate your own identity mode shift from tour commander as Sgt. I can relate to all too well from patrol into an investigative Sleuth identity mode you embraced. It is crucial for you as sensible in taking back and owning your own ingenuity and humane decency as a man of faith beyond and inclusive of being a police sergeant."

"Remember you were the conduit for Dundee, the Murri family and clan members side by side with the Kowanyama clan and family members, the police officer and the two informants and Inservational person, and the scary Kirditcha-Pama bogey man equivalent: Provoking conflicting identity modes and switching based on forces that provoked different identity modes in each eco-ethological and ethnological niche unconsciously – these identity modes emerge as defenses against threats to life. Your own specialization of adaptive assimilation and accommodation to situations threatening integrity of life and limb was forged. Symbolically this threat triggered existential defenses as well when survival was threatened."

"The key is '*adaptive functional dissociation*' as I've called it is when an officer or spiritual guide is placed in an overwhelming or intensely challenging situation and dissociates to identity modes that are shaped by the intensity of ethological survival events and is unaware that existentially the unconscious level of shifts in identity modes has occurred (Rudofossi, 1997, 2007, & 2013). This shift is evident when Dundee and Marilyn to their chagrin were not fully supported and I venture to say you too were frustrated and disappointed that this occurred. This refusal to venture into his expertise in venue geographic and eco-ethologically speaking was likely because the department felt this to be too ethereal and not grounded in empirical methods. The crux of the conflict you compromised with my good Investigative Sgt is that in your Sleuth and Tracker identity mode unconsciously and in synchronicity with legendary tracker Barry Port was already introjected into your own repertoire of skills. These skills were matched by innate ability."

"Like your fellow tracker you clearly have the overlay of pressure that triggered identity mode shifts that are triggered in you as well as those you aid so well and brilliantly. The fact your own losses of this girl was magnified in the tragic optimistic vista of your own limitations as a mere mortal which both you, and I, are! The soulful transition of faith bridges a better narrative for you as much as the Aborigine family and hopefully Dundee and Marilyn, Inservational person, and the Officer who alerted and worked with you. This is true even though you have your own faith and they have their own unique faith. As humane beings you all are able to embrace respectfully the differences and enjoin the common loss from a soulful and respectful bridge of empathy."

"Your own compassion and energy to ferret through truth and respectfully understand with insight the challenges of a possible murder and mutilation of this young lady is no less processed in a world of spirits and spirited journeys. In fact, it is made richer because of who you are which includes the rich education of your mentor in the field as a tracker, Barry Port himself. You've imbibed and enriched your spiritual life with wisdom from your own deep wells and have shed some light for others including my own to ponder and contemplate within my soulful wells as well. That is the potlatch of learning and growth and development."

"Remember the unconscious dimensions of experience do not preclude the sensibility but compliment and reinforce their endurance and evolutionary advantage. You're own adaptative resilient intuitive personality style has transformed from a hyper-vigilant and hyper-intuitive and excited personality style. Your own transformation is refreshing and this is exquisite courage and determination on your part and a small part on mine to assist you in adaptation is well worth our journey and narrative.

Your growth has succeeded and my own as well. You have navigated me as much as I have piloted and vice a versa in this long and meaningful dialogue where the twilight of faith is not dimmed but supported in the crux of culture and eco-ethological niches."

Commander Sgt. Matt Moloney: "Doc, let me assure you it is no small part that you had in my adaptation. It is difficult for me to articulate just how much I've learnt reading your work, actively listening, and intellectually absorbing your method of applying the eco-ethological existential analytic method since we've met. I am holding what you said near my clips for duty to use in my existential analysis for defenses I can unholster when and where the losses get to be too intense and overwhelming to keep holstered and bottled inside anymore and where a lager will not drown out the pain. I never thought of myself as a tracker and spiritual guide as well as copper but coming from you as a Cop Doc Navigator I will not close mindedly dispute your wisdom but let your own compliment my piloting."

Cop Doc Dan R: "I appreciate your genuine humility for sharing your feelings and processing of our very brief existential analysis of your own eco-ethological multi-layered niches of trauma and loss as complex as the wonderful clans you are working with. If it works the next chapter in our dialogues let's move ahead to visit the harsh and cruel world where a person of interest is in-deed as we say in Brooklyn North 'homicided and in cold blood' and your dealing with the whole kit and Kaboodle as only you can and do! Are we cool as in hip and not from the holster of police work only, Commander Sgt tracker and spiritual guide Matt Moloney?"

Commander Sgt Matt Moloney: "Cool, Doc that will do for me as soon as I take a sip of that Mint Tea after my strong dark Roast black and with no sugar!" Oops by the grace of the Almighty..." **Cop Doc Dan R:** "Ahmein!"

CHAPTER 8

PPS-COMPLEX PTSD: COMPLEX WEBS — BRAIN MATTER

INTRODUCTION

The imprint of traumatic loss is often woven into the crime witnessed by the police officer: I will illustrate with Sgt. Matt Moloney as a trained Peer Support Sgt Commander who has allowed our dialogue to flow into an illustration that can be used for understanding an ambulatory assessment and framework toward intervention. An illustration which helps understand the why before the how of unraveling losses stuck in the tangles of spokes. Spokes tangled can become lost in the land down under, where death is woven in tragic violence. Losses explored on one front where love unrequited is sundered in violent effigy in quite vivid and enclosed terrain: Under the front of another surface ripples another series of losses that grab hold of our collective unconscious – becoming violently conscious where complacency tacks 'It's' ticking bells on a reptilian denizen.

Ticking Organic too In-Organic and Unnatural Losses – Toward Understanding.

Natural losses are assumed and even evidence somewhat supports that for some people such losses are better received and understood. Losses that are natural are more digestible, assimilated both/and accommodated for over the space of time, because it is not with, mal-intent. But we will in case example's present the core approach my colleague Sgt. Matt and I are working through together. It is not the natural trauma event, or even the unnatural trauma event aka humans acting less than being soulful, and even less humane but the individuals involved and each personality style that really clinches 'how' and 'why' impact occurs along the fault line of losses. Losses that become gaps left unmourned, and even less understood by each participant ideographically.

Again, the idiographic method is always nested in the monothetic but it is not only as clinicians but dare we say researchers both/and scientists that the individual subject, participant- officer, aborigine clan's person, and non-indigenous person is where our method of 'how to intervene' is matched by 'why a certain intervention is best fit' than another of lesser fit?!?

An Eco-Ethological Existential Analysis – Education, Assessment and Intervention.

The Eco-Ethological Existential Analytic Approach used here is for educational purposes and to gain perspective and insight into Complex Trauma Events officers endure without identifying and underscoring the impact of these events as traumatic focal points. I coined my approach in 1997 and published my method as a clinical guide in 2007, (Rudofossi, 1997 and 2007). In presenting an abbreviated Eco-Ethological Existential Analytic Approach I use here too lasso the trauma events that tames these experiences into an educatable guide to assist you as the reader to identify areas of traumatic losses within dialogue between my police colleague

PPS-Complex PTSD

as a well tenured and trained peer support officer/paraprofessional and me. The working through the field of experience is enlightened by understanding Sgt. Commander Matt Moloney is the only active front line-first responder.

I am a retired Police Sgt Cop Doc dealing with real events that will enlighten much that is likely to be a novel approach in your way of understanding. That wisdom clarifies that the 'simple and routine' is not all that simplistically understood as routine. 'It' is never – 'all that simple' as we all come to understand as time does not cure all evils and ills of humankind and kindred spirits alike! In-deed it is the officer as the most important front line of crime analysis that is often left hidden in the layers of crime detection, Yes, I am suggesting in this book that the officer is mal-treated at times as if he/she has become invisible coordinates that analyze and gather information but remain out of the boxes they are forced to package and deliver unscathed.

If you as reader, for a moment – **'Stop**', please; **'Pause'** for a spell; and now after your pause: **'Re-direct'** your attention toward inner-sight as it becomes self-evident that all humans remain all too human. A human being regardless of any profession or occupation cannot willfully surrender their own innate humanity to becoming in-human as much as one attempts to distance him/herself from acting humane. One can pretend and even act inhumane but that does not preclude being human as in-alienable and if one dare says, a given fact! Parting with this philosophical-psychological truth before moving on to understand human loss, it is equally true that human beings can truly and factually give up their rights to enjoin others in a humane society.

The unique acts of inhumanity still do not nullify even the most heinous criminal actions perpetrated by another human being in the most inhumane manner does not nullify his/her in-alienability to still remain human to the day one dies, is no longer alive and in eulogy remaining human-essentially. This frame work returns us all to ponder as to who instigated, and why instigate, and how can it still be so curiously ignorant and adamant to hold some officers are not humane, inhuman and pretend that he/she cannot feel and be impacted by the trauma, losses and human and non-human acts of terror they experience? It is clear those entrusted with the sacred trust of caring for others endure in reality and in much greater impact the negative effects of such careless and obscurant views that dehumanize those entrusted with the front line of rescue and service such as sworn police officers and those who love them, one officer at a time.

With this in mind factually and in reality, spoken frankly we can move on to analysis both human and quite methodologically speaking:

Analyzing the impact of doing crime scene analysis calls for uncommon good sense in sorting through the sensitive sentient and emotional sensibility each officer must go through as their own journeyman.

Crime scene analysis often leaves out the psychological layers of transferred elements of the scene to the victim/complainant that survives, the officers involved in witnessing and participating in the categorizing and sifting through the viscera to the ecological affordances they experience first-hand. Further, the family members of the officers and civilian staff who often support the investigations which include the prosecutors.

If Heraclitus was right in pointing out no one steps into the same river twice, then leaping forward – the flow of the River itself is changed as well as each participant impacts and reshapes the River by making a step forward, or out of the River itself. The zone of entry by one participant at a time is crucial towards gaining an understanding of the complexity and the multiple relationships that are possible in sum. Heisenberg and Freida Fromm Reichman outlining the bounds of physics and the elasticity of the human interactional space from an emotional and dynamic level underscored the impact of the patient and therapist in a duality in which both are changed in each interaction with a growth of insight or progress – or a checkmate in stagnation, and predictably regression at times (Furuta, 2012; Reichmann, 1960 & Sen, 2014).

The River is the metaphor for itself, for each crime scene and the trauma that unfolds in the defenses against, the motivation to master and to force changes to the lowest common denominator of simplicity of cause – of course it is uncommonly sensible to appreciate that the lowest common denominator is not at times all that low, or that common as simplistic answers easily given may provide.

Crime Scene – Complexity of Forces, Motivation and Push-Pull of a River:

Indirectly and equal in distance existentially is that the one who steps into the same crime scene will ever experience the crime the same way again, and his/her understanding of the impact of that crime on not only the victim and the toxic effect from the perpetrator but on him/herself as well. Each dip into the well of a crime scene changes the observing participant as suggested earlier. I will with the dialogue with Sgt. Matt explore his experience of a homicide from an eco-ethological existential analytic approach. Keep in mind Commander Sgt. Matt Moloney is a tenured and exquisitely insightful officer familiar with and trained in my method as a para-professional peer-support officer. In this chapter we will also briefly review what could have been a homicide by an unfolding natural anomaly that he shared within a motif and narrative with a fellow Police Sergeant. This anomalous vicarious trauma in synchrony with his buddy/mate's experience felt as if it could be his own skin literally and metaphorically as Matt could feel the potential victim hooking into jagged teeth and herculean jaws of a pernicious Salt Water Crocodile looking for an opportunistic meal. The parallel crosswinds of such trauma meet in the moist and fluid waters off of Queensland wistful winds. The unwinding lull of such trauma can provoke dissociative moments when survival kicks off an adrenalin flow and evolution is primed to win when one's own life is at a no barred event where teeth can rip apart hope and promise of one more moment that can be whisked away.

Adaptive Functional Dissociation – When Dissociative Processes Makes Superb Sense!

Let's understand the use of my operational definition of 'adaptive functional dissociation' to understand Police and Public Safety Complex PTSD for our use abbreviated as PPS-CPTSD (Rudofossi, 1997, 2007, & 2013).

First, all trauma occurs in an ecological niche in which for public safety professionals captures an officer's experience when he/she witnesses the extremes of violence to humans within an ecological-ethological niche. Secondly, the context of public safety officer's personality which initiates in young adulthood shapes defenses against loss and trauma. To understand the complexity and impact of trauma the clinician needs to understand the personality dynamics within the survival value for the officer. This personality style is shaped within the public safety culture of policing, firefighting and emergency medical response teams. Again, in a veridical manner evolution occurs within in each unit and each commander is what maximizes what is selected for speciation in performance from each officer. That commander is more important than the entire culture of policing, firefighting or emergency medical departments. It again is a very personal and unit wise eco-ethological unit that brings out the innate and learnt skills of each officer, that is in maximal learning eco-ethological niches. The best reality is rather a field experiential niche-based trauma setting.

The last tier and most important for us in this chapter to keep in mind is the officer continues to work 'as-if' he/she is functioning at optimal level and with the best advantage within the unit to maintain status. Status is not defined in egotistical frames although in some cases it is such as the hyper-aggressive public safety style. In most personality styles and units, the status and shaping of responses to trauma and loss are defined by defenses as much as adaptation to such events. Meaning for most officers maintaining status within one's own unit — creates a utility and reinforcement of function regardless of internal states of dissociation and struggle with mental illness. Examples of responses to trauma include increased substance use, heightened anxiety disorders, depressive and bipolar mood disorders fine and right back on track is left out of perspective as the impact of traumatic loss hits home.

In Chapter 2 we discussed Observing Participant: The real deal is officers may never change their culture in which trauma and grief in its complications in reality while in global ways are acknowledged may not be disclosed in front of peers. This is no different than our case with Aboriginal clan emergency volunteer units who will not publicly disclose the real deal inter-relational and inter-communication reality of cooperation when working through great fires and tempest-cyclones. From an anthropological and clinical perspective this social mask is distinguished from the persons true self. The adaptive functional dissociation (Rudofossi, 1997 & 2007) is not only social or even the different defenses such as different identity modes emerge in order to function during the trauma event and unconsciously after. The Alexithymia is not only normative across males and females in police culture (Rudofossi, 1997 & 2007) but serves an evolutionary advantage which education cannot undo. Understanding the advantage culturally within an eco-ethological niche perspective is more than helpful again - it assists in creating an insight into witnessing for self and others that the officer is working in a sensibility that makes superb evolutionary sense.

Individually one can work on their level of traumatic loss in measured clinical interventions and understanding the process of what is happening within him/her which then can be amenable to change as each officer chooses in his/her own personality style gradually, gently and with respect for self and other peers. As a cop doc and scientist practitioner this makes more sense to me than trying to force change especially the naive and misinformed approach to cultural change that is endogenous and exogenously shaped such as an officer's response to trauma and grief. I am not alone as my fine colleague and peer support Sgt will illustrate to me in the following case example we work through together. Most of all we will also not neglect the core dimension of this book which is placed within a murder of an Aborigine woman caught in her own web of violence and trauma of the most intense expression.

Before the dialogue moves further, I ask you to consider the following factors which is far from exhaustive when being allowed to peek into the domain of complex trauma and grief as experienced by tenured police professionals. Looking beyond a general description of police officer's eco-ethological niche and even the macro-cultural roots is a fact often overlooked and overshadowed when science tiptoes around the real impact on the individual while reconnaissance into traumatic loss follows legal and administrative worries to frame the boundaries of intervention to prevent losses from a political and economic framework. Clashes with the larger culture in which the traumatic loss is experienced by one officer, may bring little if no losses and trauma to another officer as she/he experiences that event that may be described as traumatic by outside onlookers. Yet, the actual point of impact and the event that does become an ongoing motif with the narrative positioning which is dynamic may oscillate, stagnate and freeze, or be placed in a fluid and adaptive navigation.

The idiographic push and pull and dynamic impact for the specific officer in question and the overall wellness for the team as a unit is the crucial description, understanding and eventual insight that must be unqualifiedly pursued by the scientist-clinician who is hot on the trail of the mapping of traumatic loss as veridical, as secondary and even vicariously experienced each time by the officer in question. Further is each time the officer is experiencing the event in his/her mind and as eidetic memory is stored it changes in fluidity and permeance as a fulcrum from which all other events will be processed. The import of this point is crucial for officers and those who love and work with them in order to create an inroad toward healing and repositioning each officer under the hard-core shield whether silver, gold or ornate as rank and status increases at a fundamental level of understanding and insight.

Excluded is the first experience with a particular type of trauma an officer has to deal with that may be particularly harsh: That traumatic event is not usually acknowledged in the larger police culture and yet uniquely impacts on the officer in some manner that is not only unshared but in an existential sense is unknown to him.

Within the ecology of traumatic loss in which one or more police officers are dealing with a very real unique human being who is still alive and dying, or has just died when they arrive or shortly after many unique aspects may resonate in a shared communication that is acceptable within each unit, and even within a larger sense of policing and yet more silent questions remain hidden to the officer and her peers: Such questions are:

1. Why does one specific aspect of the event make such a profound loss on one officer and not another, such as my finding I am responding to a jukebox radio memorabilia with intense sadness and not responding to the dead guy shot in the corner?

2. If that loss is not really accepted as an 'acceptable loss' from a cultural and existential perspective, such as a 'homeless skanky person' who is beaten to death and has done numerous con games: How can I actually begin to mourn my loss (es) with any support and acknowledgement from my peers?

3. What is it that makes a particular type of loss so profound for one officer and not another officer within the quiet and private sensibilities he/she has constructed for his own navigation within the eco-ethological niche of his existence on a day to day level of experience: For example am I ruminating when alone as to why that woman was born into extreme poverty and what could her life have been if someone had given her a break to scaffold onto a better means of self-respect and preservation than resorting to prostitution?

4. Further, how can that officer be assisted in acknowledgment of the actual loss and its impact without disrespecting the overall culture and that officers fear of being looked at as weak, or mentally ill: Such as showing fear and worry for a guy who clearly deserving getting the beating he got by stealing another fellows car and

getting chased by him and his friends as he fell into the gutter and cracked his skull and is now being rushed to the hospital in a comatose state?

5. Do officers at times truly identify with the aggressor in a nondescript way by the process of mimicking: For example, I can see I hardly feel any emotions in processing a double felony robbery with a victim shot and likely to die *since she was a pot head along with her coke head boyfriend* who is also shot and likely to suffer from traumatic brain injury?

6. Does the victim who is dead on arrival at times become deserving of violence as culturally defined when he/she is found involved in some way in certain crimes from drug smuggling, and human trafficking: As a mule who was carrying dope in the most dopey way in a condom swallowed and it exploded in her abdomen and is now writhing in seizures and likely to die as a result of being so low as to do this for the drug cartel?

7. If the question above indicates the victim found DOA was implicated in drug smuggling or human trafficking, is it clinically accurate to label responses of anger related to the cultural and socially acceptable norms within that police ecological niche based really an index of an anger problem, or not?

8. Is the label given officers who judge criminal behavior harshly and those that commit such crimes as 'Animals' for example truly a correct fit identifying an 'Authoritarian Officer'? Is that officer truly inhumane and elitist without compassion for a perpetrator or is he/she stigmatized and judged too harshly – perhaps. Is it truer that there no marking on the officer who is made to appear less humane in the context of repetitive trauma experienced and in defending his own sense of vulnerability and harm is articulating this loss in a transformed manner of aggression as acceptable rather than loss which is not as easily acceptable?

9. Is it not true that the outlet of anger and dissatisfaction expressed as ventilation which while unhealthy if this anger is permanent, is not so unhealthy if it is short lived, irrationally expressed at first

but as all fallible human beings put in perspective later in his/her life experiences without any toxic and lasting effect?

10. Do Officers that dissociate and process loss in a way that distances himself/herself from 'It's' impact in the here and now, have to deal with 'It's' impact later with a synergistic intensity of complex grief?

11. Following the above question, is it true as a cop doc that my point of adaptive functional dissociation I coined is adaptive when it is understood and temporarily placed within an eco-ethological niche perspective?

12. On the other hand, is it also true that mal-adaptive functional dissociation occurs when an officer has created an existential distance from 'It' by insisting 'It' is what it is and that all is ok when 'It' clearly is not as a way of dissociating to function while mal-adaptation is blowing the cover of health by implosion through these existentially functional defenses?

13. Is the Aborigine Victim/Complainant family member who survives the intense trauma of the homicided victim less likely to have complex trauma symptoms than the Officer who is tasked with investigating the crime scene and profiling of the victim?

14. Can Police and Public Safety Complex Trauma symptoms that are heard, watched, or felt but not directly experienced instigate a similar impact as an original Quantum Intra-Psychic traumatic loss experienced and lived through directly by that officer who responds to the ongoing event in person if the witnessing officer is a member of that intra-psychically injured officers' unit?

15. Is there a potential pathway to lessen the intensity of suffering from Police and Public Safety Complex Trauma and Complicated Grief Symptoms and Disorder without formal therapy for the investigating officer both/and surviving family member: If some pathway can ameliorate symptoms experienced by an investigating officer can that officer as part of healing extend his unique and first hand wisdom to the Aboriginal clan member so impacted by the event as a witness, victim participant or complainant for the victim post-trauma event?

16. Can a professional peer support law enforcement officer assist as a gateway to deterring suicide, depression and complex PTSD in their initial intervention through an existentially aware approach that proscribes a specific one fit all prescription for field practice with another peer officer and by extension the indigenous citizen so impacted by a serious crime and its eco-ethological vectors of violence and losses?

THERAPEUTIC VISTAS OF COMPLEX TRAUMA INTERNALLY WITNESSED AND EXISTENTIALLY ANALYZED.

The answers to the sixteen questions above and perhaps more that come to mind and not answered fully will be answered at least in part. Some questions I have answered in other works and some remain unknown: All are worth asking and as the reader you may seek scientific means of understanding by describing and testing further questions and in part answers derived.

The means in which these answers will be delivered in this last chapter of this book as in earlier chapters will be through dialogue with my esteemed and tenured Queensland Police Sergeant and Commander, Matthew Moloney and myself. Kindly remember that the actual events are not only psychological narratives woven to illustrate the critical focal inroads toward understanding trauma and loss within Aborigine culture and the non-Indigenous culture but also the history of a humane being's life that transcends culture, eco-ethological factors and niches, and the learned and novel partial insights we are gaining, but the contracted space in which each human being lives – his/her life.

Commander Sgt Matt Moloney: "Dr. Dan I know as a Sergeant and street cop you dealt with many gruesome and painful situations where the ecology of death rose to meet you with a wave of smells that were overpowering. I also am sure in order to deal with victims and crime scenes you had to do preliminary investigations and cover the bases of securing the *inner perimeter* which includes coppers and other police professionals from scouring over the evidence and ruining potential leads as they may leaf through at times carelessly with no malintent but still spoil the fruits of evidence acquired."

Cop Doc Dan R: "In other words you had to hold back those officers who at times may with curiosity, sloppiness, alleged ingenuity and even some ego tip toeing move through the evidence scene in order to cull through to the most important aspect of the crime scene from my biased viewpoint which is what motivated the perpetrator toward committing the crime psychologically speaking. When speaking frankly from a psychological perspective I include correctly the physical evidence and the mental, emotional, existential and physiological evidence of strength used, passion, creativity or lack thereof for beginning layouts of importance. Disrupting your overview as a Sergeant commander and the detective as well by uniformed members regardless of desire to assist is creating an unnecessary – mind block from A-Z. Correct?"

Commander Sgt Matt Moloney: "Correct from A-Z Cop Doc Dan! That is not including as you know too the outer-perimeter where all others come to drink out of the limited pond of evidence and peak in to see what is happening inside. I would say morbid curiosity and also a need to get involved and to say they were there at the famous, or should I say 'infamous crime scene'?"

Cop Doc Dan R: "Yes, I am totally with you and in fact, those who would like to foot the tab and bill on what we call the 95 tag in the NYC Police Department as memento to paint sensational in hue and cry. The 95 is the toe tag that accompanies the person now deceased. That tag along is a memento whether the cause of death was: post natural caused trauma; post terror attack; post-accident fall; vanilla homicide-where perp wacks another guy for 'no apparent reason', suicide in a fit of passion, or suicide as a long drawn out exit door is left in its finale – closed and shut! Some select tabloid journalists report and synopsize such crimes and criminal's way too soon. Others get the bare boned facts but with no, or little evidence save wild conjecture at best, and pure guess work at worst as to the why underlying each crime and 'It' as the frame and scene that wraps around the crime it-self."

Commander Sgt Matt Moloney: "The crime scene of the DOA, or as you Yanks abroad call the Dead-on Arrival victim is what is so hard to process. Remember we discussed the Aurukun indigenous community on the Western side of Cape York as a truly remote geographic region. Its about three quarters of the way up. It's a truly indigenous community where the people of the area still speak their traditional tribal tongue. That tribal tongue as language is called Wik-Mugkan. The overall language of Australian non-indigenous folk's clash with the cultural nuances, and rituals at times that the Wik-Mugkan present. Unfortunately, this clash of cultures has all of the issues that remain between industrialization and rural fortitude in Australia that is still aflame as discussed earlier in dealing with cyclones both/and fires. At times the media and also the larger elite centres in society present Australia as if the process of colonialization is over and done with – Doc, it is not done! Not done by far in some ways and means of society – it is still a struggle. 'It's' (pause) still quite embroiled in Aurukun. I had done three tours of duty here over four years and after a while to tell you the real deal is the murders really do all start to blend into each other!" (Silence).

Cop Doc Dan R: "Sgt. Matt that was a real pause and I heard your silence loud and clear as the passion you feel. In your educating me about your own unique experience in Aurukun as 'embroiled' and having aspects of 'acculturation' colliding with micro and macrocosmic divides I am hearing some aspect of 'It 'being overwhelming. I may be wrong and if I am please correct me that the wave of upset you are dealing with is one again of your own passion and commitment to stave off the crimes you've dealt with and on the other your true compassion and empathy for the folks you work with. [Pause] The clash is when crimes occur again and again and the same results almost seem invariable no matter how hard you try to re-direct violence from your post as police officer and commander to a better outcome. That is in part the 'It' that embroils your soulful wrestling with the angel of violence and death. Does that make sense at all?"

Commander Sgt Matt Moloney: "I had shared with you my long interaction with Leoni who has been in and out of mental institutions and as you copper's in the US call it collars, we call it pinch and the general public call it arrests: Both are revolving doors with closed windows and sponge like walls that absorb endless confusion and chaos. I shared with you the dude lets call Ronald who was doing perverse acts with young girls for money including self-harm on his own digestive track. I need not get into the details here correct? [I nod my assent]."

"Well after she assisted in this case and others, she truly earned being an informant for me and some other coppers who learnt to trust her as best as we could. I will say for the readers to understand the level of perversity Leoni dealt with as a ten-year-old was that he would ask her to shove bottles up his arse while he pleasured himself: If Leoni brought a friend, they would get paid double. Ronald was filmed and also admitted to his behaviour and was sentenced to jail time for multiple events like this to which he confessed to us. In the assistance she gave and over the following decade I worked in doing law enforcement I formed a bit of a bond with Leoni. As Leoni transformed into an offender, I still shared information with her and I was also able to get her treatment even after she was arrested and placed into a rehabilitation centre, a number of times. Each time when we caught up and had new interactions due to her being pinched or having mental breakdowns it was like two old acquaintance's catching up."

"Well this one time I was in the middle of a pile of reports and paperwork completing the tour and I get some desperate calls as Leoni was locked up for something by an all-male police crew and she was given the lightest pat down. Leoni had her mobile phone on her that was secreted in her vaginal area and quite understandably not picked up on initial search at the time of arrest. She had become abusive to the arresting officers and because she was a slight defendant, she was left restrained but uncuffed in the wagon that carried her to the station house. In the back of the police van she began yelling to let her out and when this was not responded to immediately her verbal entourage exploded into hysteric and violent writhing whereby that cell phone became a jagged edge instrument to stab herself. In a menacing and threatening way Leoni had began to jab her cut piece dissembled from the phone into her thin wrist causing the blood to flow. The strong red stream was not profuse bleeding but enough to get the officers to begin to try to negotiate with her to let down the jagged edge homemade weapon. She tuned off and away and said, "I need to talk to Matt only!"

"The message was clear and highly volatile that if Matt was not here soon, she would proceed to destroy herself. Well as providence would have it, I was within five minutes and dropped all I was doing to respond to Leoni. I saw Leoni at the entrance and she was clearly on some illegal substance at the time. She was hysterical and high as well. She barked out to me in no unclear terms, "I'm serious Matt!" My response was to assure her I was there for her and in the calmest voice I could speak in I asked her what was up and then silently listened taking the submissive position I could present to her. She let me know she trusted me and had liked police even though at times she got pinched this time she felt was unfair and she just had reached her point of no-return. She had pointed out that real friends do not pinch other friends and that she was hurt and disappointed she was targeted for arrest. In Leoni's mind she did the math equation which held a solution card which you detectives call a get out of jail card which solved the problem by stating she did not deserve to be pinched."

"I let her know that I did understand her upset and feeling of being so rejected that she felt threatening suicide would awaken the coppers she just wanted to be let free and had no hate of coppers. She had a lot of dealings with police and she had a real bond with me which was a bit true from my perspective too. I came closer than she allowed other coppers to come to her and while I saw blood as my peers, I realized it was superficial and her blood was congealing already. It definitely was nothing more than superficial. The Perspex was jagged and was still pressed to her wrist, while she was talking to me her attention shifted to me and not her Perspex. When she slightly relaxed her grip the point of contact to her skin moved to a less jagged edge and if she moved for a microsecond her edge would do little harm. I took full advantage of that moment and was able to subdue her and get her in custody and to treatment as well post custody. It is key to understand Leoni had the motivation to commit suicide and was truly escalating to this level she did not have the full means to do so."

"It was not only her upset at being pinched as in the past, it was the intense heat of the day, the 'ice' perhaps, and her ensuing panic which added to her confusion, chaotic thinking and disordered behaviour. A crowd had gathered to add more fuel but Leoni had calmed when seeing me and as she knew and I did she needed some medical-mental health treatment and detoxification which I proceeded to get her. I had gotten the female officer to fully search her and also in follow up we had spoken again and again with me listening and her smiling and me getting my wave as last time we crossed paths. I can't say Leoni will live happily ever after as she is in and out of Gaol, and in and out of mental health institutions, on and off of streets, and her ever growing brood of children are in and out of care following in mothers' footsteps. This did not end in death as others have and did as step into and out of life as you NY Coppers say in a heartbeat, and all alone in the asphalt jungle" [pausing for a moment].

Cop Doc Dan R: "Let's Stop and use your natural occurring 'Pause' as we consider the importance of pausing and realizing the victim, the officer responding, and investigating the crime and crime scene is also the same *unseen hidden experience of the officer such as your exquisitely empathic self that is* experiencing the victim as another human being – no matter how washed over and painted over with distance, objectivity and scientific enquiry: Victims are truly another human being as he/

she lived; lives on in the witnesses and complainants minds each time narratives flow; losses frame who that person was through actions, deeds, behaviors, emotions fleshed out and given blood, sweat and tears in each narrative as the River ebbs and flows its font of movement. The Officer as you shared with me does experience. Experience existentially in silence the untold part which like a sponge absorbs the essence of this other person's life – unknowingly and unwittingly unconsciously as a gift and more oft, at times a painful loss."

"That is all left behind serves as evidence when worthwhile from the dimension of physicality both/and or psychological reconstruction of the crime scene. But the artifacts remain guidepost clues: Coordinating color patterns that can offer texture and foundation of what is left behind as witness to the victim's life – life produces substance and centers on what was meaningful existentially. Remembering as often forgotten is when meaning does not seem to exist and chaos has taken its post in a person's space within allotted time. Nothing has substance for what has evaporated into a vacuum in squalid messes, disorganized rooms we can find 'possessions left to be cleaned'. Before cleaning up artifacts inestimable in the value of another person's life that may have become de-centered can still offer the clues that flowers from patterns of chaos beckoning inner-sight from the vistas lost."

"A crumpled picture, a pale thin and gaunt face malnourished, a discarded love poem in the trash with mold forming, a frame with no photo to hold it staring emptiness at love unrequited. All are clues as to a life whisked away into the vapid arena of an ecological niche devoid of what was once purposive and now aloneness pervades. Such as the aloneness and the futility of dancing as you did so elegantly and regale with Leoni who now unwittingly indefatigably continues on in her own unique move by move iteration of her own tragic trauma with her own children as pawns of the asphalt jungle of concrete and cobble stones."

"This aloneness is not without clues it serves as a tome of what is helpful and offers a glimpse into the reality faced by the victim's actual stance of withdrawal, surrender existentially and not caring enough to order the chaos long before the strike of the perpetrator predation occurred. For Leoni it maybe she has learned to mimic the offender and repeat endlessly what she cannot remember and afford to in sexual and physical abuse and exploitation? Questions again arise for us to consider: "Perhaps this was a bait and allure of the predatory human being that was anti-social? It is nonetheless a record to be read quality wise even if the quanta of hard-core evidence in your face does not fully follow – soft evidence can be felt and explored as well, cannot it not? Does this make sense and what does come to mind in this context my good Commander Churchill Scholar Sgt. Matt Moloney?"

Commander Sgt Matt Moloney: (Pausing in mindful reflection). "The fact that comes to mind does merge with your thoughts Doc. Let's go to a darker place than Leoni for now if ok?" [Pausing and nodding my assent] "I think we had close to three murders in three weeks in Aurukun. It was close to fifteen years ago but as you know crime holds no vacation although it can change its territory. Give or take, Aurukun must have about a thousand folks in its population. With a crew of four police officers we had small occasion to catch a break and rest well. It is interesting that the case of homicide I remember actually fits the bill and answers in the affirmative for your questions here."

"I remember the vivid details very well. The murder scene was chaotic and grotesque. I can also rehear the police call, mind you this with a very busy schedule and having seen or witnessed many murders at this point. No rookie here [grin and laugh audible slightly angst driven and quite genuine in expressive hue.) The callout was memorable. It was tragic and yes, the lack of meaning when I re-think of your question makes sense to me after all this time. You hit on the nail of the Aurukun ecology and as you ask us to look at the ethological motivation which was to be perfectly frank Doc, and summed up in one word, *sub-standard*! The reality in Aurukun is the housing is sub-standard because the homes are transient and flashes of existence at times that co-habit with humans and places that remain run-down because not enough time to develop real abodes strikes the hearth of the citizens lives. It is complex! Most houses are filthy. The walls are covered in greasy marks with hand and finger prints all over. Grease overrides the prints as one person tries to clean up the other persons marks that brush the walls. I am thinking of how to effectively do an eco-ethological existential analysis. As I recall. in capturing what is an ecological niche and the clues that tangibly impacted on me – yes, these memories left an indelible mark in my mind: Is that correct Doc?"

Cop Doc Dan R: "Yes, that is correct as you've got the ecological-ethological analytic needs assessment – 'Down pat!" Please continue to keep in mind that there is no right and wrong here. It is worth pausing to let you know that your own shared experience which I am privileged and by extension so is the reader of our book to learn and understand better as you draw and colour in the hues of your vision. What is case in the hues although not always fully logical, methodical or discrete flows from the vista potentiated in your own mind: Simply put forward good Sgt is that what comes to your mind, even if only to instruct our readers collaboratively is well worth the print: You with me Sgt. Commander Mate?"

Commander Sgt Matt Moloney: "Yes, I am with you and to be honest for me it is a relief to be on the same page. Dr. Dan the way I view your eco-ethological existential analytic approach is it is an ultra-violet light of police psychology and psychology in general. What I mean is that it has helped me in my perception to gain a foothold and mindful method of what was previously unknown to me and many of mates I have shared your clinical method and intervention with. It has helped me perceive things and get some idea of what I see, others see and to get a better handle on a very important and neglected piece that keeps coming back in a day and age where all questions are answered with how to solve the problems at hand, but not why those problems exist?"

Cop Doc Dan R: "You have hit the exact point of my therapy and also what Professor Neil Postman called Eichmannism which is in his book titled crazy thinking stupid thinking – as the triumph of technique as Jacque Ellul pointed out earlier, (Postman, 1977). Postman's admonishing gist is well worth the effort to read and is responsive to your rich insight into the process of what we set out to do together – as this supports and encourages our readers as well."

"I opine that when technique over substance triumphs as the Arch of Triumph as Arc de Triomphe wails and falls into extremes. When science portends to know it all the lectern becomes a place of dry wood ready for the kiln of pedagogy at its worst. When the scientific world can balance that both the 'why?' informs the 'how?' at times, at other times can be altered into what can be done and at others is subject to witnessing what is done and why with how acceptance and shared values can depart from agreement without war then equanimity is the balance of what is right and wrong as a balanced compound. So, let's return if that works to your experience of the Aurukun as to the why of all experiences one murder hung the balance of your attention in infamous relief to be explored together: Game on my fellow and good Sgt Matt?"

Commander Sgt Matt Moloney: "Game on Cop Doc Dan R! (Said with the strong deep undertone of passion and zeal). Going back to the murder in Aurukun the ecological niches in this one community is a string of homes that are left in disrepair and to be frank are filthy. The walls are covered in greasy marks from hands and people constantly in motion – brushing the corners of each room as they intersect into one another. Showers, baths and toilets are hardly cleaned and due to the rarity of good hygiene are biohazards. Kitchens are an entomologist's dreamscape as many varieties of insects abound and not just palmettos and roaches but all types of unique and nasty pests. Mange has afflicted the dogs and they too suffer from hair loss. Cats follow foot and paw in line with their domesticated canine fellows – cats have their own unique complications and diseases including but not limited to potential for becoming rabid by Bats that they encounter, and becoming carriers of diseases that can impact on those who are indigenous and non-indigenous Human-Being's with equal pernicious illnesses: Basically, mangy and hairless dogs and disease-ridden cats live and sleep with the people together."

"If I had to give a comparison to other areas I have seen, Aurukun houses in some cases are worse then what I have seen in third world regions. Yet the house where the murder took place was not atypical it fit it in quite normally for the area with bare cement floors and windows smashed in with band aid repairs. Damaged walls, no curtains surround the houses that remain decorated with mess and filth as the trimming and that is no exaggeration. It is a very depressing place to die. [Pause] I mean it is a very sad area of town that has no area that one could even scratch out to die with dignity as a human being. That is the reality. I don't fully remember the exact address if you asked me as to what number the apt building was at exactly although I remember the details as I have shared with you. I have tried to block 'It' out as much as I can. Blocking out any memories from seeping into my awaking moments, or my falling asleep moments too." [Silence and sadness pervade with the elegance of 'It's' impoverished feeling made loud in its unspoken statement].

Cop Doc Dan R: [My pause and silence in tune with Sgt. Matt's, leaves room for what will follow]. That is at least as I anticipate what will follow is details of the murder. But before rushing in as almost all police get habituated too, my pause intentionally allows us both to first acknowledge the sanity of many difficult feelings Matt has at present is primary, not secondary and his feelings and ideas count without me devaluing his own way of getting a grasp on the trauma he has pushed away, under and with intent. It will lead our exploration into what 'It' is that is truly traumatic for Matt]. "Sgt Matt it is that harsh reality that as you share with me adds to my own personal memories of young to elderly people murdered in the squalid and impoverished NYC projects. The harsh loss left me holding in many moments of loss, anger, and anxiety over the futility of violence. The 'messy' and 'filthy' business of criminals and activities of criminals. The shitty messes that include devastating tracks to follow. If I can suggest, what seems to lay under the surface of your very descriptive expression of the shit layering what ought to be home – is nothing like what a home is supposed to be. Clearly what is left is cold, dank and aloneness. It is important for us to validate and describe as not only truth as you see it but in a healthier way to capture the ecological niche with ethological survival motivation for these folks as real".

"Disease and biohazards are truly anti-human and have no borders to hold them within when they strike people and pets alike. Sometimes it is just that so many questions emerge when you and I pause. In our pausing we can reflect at how fellow human beings become disenfranchised from their own experiences. It is something we can both keep in mind as I lean my big ears down to listen to your own feelings and attitudes towards what is too follow if that works for you good fellow Sgt and Commander Matt?"

Commander Sgt Matt Moloney: "It does work for me Doc! I am visualizing right now the actual crime scene itself. What had happened was a man had come home and found his girlfriend engaged in an act of adultery. The man involved fled immediately. He exited by jumping out a window closest to the enraged common law husband. The third wheel guy left the woman to take all the rage the husband had to give out. The woman stopped her sexual act with him and in its place took all the wrath of her husband head on. What we reconstructed was a kids BMX bicycle rim and wheel was lying nearby, and in need of repair, the husband picked up the wheel and began in a blind rage to hit his wife in the head. He didn't hold back and in fact continued to hit without any restraint: He didn't only hit her once but multiple times and with full force for impact! She fell to the ground as he kept hitting her again and again. As he was pummelling her to death the actual rim itself cracked into many splits. Some of the spokes sticking out of her brain actually resembled spaghetti – that is steel spaghetti – you can't imagine the scene! 'It' is truly almost indescribable. I mean it defies what most can see and hear in reality!"

Cop Doc Dan R: "I can imagine the unfolding scene as you are describing the enormity of violence against this woman for her sexual indiscretion with another man outside of her marriage. "It' is larger than life and sounds, as much as images understandably are hardly worthy of descriptions that could capture the horror and imprint of your witnessing this traumatic murder! The enormity if we can for a moment pause and allow the truth of how immense the pain and loss is to witness a murder for any reason. Can you go on in your very descriptive capture of the scene as 'It' is unfolding?"

Commander Sgt Matt Moloney: "Doc, he kept hitting and hitting and hitting and hitting! The rim not only broke into shattered spaghetti like spokes but the woman's skull did too. (breathing and pause) The reason headwounds always bleed out is that the brain needs more oxygen and fuel than any other organ. Blood going into her brains as with all of us is always oxygenated. The really bright red rather than the duller crimson colour and less glossy de-oxygenated blood that is leaving her brain. The blood that leaked out of this poor unfortunate woman came out of her brain. I remember the picture was of a mostly really bright red pool of blood."

Cop Doc Dan R: "It seems like you had to distance yourself from her again by describing the crime scene segments of this woman to poor unfortunate woman who now lay dying and virtually dead although some aspect of life may have been oozing away. The scientific description does help give some feeling of distance and removal of your feelings from the tragic imprinted photo like memories you've catalogued in your brain at the time as a police supervisor. True?"

Commander Sgt Matt Moloney: "Yes, true and even more so I remember experiencing the reliving of her moments before and while dying as powerful blows literally cracked open her skull and the steel spokes acted as little prongs that were penetrating her brain. Steel rods that gripped into her grey matter. It was like a fork digging into organic gel. The hammering action he used meant that the rim in his hand went up a wide arc and was moving quickly. Centrifugal force resulted in the bits of brain, blood and gore being forced away from the axis of his hands rotation. The blood and brain and skull matter with the bits of metal were splattered. The spotting and splashes were not just on the floor but up to the ceiling and walls and onto the roof. How is that for some crime scene to witness? So sometimes it seems like it is what it is does come to reality like this poor unfortunate cheating adulteress."

Cop Doc Dan R: "It sounds to me like 'It' is not just what it is but as you and I can see what and how you are fleshing out what 'It' really is comprises your own stored vision and memories that are imprinted and stored in files in your brain. This makes sense as keeping score is an actual guide known as the body keeping score of such events (Van Der Kolk, 2015). It seems like as you are describing this tragic event here Sgt Matt you were in your procedural identity mode analysing the crime as it was unfolding with all the intimate moments of violence. Aggression enflamed with what was once passionate attachment and now with equal ardour had become passionate rage at the affair witnessed in progress by the murdering spouse. What comes to your mind without censoring the events and those tragically and intimately involved?"

Commander Sgt Matt Moloney: "I remember looking at all the blood and splattering on the wall and visualize this as a Jackson Pollack painting. Talk about abstraction and weird stuff. I think maybe it's weird and maybe, oh never mind."

Cop Doc Dan R: "I do mind and never push away what is deep inside your mind. I don't think weird captures your inner-sight into the abstract patterns you've woven as a motif to frame the horror imprinted in your brain. The weaving is not conscious but an associative web in which you posted a frame of reference to navigate out of the sheer inanity and intensity of pain – pain that encircles your core self. Inner-core to outer-core existentially framing the artist within you. Uniquely appreciating haphazard spraying of blood and brain matter in a way that is made sensible to you and me as well as our readers on the fence:

The complex web of unconscious motivation to make sensible what is to horrid to confront in all of us – the drive of aggression and sexuality – not sublimated like Jackson Pollack but in bestial carnage as counter-erotic and a bloody mess of sex and rage. Does this make sense in interpreting and understanding your own response artistically as not weird but even ingenious without being conscious of the drive to create and noetic to colour the grey with intensity and plasticity not concrete chunks of gory bloody chaos?!?"

Commander Sgt Matt Moloney: "Intensity of the hammering action of his hand was like a sur-real scene from a slasher movie. It became a particularly primitive slaughterhouse run by people who did not know how to kill, quickly and humanely would look like. It is too disgusting and revolting as you point out to process as one would even a slaughter house."

Cop Doc Dan R: "As you passionately described earlier, he was hitting, hitting and hitting four or more times which tells you as it does me that the words are the extensions of coordinates to make sense of your own eco-ethological sense of this very real niche you are now confronting with me 'nice and easy' as we slowly uncover the veil. Kindly go on good soldier Sgt Matt."

Commander Sgt Matt Moloney: "She couldn't have been dead for long as we arrived on the scene and found her, but the murder was done. We were later told by forensic experts that her blood splatter patterns indicated that the most likely situation was her skull had opened up while she was still alive and conscious to whatever degree. Unconscious was swallowing her level of awareness but she was still alive. With her heart still beating the blood gushing out of her as her heart stopped beating gradually. As she went into cardiac arrest, she was bleeding out but at a slower pace and slightly less voluminous rush. Because she lost so much blood, her dark skin was really translucent, so much so that I felt as if I could literally see through her skin, although this I think was an optical delusion."

Cop Doc Dan R: "It is interesting you called your vivid impressions an optical delusion – in a way it was perhaps what is known as a hypnogogic hallucination we all have quite normally from time to time when exhaustion and sleep deprivation occurs upon waking. It appears as an after-image and considered to not be a genuine hallucination but results from the attempt in part to make sense of the unconscious when the patient returns from an unconscious dream like state. Staying with me I conjecture this may have happened to your own perceptual process of again this almost overwhelming traumatic situations when she clearly held some level of attraction in her mulatto hues which became translucent and yet repulsive in the bloody mess of her now broken being dead as dead could be. The skull being opened as alive is as primitive in its impact can be for you as you vicariously imagined all too well as if you could hear and smell the malodorous smells – you visualized this all as you described you're seeing the abstract of Jackson Pollack and the slasher films of your adolescent years and as she the victim becomes a humane being who is so tragically being redeemed in your own noetic unconscious as you identify her as a fellow humane being. This is a reflection of your own essential self-image. Meaning what to you?"

Commander Sgt Matt Moloney: "I imagine my own intensity of a surreal crime scene to revolting to process for this poor innocent woman even if she got off with another guy, she did not deserve this extreme violence he laid on her."

Cop Doc Dan R: "Yes, and very well said and understood in one dimension of your own experience but in another realm of your own experience it illustrates to me as I hope you can witness your own unique humanity by seeing her own evolution as a distant pathetic victim to a real humane being at a great cost to you. But the cost of your discipline is one that redeems her from a soulless discarding of a crime scene after prosecution work is done to a soulful noetic dimension as our dialogue evolves spiritually and her humanity is clarified in reflection of your own unique creative and genuine compassion. If you could internally witness this reality rather than interpret it as weird as it is truly your courage and creative drive that assists your journey good Sgt! Further the sur-real and abstract go together as both attempt to make sense of what is truly unsensible as the brutality, hatred and rage against another human being for whatever reason. The delusion is the illusion that others remain inhuman rather than confront what was and is truly evil in action and theory the killing of others for the satisfaction of a drive that leaves the driver and those driven into dead existentially or physically after bleeding out their grasp on what being human really means by holding back their own anger and rage. Seeing others do such uncontrolled violence at some point may leave you as most of us wondering could I ever get to this level of losing control?"

Commander Sgt Matt Moloney: "It is about losing control of our ability to help and even effect any type of rescue for this lady. It was left for us to call in the experts as we secured the crime scene and gained as much evidence protection as possible. The health care staff from the clinic threw up as the medical professionals issued a "life-extinct' certificate for this young woman obliterated physically in a rageful violence attack. I believe he may have thrown up into the crime scene itself as it was a visceral uncontrollable response and not disrespect of any sort. This is what it does to human beings, that is this type of crime."

Cop Doc Dan R: "Yes, it does Sgt. Commander Matt Moloney and it pains you and I to listen actively to listen to this young lady's life whisked away in a tragic explosion of violence that was let loose in uncontrollable rage addiction that once spent will destroy both the recipient and the giver of such aggression. It is a double homicide as one died that day and the perpetrator relinquished his freedom and humanity in those moments which may or may not be redeemed while he victim is now dead and will remain dead. This tragedy was lightened when you clearly cared and did your best to use metaphor and emotion to express your hidden loss but loss nonetheless. Now you have expressed it and realize her value and yours in a mellifluous manner for prosperity and memorialization.

Perhaps at some time we will revisit this idea of memorialization that is more visceral and abstract in a poem for example and ritual or some other medium you choose to use? Does that make sense?

Commander Sgt Matt Moloney: "Yes it does and I do say it is a relief to re-direct my attention to a different perspective of what was only horrible and imprinted in my brain to an alternate sense where I am in control of what I do remember and have allowed expression now. My own with you as my witness, calling her Penelope for her perilous life and death which still is meaningful."

Cop Doc Dan R: "While you analyse your own investment and expression now as giving the lady, we can call Penelope for the perils endured and the tragic moment of her demise without ending her entire existence. Not allowing obliteration to set its cast and mould this lady into being objectified is a rich way of memorializing her for now. In other words, by your clear struggle itself in placing Penelope as a human being who was brutally murdered even within a domestic violent situation is a way that you have given her empathy, respect and dignity as another human being. In situating her as a woman who is worthy of being remembered not in the brutal crime scene which was her final scene you witnessed and protected. Further it was in your sharing with me that helped you and I also make sense not of the insensibility of her death but that her life, her last suffering brought meaning to you, me and readers who are now aware of the struggles and creative defences you've shared. The defences are not only within the eco-ethological you have dealt with but hues you've brought to vivid expression. You seeing her translucent skin will awakening as in a hypnopompic hallucination as we posited as one way of looking it; in another is your transcendence to face her existence and your own witnessing of your valuable intervention as modest, but real. Preparing her body and transitioning for the morgue and evidence of the brutal crime counts in achieving justice for her. Finally, the good you creatively have woven as a wreath of value and dignity to someone who fell hard and fast is a way to extend your centre outward in ripples that open the space of loss with meaning well timed! Is this sensible to you my colleague and fellow Sgt?"

Commander Sgt Matt Moloney: "It is and much valued and appreciated. I do believe I can replace the horror of her murder into a better place in my mind without this guilt and repulsive feeling. Maybe at least less of that repulsive feeling and as the offender we collared he came quietly as most due in Aurukun after the homicide. He needed protection from the community and that to was what I provided. I understand the importance of doing an Eco-Ethological Existential Analysis it does help to place this homicide in sharper focus and perspective for now. One question remains here for now Dr. Dan and that is how can you summarize the crime scene itself in a way that makes sense of what I experienced and many more times with other crime scenes although this one was particularly hard to even recount as you know too."

Cop Doc Dan R: "If I had to summarize a crime scene itself, that is from a noetic and existential frame of insight, I would say it is a layout that helps you and I understand a crucial moment in another human being's life."

"The crime scene is not just a specific crime as committed by a suspected criminal that is being sought as the proper owner of that crime and his/her egregious behavior: For our purposes I am interested in 'It's' impact becoming more humanized, by understanding how and why each investigating officer is affected by and through his/her unique lenses which includes experiencing the crime and the criminal sought from identification to hopefully solution."

"I also seek the impact of the victim, his/her associates, that is close to the victim, as well as the perspective of the individual who is now brutally murdered or assaulted as well. The more the police officer understands the victim's perspective the more the impact of another person's essence is respectfully ensured prosperity. In ensuring the essence of the victim's perspective and life, perhaps peace as much as is humanely possible is closer to being achieved rather than the horror of the crime as brutal and imprinted in the brain. That is, once we understand the analysis of the victim as another human being who lived, breathed, and whose life was abruptly ended while valuing what the police officer has done in helping in small to large measure in finding peace for the victim by seeking justice in solving the crime in this existence as life is lived and any other possible life as of yet unknown in the hereafter -faith can embrace in possibilities playfully and meaningfully explored."

Commander Sgt Matt Moloney: "Your psychoanalytic and existential approach within a cognitive behavioural layout has helped me deal with the heartfelt issues while the eco-ethological niches help me understand deeper layers exposed to that ultra-violet light without the toxic effects that boiled in my blood. My blood is not boiling anymore it is percolating at times to a simmer although the memories are still there at a lower level without as much revulsion and shock and certainly, I can handle remembering the scene and now diverting to the real Penelope as a human personification of the girl Wallaby I also lost so suddenly."

"In the losses there is a theme that weaves through the sudden loss of your Wallaby pet that felt as we explored as a surrogate daughter stolen from you as a copper when Penelope the lady who got caught in an affair was dealt blows and violence nowhere acceptable and in fact tragically a loss for you and the world and in fact destroying the human being who also committed the horrid crime. Tragic losses all trappings that shroud the losses as your brain kept score. We had looked at Dr. Van der Kolk's work titled, "The Body Keeps Score' (Van Der Kolk, 2015) and it does within the challenges of what we have derived from our own eco-ethological existential analysis (Rudofossi, 1997 & 2007). But the insight into the impact of the eco-ethological and soulful therapy has been the right dose – as you say often Doc, imperfectly perfectly good. This is as good as we humane beings can aspire too! I mean that whole heartedly – thank you!"

Cop Doc Dan R: "Your quite welcome. If I can ask you before we close this dialogue, can you share another event as hard on your as this tragic moment where Ms. Pauline was murdered in a less than sensible murder by her own mate? Any single or repeat murders come to mind that have been impacting on you emotionally and spiritually from a while ago, or closer to now?

Commander Sgt Matt Moloney: (Pause and long silent moment of wincing pain in contemplation that is non-verbal but gesticulative of fear and anger. Intuitively from my clinical sense I actively listen in the loud emptiness of space articulating its long wait for expression to confirm or disconfirm my conjecture).

"The bite of this is hard to swallow Doc: Remember this is a shared trauma as a peer support officer without portfolio where a fellow Police Sergeant experienced a horrible event and I mean it was a horror situation he faced. The perpetrator was one you can't collar and charge in central booking this stormy offender was a Salt Water Crocodile and it is very weird but this bothered me as if I was him in the water with this monster crocodile. We will not name the Sgt involved if Ok, Doc?"

Cop Doc Dan R: "Commander Matt the experience of this Sgt with the Crocodile is fleshing out a reality for you and me to relate to and then to translate for others. That translation is not lost if we do not disclose his identity. The impact of vicariously experienced events can become eco-ethologically laden does not diminish the lasting endurance of complex trauma but may emotionally, mentally and spiritually impress different memories. Those memories may include traumatic and losses laden with 'It's;' deleterious effects as the most complex puzzles to gain insight to by doing an eco-ethological existential analysis. Can you relate that crocodile attack I assume to what I am suggesting?"

Commander Sgt Matt Moloney: "Yes I can relate this Crocodile to such trauma and will now but with one qualification the attack while feral and ferocious did not end in death but it was the potential destruction and horror of being eaten alive that was so distant to me, I hardly want to ever remember what I listened to intently with the curiosity of a teenage guy looking at his first playboy centrefold. It was January 2007, mid-monsoon season in the Torres Straits which is located in the Northern tip of Australia. It is also as close to the Equator as you can get. The heat index is hardly bearable and the humidity is stifling at best."

"The excitement of different means of travel and transport for police from air, land and sea was fully stimulating and added to the fantasy of exploration of countless islands, reefs that are fresh and unexplored for this Sgt and of course me as well."

Cop Doc Dan R: "The excitement you heard in the two couples that day sounded like your own unique twist when you have explored other places with your wife as well. It seemed the moment was meant to be seized – Carpe Diem rang deep and blue in you as well as the Sgt. and his wife which you identified with yourself here as peer-support and witness."

Commander Sgt Matt Moloney: "Doc, I can relate as the Sgt as my peer expressed to his wife and rushed to explore and fish in the uninhabited islands in their six-meter boat, that is for you who use feet, around 18 feet long. His venturing out on January 9th was to fish and explore such an island. So, he and his wife joined up with another couple going out Southeast to visit submerged rock and reefs. The reefs were around 40 minutes steaming from Thursday Island. It was a regular January day: hardly a breeze, a glassy sea, and no cloud as cover, made where the horizon actually met the sea itself non-distinguishable. It was stunning conditions that welcomed the couples!"

"However, no fish were to be caught here and after a few hours both couples steamed over to Little Adolphus Island. It was here that spearing for crayfish was attempted, for a catch could mean tender and tasty morsels of picnic lunch. I should note quite wisely the reconnaissance for turtles and hatching eggs was done well to ensure the apex predators such as tiger sharks would not prowl the waters. The coast was clear and no turtles or their offspring were hatching to attract the sharks. The sense was it was sur-real with the conditions inviting a lovely day."

Cop Doc Dan R: "The reality here was the day was shedding its normal veneer and had been scouted as if he was doing a recon job for Tiger sharks. Tiger sharks known euphemistically as the large junk sharks Navy personnel call them because although they relish sea turtles as a staple food, when not available a garbage can, seagull, dog, or human swimming or floating nearby, may well do – no need to cruise on ceremony for the Tiger shark. Clinically it is more than passing interest that you said his experience was sur-real, my clinical ear is piqued with using the term sur-real: Trauma intuited becomes clearer in a more sanitized way by using sur-real in a pre-cognitive both/and emotive dynamic frame. Go on please good Sgt Commander Matt."

Commander Sgt Matt Moloney: "The one couple who joined the Sgt and his wife had ventured out into the deeper waters where the Coral dropped off precipitously. Although it was rife with danger such as a rogue Tiger shark being more likely to follow the Coral depths they stayed in a safer area near the shoreline – at least so they thought. I guess your intuiting what is to come is pretty interesting as well to me."

Cop Doc Dan R: "It's an intuitive sense from experience and clinical sensory coupled with being a Cop both//and Doc. We can return to this later if that works." [Matt nods, yes.]

Commander Sgt Matt Moloney: "The Sgt I know as a peer support was inspecting his first coral for crayfish and found none. Then he shared with me, that he had scanned for a good ledge to explore further for his next dive. Suddenly and without any hint of danger he got hit, and I mean hit hard! The hit as our fellow Sgt. described it was being hit incredibly hard across the back of his head. As he described, I winced. It was if I could not only see him there but I felt being there with him and it stung. Weird as I am recounting his being hit hard, I am feeling somewhat numb but also chilled as if a cold air has come across the room."

Cop Doc Dan R: "Go on please."

Commander Sgt Matt Moloney: "It was as if a hard branch of timber had just been smashed against his head. I feel pain as I am sharing this with you Doc, but the timber smashed in reverberations against the rear area of his skull. I felt a strange pain in my own head as he elaborated."

Cop Doc Dan R: "What becomes clearer is once again as we assessed your experience as you encountered the shark earlier is now repeated as he is sharing his being hit by the Tiger shark and not only hard but real hard. This is vicarious experience where you are not directly experiencing an event but by safely looking at it unfold in your mind's eye it feels so real, it is sur-real or mimicking reality as your peer Sgt. you identify with experiences the shock and impact of attack I assume."

Commander Sgt Matt Moloney: "Doc, your right in all you've shared in my experience as I was more than listening but I imagined without wanting to being there with him. But on one very important account, you are incorrect as it was not a shark. Not a tiger shark, as I intimated and thought myself. You will see if you hold on for a moment."

Cop Doc Dan R: "I stand corrected my good fellow Sgt and scholar, thank you for correcting my jumping ahead here, even for a moment and being off-centre as errors are as important as correct identification in learning ways of doing what we do, even better and with improvement. Please continue and educate me about the animal involved and what our good peer Sgt. was hit by?

Commander Sgt Matt Moloney: "At first my friend told me had no control and feeling of any of his senses. He remembers realizing he was floating in the sea as darkness surrounded any perception of light. No sight. No hearing. No pain at this point. All seemed to be nothingness. He described 'It', as indiscernible but he actually said as I recall it resembled if anything he could identify as if it was an inky blackness. A nothingness that is that surrounded him."

Cop Doc Dan R: "That inky blackness was a distancing from the actual horror imprint in his brain and in what is sensibly a synchrony with your own life-threatening attack forward by the shark on you – escaping from the sheer pain and fear of being eaten alive is the knockout punch for all senses. Does that make sense and can you relate this or not to what further happened to your Sgt. Mate as you recall?"

Commander Sgt Matt Moloney: "Yes, he was completely shocked and confused and had no sensory perception. He was trying to fight back and grasp onto survival or death as quickly as possible. He was trying like all Hell to work out what to do and to assess what was going in. His senses came back as he felt his head and saw 'shards of light' could hear the bubbling water, and feel enormous pressure on his skull area. He then awoke to the realization he was attacked by a shark that bit his head. He grasping in desperation tried to identify the one vulnerable area which was the eyes. He held the spear gun jabbing aimlessly hoping to strike and maim the unknown shark."

"He recounted the seconds where he felt his body being towed down towards the sea floor as the animal ignored his protestations which were desperate now. In an instant he said blinding sunlight ventilated the darkness and allowed him to rise to the surface and blow out hard and long as his longs were screaming for air. As he started to awaken from his plight the warmth of deep red blood was flush against his face as the sting of salt interspaced with pain of bite marks was interrupted with the sight of what froze the Sgt in disbelief a crocodile. He pointed his spear gun at it instinctively with little hope of conquering this animal. Instead of the crocodile attacking again he lurched away from my mate. He was using his massive tail to power away from me ripping up the sea as he went. My mate told me he saw the croc was a young animal approximately 2.5 to 3 meters in length, brown in color with a yellowish strip down his side. He got approximately 4-5 meters away from the Sgt. and doing a slight right hand turn back and then disappeared underwater."

Cop Doc Dan R: "Woah. It seems like the Crocodile was a monster in comparison to human standards. He was a crusher on top of your buddie's head. I know I felt the pain as your description fleshed out before my minds eye. Did your minds eye see the Croc too? As you are recounting the impact of this reptilian dinosaur that lurks in the sea under the same waves that surface opaque on top and alongside the dreaded shark can you actually feel and sense the power of his massive tail ripple through the tides?"

Commander Sgt Matt Moloney: "It felt as if I lost myself when I was listening to him and could feel his fear and pain too." Silence. It was like he said, Oh Shit! But in reality, he couldn't even say that at all. He was silent in painful reflection of his own death.

Cop Doc Dan R: "It was again emerging 'as-if you again were encountering your confrontation with the monsters such as the Bull Shark checking you out eye to eye, face to face and in the shadow of deaths inkwell of fear blocking out the light. Fear became fleshed out with all the mustering of courage you had while still having that 'oh shit' moment if I got it right! Oh, shit like how can I get through this mess as you did when you encountered your shark and the near miss on your life."

Commander Sgt Matt Moloney: "The sea quickly settled as the Sgt shared with me that he waved his arms at Jane. She however unlike my situation started to move rapidly toward her husband as she too fell into horror herself. He began screaming, "Croc in the water, croc in the water".

"Doc, our Sgt, remembered dropping back down into the water and sticking his head under the water scanning to the left and right, behind and front again, he remembered taking a deep breath and doing this ritual again and again. He explained that his fear was that the Croc mercilessly would come back and finish him off as food."

"In sum he spoke about his feeling hopelessly ineffective, and also helplessly prisoner to the ferocity of such a predator and being prey. This fear he had, turned on the primal panic button within as a victim of this predator. Terror and fear were totally new to him at this intensity and level. He told me that inside he was standing by as he actually fought to survive. But to be honest, as he put it, he was awaiting being eaten alive. Finally, by the fourth scan back and forth and up and down the

Sgt was brought to rescue by Jane. His wife grabbed him by the back of his wet suit and dragged him into their boat."

Cop Doc Dan R: "The imprint as we saw earlier is still with you and understandably the frantic checking back and forth reminds me of the hair grooming and checking that officers do with one another when they feel very threatened and as if danger lurks under every shadow and surface. Here the horror is when one's worst fear is realized, whether in part or whole that type of confirmation feels 'as-if' the world could melt into a sur-real drama as trauma endlessly in **'It's'** iterations of left to right and right to left; up and down until the roller coaster is stopped in all its hyper-vigilant flavour and intensity. Does this interpretation make sense in part for now?"

Commander Sgt Matt Moloney: "It does as I know the need to deny and escape is overwhelming at times. I think us talking it through and working on it as I am owning now is sensible to me. Sensible in so far as our Eco-Ethological Existential Analytic Analysis and attitude does help me regain some sense of order and control. I did not feel until now that this horrible and cruel crocodile is really some animal that is geared toward eating any animal within its domain which I know the Sgt. was as was I. The fear is very real and is almost thick as a cloud of ink as you suggested and I can convey this to him. 'It' is *'not what it is'* as you've pointed out in many of your lectures and books. I feel better even saying that, this Croc like my shark was an Apex predator but in my line of view it was fire ready to eat me alive and I was terrified. That is normal to say now. Right?"

Cop Doc Dan R: "It is as you say, exactly what is needed to understand and work through to its core emotional weight and the evolutionary sensible perceptions but with disputing the irrational foundations of thought that harms and causes much hidden loss and pain that cannot be directly expressed to easily. That lack of ease is often the easier way out and one I often have to work hardest at clarifying and confronting with the officer patient. In understanding the Eco-Ethological niche of the Croc was violated little empathy can be expected by mere mortals as much as the Sea Tortoise who crosses the line and is left grappling in the Jaws that can crush a Wildebeests powerful femur bone and shaft which is as strong comparatively to a Traffic pole. Imagining you could be eaten has caused much fear and anticipatory loss as to powerlessness and confusion in understanding how this could happen. But help me out here, how did this happen to our peer Sgt and to you as well with the Shark?"

Commander Sgt Matt Moloney: "It was in both cases taking risks I believe now that may have been better thought through as the excitement and the temptation to see new vistas in unchartered waters as well as waters where Apex predators' dwell is taking risks that may be foolhardy and also way too high a chance at playing roulette with our lives."

Cop Doc Dan R: "Perhaps in saying and using the word 'fool-hardy' you really are saying to yourself, Geez, how much of a fool I've been to risk all and what a great risk I've taken which is way over the top. But if you examine your behaviour and our other good Sgt. peer it is observable both you and he did do some preliminary checks and equally both/he and you may not have ever faced the challenges you did and the traumatic experiences needing some further work on. Does that strike you as being correct?" [Nodding, 'Yes' by Sgt, Matt]

Commander Sgt Matt Moloney: "Finally, Doc, one more point I don't want to neglect was the Sgt and his wife Jane picked up the other couple who witnessed the Croc swim past them underwater. It was the Croc who clearly was 'put off by the fighting back' and just swam off and away. The Sgt sustained multiple injuries, a hole in his left cheek, his left ear was torn in half; lacerations to the back of his skull; lacerations to his shoulders. After he returned to the water so he could prove to himself he could still do it. He ended his experience with the frank admonition that, "I don't dive much anymore because it just isn't the game now."

Cop Doc Dan R: "Game on for both of you brave chaps – became game off for the Apex Predators: Sadly, they don't care for our sense of fairness and rules – terror mongers of the Seascape! [Slight giggle by both Matt and I]. Although we are clearly anthropomorphising our Sojourner's of the sea and they have every right to be and do as they do; yet, to ignore our decreasing new experiences and found ways to decrease the risk of death and serious injury after the fact would be playing the hardy fool. It seems like you and he almost were on the same warring path of being taken as a food item, as I recall you shared with me earlier in your narrative about the near miss by the Bull shark was similar in the letting go. More so both of you have learnt invaluable lessons that also are kept in your tactical approach to diving and exploration. By the Sgt. going back in to dive validates courage and understanding by not stereotyping himself as being stalked and targeted but taking adequate protective measures and not being paralysed with fear and withdrawal."

"If so, it is preferable that you may choose to not take the risk when the chances are stacked up against you. That is when an increased risk of facing a predator is present, as in police work an increase risk to enter too soon is present at times you can pause and prep up than to blame and judge yourself or your peer if the shit hits the fan, does not make sense. In fact, from an Eco-Ethological perspective as curious and intelligent humane beings making a risk assessment is not as neat and snug as a mathematic equation."

"Existentially you and I may peer into the souls of us all and say as you love to say and I fully and wholeheartedly agree with Churchill and you as his scholar, 'There go I, but for the Grace of G-d, go I!' But in saying this I think you and I agree there is no fool-heartedness and blaming anyone including our Salt Water Crocodile or Bull Shark: I imagine being as they are made to be, without attributing malevolence as a human construct to a Reptilian, or Shark is a construct as far as we know at this time, they can't share with you and I. The rage you've seen in a human for disloyalty, disrespect, or offenses is rage much harsher in motive then the Croc or Shark who simply takes a bite of desire to satiate the appetite to fill their abdominal track. If this is so than I guess the need to diminish collisions where adventurer does not become a food item has more to do with good strategy but not being less wise or more foolish?"

Commander Sgt Matt Moloney: "Yes that is true as you say!" [Smirk and smile]. Hum... Doc that makes sense I get your point where my earlier recounted trauma and this peer Sgt was hard luck with a superior grace to pull us through. The human trauma further was no more our responsibility as I never also triggered that rage of harsh ego but did much to help clean it up. Is that what you meant?"

Cop Doc Dan R: "From a Socratic perspective quite so and a millennium before Socrates method was the method of the Talmud where a question yields an answer. An answer as a 'pause' following another question to clarify that former question with a later question, whereby a metaphor captures an analogy and the story teller richly weaves a wisdom that is not prescribed but emerges in a synergy after thesis and antithesis without boundary but steps to the ineffable richness of each individual as rich as you my colleague and commander Sgt Matt Moloney.

"Such is the fabric of the complexity of our lives and the impact of wisdom to grapple our own trauma by the flame of our indefatigable humane spirit of being without having been done by the being of excuses as wrapping human anguish by saying woe is I, but rather I am over wallowing in woe and have wrought wisdom over woe as the hope within our tragic moment of time is overcome by the hope in the respectful eternal light that is supernal as superordinate faith as much as the Jew in the Shtetl and the Aborigine in Australia and the Native American in the field of dreams eluding capture. For as the Aborigine know in their ingenious wisdom that the dream story is metaphor and as Joseph Campbell.

l has warned us the metaphor if we understand it correctly is the reality one lives by and which one, we chose is a free for us to do as the culture and religion we affiliate with and call our own – each person with tolerance and respect for the other in his/her own way. This is the first step towards solving the problem as metaphor taken as the community and reality for each community large and small. It is a non-reductionistic wisdom and one that covers science done right which is never controlled by one of its pieces as a Pie's taste always is absorbed by its genesis as a unity no matter how much division is applied to breaking it from a whole: The peace of the entire human pie, in analogy and visualized as metaphor is as ineffable and elusive as its homonym 'Pi' which in its modest simplicity is eternal as the human Pie indivisible by force. After all, this analogy is a metaphor and story where healing from the trauma of supercilious arrogance by any one group forcing its momentum to conform on another is only met by determination of its base being imprecisely unknown as the uncertainty principle of Heisenberg and less operational."

Epilogue

The closing of a tome often has led to a promise in which one window peers into the shadow of another: That vista must close and the epilogue is where its last ray of hope glimmers open. In the case of genocide – two routes are possible among many. One route is the physical annihilation as murder of a people. Another is cultural and spiritual assimilation and accommodation with no conserving of the real values of the people under siege save a paltry token of the essence of that people that perished.

An exquisite example regardless of renaissance was the destruction of East European Jewry. I am very intimately aware of that tragedy and the impact of that loss, timeless in its damage both/and *incomparable in the depth of its crater.* In no way would I dare to compare the Holocaust to any attempt to assimilate a culture but it is critically important to understand by forcing culture to change, conformity can only be disingenuous and bound to failure in its compliance

Yet some sparks and splinters can ricochet unto a new ledge where some flammable wood ignites a makeshift candle: Ledges sketched along the edges etched in Chiaroscuro outline the reality of boundaries. Boundaries which are linear and unidimensional by not including all parties are schisms waiting to implode – sadly many rehabilitation utopias are myopic in this regard. Myopic not in visionaries lacking motivation, effort and even honest commitment but the sundry reality where ideals are overwhelmed by real differences. No less then marriages begun in love and ending in divorce.

Some bounds kept in this book have been lightly and gently coaxed into petals that gently allow the dew of growth to drench the fecund seeding of creative solutions.

Solving clinical problems that proffer hope and optimism within the tragic cost of assimilation whereby progress of new domains sadly portend the death of older domains: Such is the cost of life and living – done wisely with genuine respect for wisdom as timeless as new sprouts. Nascent growth in the compost of deaths desiccating nourishment is eternal in its morphing out of endless cycles of resurrection.

New sprouts within the older host that is dying and crackling in the winter breathes of its last grasp. Its last grasp – grappling as a seed rebirths a new sprout grafted on our legendary ledge. The ledge of imagination daring to try to rectify with new vigor, from an indefatigable soulfulness to survive.

The plentitude where earth in the dank corners of a wintry night connects in a few drops of a homeless mans coffee spilt onto whilst while wind brings hope eternal as miniscule earth shifts onto seed and watered by almost rancid coffee -etch out life. Accidents are events that synchronize in wisdom beyond our reach and held in the pale of the finite pleading for the infinite in the senseless reaches of editing out wisdom as knowledge is cast in concrete walls.

Scientists who cut the edges know poetry begs the reality of the ventilation of branches mushrooming out of fiction-scientists playfully weave. Too many examples exist to the knowledgeable such as B.F. Skinners Walden II birthed out of Henry David Thoreau, Walden. H.G. Well's the Island of Dr. Moreau and Dr. Mengele's Experiments on Twins in the name of National Social Democracy in which one nation espousing the gilded glitter that Beacons despair to the peoples who simply don't fit into the assimilation plan where politics are corrected by the force of law and the law of the lawless legislated. However, being the epilogue – refrain is called upon for this moment as the promise of clarifying and confrontation is temporary shelved.

Epilogue

Done in pomposity and arrogant ignorance of the genuine wisdom of a people although perhaps not in sway and rhythm of the fads of the day are bound to repeat and with zeal exponentially in the mendacity of audacity as bodacious as they march on in blind bliss of their homogenous mirror-echoing the image of the same narcissistic tune. The tune of merging all cultures and advocates who change all agendas into one is perhaps the manic addictions of our times where mental health as a science has prevaricated its future to an illusion of steel flowers politicized and the lichen must perish in the foliaceous brush.

The world is a very large place with one species that have invaded all others and yes that is the one each of you as I can see if we peer into the mirrors of our own image too long. It is so much richer to examine the extremely crooked thinking of our times which in the past hundred years have led to the darkest age's history has ever witnessed as in our bliss we rant we are yet in the year 2019. Never has blood-shed and the attempt to conquer the ability of critical thinking been stronger and more forceful.

Perhaps a solution is examining the death drive and Destrudo which is a nirvana of stillness where in the name of diversity and inclusion no ability to embrace historic resistance to a holocaust that is spiritual is exactly what progress has brought us to in a universal suicide of culture and tradition.

The culture and the wisdom of the forgotten language of the unconscious has never been more precious in a world society of self-absorption. The ignorant yell at the insightful and tell them by force to shut up. But their echoes will drown their own reflection where self is made into ideal idols without soul. It is hard to allow the light into the shadow to illuminate the reality we have made. Enormous caves with no air in which to breathe freely. Like the bats that sojourn in caves with us we have lost our vision and sight to vistas as Jasper post holocaust warned us against and have been hanging like our bat friend's upside down using the radar that only reverberates to the scratches that now lead the way out by facing the insight, we first must embrace is inner-sight to realize what is potentially outer-sight to be sight blighted out in the darkest of ages portrayed as the lightest of all beings as culture is murdered without a drop of blood. The sequel to this tome is possible in which the dialogue will continue across two continents and promises to be as poetic and philosophical without the trapping of sophistry so commonplace today as trees are spared but cyberspace is left as the last bastion of the voyage where the Abyss has swallowed thinking and the seminal mind in the quagmire of a dried lips that cannot bare the potency of creativity.

In a crushing reality that rattles the future of the Aborigines and I will add the culture of the Blue – Public Safety Officers Sgt. Matt Moloney as a Churchill fellow wrote a Fellowship report which after we meet in NYC and I had been interviewed he made his unique validation of my theory of traumatic losses, via Complicated Grief and Complex Trauma as 'It' impacts on officers and their families: Nicely validating and supported by the research funding his investigation conducted with diligence, honesty and integrity of Matt Moloney. His contribution was to add my concept of racism against police and public safety officers and do the first study that validated Centurioncide independently. The fact that harsh criticism of police and police agencies at the time of his fellowship visit to America was also enflamed by the murder of police officers in the line of duty did not deter him. The realization that the Eco-Ethological Existential Analysis appealed to the scholar and researcher Sgt Matt was in his own words reverberates past the echoes of those whose myopic vision dismissed that of officers,

> "The well-articulated recognition of the problem where all people involved including those dealing with and judging police recognize the humanity of police involved as fellow human beings that also have the same sordid issues and problems as the rest of mere mortals is what your term and concept of Centurioncide makes crystal clear."

As I shared with such a promising scholar and police colleague who was outside of the United States that found a consistent stereotyping of police, Sgt. Matt Moloney resonated with what I had written elsewhere such as the stigmatization of police from academia, legal fraternities, and the media as well as other branches of government that were willing to scapegoat our community without thought as to the consequences of such narrow-minded short-sightedness. Further he added in his own style that socio-economic lower status community members are not all against police officers and their families and oft times, more conservative in approach.

In fact, Sgt. Moloney in his report summarized that without stereotypes that reinforce that all minorities are against police and public safety is not only a reductionistic and racist approach but treats minorities as being incapable of dissent against the sweeping fads of political correctness dictums. National socialists as well as communists have tried to reduce the individual men and women to stereotypes. Any attempt to advocate a standard for all men, all women and all members of any one group in the majority and minority in the authors view is one that oversteps the lines of justice.

Policing, law, media, academia and all professional rights ought to seek justice for all and not blame any group for any unjust acts of its participants. With Dr. Viktor Frankl I will applaud once again the truth that to blame an entire people for the acts of a segment of its population is unjust. It is a message subtle to some and more pronounced by the sensitivity of some others as to how far this message is driven to you as our readers.

Independently Sgt. Matt had taken the Eco-Ethological Existential Analytic Method and had come up with validation for what I have titled Centurioncide depicting the racism against police and public safety (Rudofossi, 1997, 2007, 2013, 2015, and 2017) in his work which focused on the dehumanization of police which in his own unique study of Queensland and United Kingdom is a linchpin in scholarship and impact on elucidating Centurioncide for the continent he has traversed and still does. I believe fully his research ought to be placed on required reading lists for students too practitioner's in criminology, forensic psychology/ psychiatry and law as well as homeland security to glean evidence of such hidden racism I dubbed Centurioncide and my colleague has validated as a critically minded and astute researcher. I have my students read his report as well.

Our next work, should we do one more tome independently or as a team again promises to tackle such an issue as Centurioncide in a ground shaking tremor that is concentrated in a tome. It may be a quake that rattles the earth of convenient myths that are replaced by myths that one can-built legends and culture on. That is always respective of truth and that makes a read quite worth the while. To be continued as we say in treatment of disorders -- both large and small -- with the optimism that in the tragic always lay the outline of hope: Humor inherent in the comic condition of life moving forward as the serious stop point clenches downward, or tilts wayward, or re-directs onward and forward to the next destination toward landing, as our pilot, takes- 'Pause'...

REFERENCES

Aristotle (2014). *Nicomachean Ethics: Cambridge texts in the history of philosophy.* Cambridge U.K.: Cambridge University Press. [2ND Edition].

Benner, A. Forward written in Rudofossi, D. (2007). *Working with traumatized police officer patients: A clinician's guide to Complex PTSD Syndromes in public safety professionals.* New York and London: Taylor & Francis, Routledge

Benchley, P. (1974). *Jaws.* New York: Doubleday Publications.

Bettelheim, B. (1976). *The uses of enchantment: The meaning and importance of fairy tales.* New York: Alfred A. Knopf Publishers.

Boas, F. (1955). Primitive Art. New York: Dover Publications.

Brenner, C. (2005). Personal correspondence during clinical supervision of psychoanalytic training as training analyst supervisor at New York Psychoanalytic Society and Institute.

Brenner, C. (1957). *An elementary textbook of psychoanalysis.* Garden City, New York: Doubleday Books

Buckhardt, W. R. (2005*). Patterns of Behavior. Konrad Lorenz, Niko Tinbergen, and the founding of Ethology.* Chicago, Illinois: University of Chicago.

Cook, J. (1773). *An Account of the Voyages: First Voyage.* London: Hawkesworth Publisher.

Cousteau, J. & Cousteau, P. (1970). *The shark: Splendid savage of the Sea.* New York: Doubleday & Company.

Durkheim, E. (1915). *The elementary forms of the religious life.* London and New York: George Allen and Unwin LTD.

Eco, U. (1979). *The role of the reader: Explorations in the semiotics of texts.* Bloomington Indiana and London: Indiana University Press.

Einstein, A. (2010). *Ideas and Opinions.* New York: Three Rivers Press.

Elkin, P.A. (1964) *The Australian Aborigines.* Garden City, New York: Doubleday & Company, Incorporated.

Ellis, A. (1973). *Humanistic psychotherapy: The rational-emotive approach.* New York: Julian Press.

Ellison, R. (1952). *Invisible Man.* New York: Signet Publications.

Feldman, D. M., Feldman, F & Smith, R. (2004). *Playing sick: Untangling the web of Munchhausen Syndrome, Munchhausen by proxy, Malingering and Factitious Disorder.* Boca Raton, Florida and New York: Taylor and Francis.

Frankl, V. (1973). *The doctor and the soul: From Psychotherapy to Logotherapy.* New York: Knopf Doubleday Publishing group.

Frankl, V. (1978). *The unheard cry for meaning: Psychotherapy and humanism.* New York City, New York: Simon & Schuster Publications.

Frankl, V. (1988). *Mans search for meaning.* New York: Washington Square Press.

Frankl, V. (2000). *Mans search for ultimate meaning.* New York: Basic Books.

Fromm, E. (1957). *The forgotten language: An introduction to the understanding of dreams, fairy tales and myths.* New York: Grove Press, Inc.

Fromm, E. (1981). *The anatomy of human destructiveness.* New York: Random House Publishers.

Furuta, A. (2012). One thing is Certain: Heisenberg's Uncertainty Principle is not dead. *Scientific American.*

Goffman, E. (1975). *Frame analysis: an essay on the organization of experience.* Cambridge, Massachusetts: Harvard University Press.

Goodall, V.L.J. (1971) *In the shadow of man.* Boston, Massachusetts: Houghton Mifflin Harcourt Publishing Company.

Goodall, V.L.J. & Bekoff, M. (2002). *The Ten Trusts: What we must do to care for the animals we love.* New York City, New York: Harper Collins.

References

Goleman, D. (1995) *Emotional Intelligence: Why it can matter more than IQ*. New York: Bantam Books

Griffin, R.D. (1981). *The question of animal awareness: Evolutionary continuity of mental experience*. New York: William Kaufmann, Incorporated.

Havens, L (1993). *Participant Observation: The psychotherapy schools in action*. Northvale, NJ and London, England: Jason Aaronson Inc.

Howells, W. (1963). *Back of History: The story of our own origins*. Garden City, New York: Doubleday and Company.

Jasper, K. (1959). *Truth and symbol*. New York: Rowman and Littlefield

Jung, J.C. (1961). *Memories, dreams, Reflections*. New York: Random House.

Jung, J.C. (1991). *Psychology of the unconscious*. Princeton: Princeton University Press.

Jung, G.C. (2010). *Synchronicity: An acausal connecting principle*. Princeton, New Jersey:Princeton University Press. [Volume 8 of the Collected Works of C.J. Jung.)

Kant, I. (1929). *Critique of pure reason*. St Martins Street, London England: Macmillan and Company, Limited.

Kennington, T. (2013). *Bull Sharks*. Cherry Lake Publishing.

Kitaeff, J. (2007). *Malingering, lies, and junk science in the courtroom*. Amherst, New York: Cambria Press.

Kitaeff, J. (2019). *Handbook of Police Psychology*. Second edition. New York and London: Routledge Taylor and Francis. In Press

Lao, Tzu (1989). *Tao Teh Ching: The classic of the way and its virtue*. United States: Shambhala Dragon Publications.

Lasch, C. (1978). *The culture of narcissism. American life in an age of diminishing expectations*. New York: W.W. Norton and Company.

Lech, B.R. (1991). *All the drowned sailors*. New York: Jove-Berkley Publishers, Inc.

Levin, V.A. & Sheridan, S.M. (1996). *Munchausen Syndrome by Proxy*. Wiley Press

Lilienfeld, S.O., Lynn, S.J., Ruscio, J. & Beyerstein, B.J. (2010). *50 great myths of popular psychology: Shattering widespread misconceptions about human behaviour.* New York: Wiley-Blackwell.

Lilienfeld, S.O., Lynn, S.J. & Lohr, J.M. (2013). *Science and pseudoscience in clinical psychology* (2nd edition). New York: Guilford Press.

Lorant, S. (1959) *The life and times of Teddy Roosevelt.* New York: Doubleday Publishers.

Lorenz, Z. K. (1969). *On Aggression.* New York: Vintage Publications.

Lorenz, Z. K. (1986). *Evolution and modification of behavior.* Chicago, Illinois: University of Chicago Press.

Mead, M. (1973). *Coming of age in Samoa: A psychological study of primitive youth for Western civilization.* New York: American Museum of Natural History. Foreword by Franz Boas.

Morris, D. (1999). *The Naked Ape.* New York: Random House Publishers

Morris, D. (1971). *The human zoo.* New York: Dell Publishers

Nordoff. C. & Hall, J. (1947). *Mutiny on the Bounty.* New York: The Heritage Press

Oliver, L.D. & Oliver, M.S. (1951) *The Pacific Islands.* Cambridge, Massachusetts: Harvard University Press.

Parisi, N. (2018). *Rod Serling: His life, work and imagination.* Mississippi: University Press of Mississippi.

Pistone, D. J. (2004). *The way of the wiseguy: Donnie Brasco (AKA Joseph D. Pistone).* Philadelphia, Pennsylvania: Running Press Publishers.

Personal Correspondence (2017) Rabbi Rudofossi with Biala Chief Rebbe Rabbi Rabinowitz and Rabbi Moshe Hillel Sperber *on the significance of Howling Dogs as Omens of Death.*

Popper, K. (2002). *The open society and its enemies: The spell of Plato.* London & New York:Routledge, Taylor and Francis.

Postman, N. (1984). *Crazy talk, stupid talk.* New York: Random House Publishing Group.

References

Postman, N. (1985). *Amusing ourselves to death: Public discourse in the age of show business.* New York: Penguin Publishing Group.

Plato (2016). *The Republic of Plato.* New York: Basic Books. [3RD Edition]. As translated by Allan Bloom and Adam Kirsch

Postman, N. (1977). *Crazy talk, stupid talk: How we defeat ourselves by the way we talk and what we do about it.* New York: Doubleday Publishing.

Reichmann, F.F. (1960). *Principles of intensive psychotherapy.* Chicago and London: Phoenix Books – The University of Chicago Press.

Ross, K.E. (2008). *On life after death.* Potter Ten Speed/Harmony Publishers.

Ross, K.E. (1970). *On death and dying: What the dying have to teach doctors, nurses, clergy and their own families.* New York: Collier- Macmillian Publishing.

Ross, K.E. (1997). *Questions and answers on death and dying.* New York: Scribner Publications.

Rudofossi, D. (1997) The impact of trauma and loss on Affective differential profiles of police officers. Ann Arbor, Michigan: University of Michigan.

Rudofossi, D. (2007). *Working with traumatized police officer patients: A clinician's guide to Complex PTSD Syndromes in public safety professionals.* New York and London: Taylor & Francis, Routledge

Rudofossi, D. (2013). *A cop doc's guide to understanding terrorism as human evil: Healing from complex trauma syndromes for military, police and public safety officers and their families.* London and New York: Routledge Publishers.

Rudofossi, D. (2017). *Cop Doc: The police psychologist's casebook – Narratives from police Psychology.* New York and London: Taylor & Francis, Routledge.

Rudofossi, D. *Cultural Competence for Clinicians and Civic Leaders Encountering Complex Trauma and Grief: Centurioncide -Police and Public Safety Officers Endure in the Line of Fire and Death in* Kitaeff, J.

(2019) *Handbook of Police Psychology.* New York and London: Taylor and Francis, Routledge. [2nd Edition].

Salmen, L.F. (1989). *Listen to the People: Participant-Observer Evaluation of Development Projects.* (World Bank). Cambridge, England: Oxford University Press.

Scherman, N. (2004). *Perek Shirah: The song of the universe.* Brooklyn, New York: Mesorah Heritage Foundation Publications.

Sen, D. (2014). The uncertainty relations in quantum mechanics. *Current Science.* **107** (2): 203- 218.

Serling, R. (1990). *The twilight zone: Complete stories.* Los Angeles, California: TV Books.

Selye, H. (1976). *Stress: In health and disease.* Boston and London: Butterworths Publications.

Solevetchik, J. (1984). *Halakhic Man.* New York: The Jewish Publication Society.

Solevetchik, J. (2018). *The lonely man of faith.* New York and Jerusalem: Maggid Press.

Stein, M. (1998). *Jung's map of the soul.* Chicago and La Salle, Illinois. Open Court Publications.

Turnbull, M.C. (1962) *The forest people.* Garden City, New York: Double Day & Company, Incorporated.

Van Der Kolk, B. (1987). *Psychological Trauma.* Washington, D.C.: American Psychiatric Association Publication.

Van Der Kolk, B. (2015). *The body keeps the score: Brain, Mind, and the Body in the healing of Trauma.* New York and London: Penguin Books.

Williamson, C. & Harrison, R. (2004). *After Captain Cook: The archaeology of the recent indigenous past in Australia.* Walnut Creek, California: Altamira Press.

Winnicott, W. D. (1981). *Playing and reality.* New York and London: Routledge Publication.

Winnicott, W. D. (1985). *Deprivation and Delinquency.* Islington, London: Tavistock Publications, Limited.

References

Winnicott, W. D. (1987). *Holding and interpretation: Fragment of an Analysis.* New York City, New York: Grove/Atlantic Incorporated.

About the Authors

Dan Rudofossi, Psy.D., Ph.D., Licensed Psychologist and Retired NYPD Sgt. /Uniform Psychologist

Dr Dan Rudofossi, a licensed clinical psychologist and police sergeant/ uniform psychologist, (NYPD Ret.), is currently an active police surgeon for Amtrak Police - FOP NY and assesses and treats a number of police, public safety, and various other patients suffering from a gamut of mental and behavioural disorders. He has written six separate guides ranging from Assessing and treating Complex PTSD with police officer patients to a guide for officers and clinicians working with the mentally ill person on the street. He is a novelist and poet who publishes with a focus on police culture, crime, and personality. Dr. Rudofossi has extensive experience as a Professor at NYU, John Jay College of Criminal Justice, and currently as a forensic licensed psychologist at St. John's University. Dr. Rudofossi conducts professional forums on Police and Public Safety Complex PTSD and his integrative therapeutic approach —the Eco-Ethological Existential Analytic Method, which has gained acceptance by some major universities, departments, and clinicians. As a series editor, Dr. Rudofossi recruited and assists Sgt. Moloney to bring rich and practical wisdom of his experiences into a guide to be used by clinical students, practitioners, and expanded audiences.

Professor Rudofossi has given hands-on guidance in applying his methods and techniques in assisting the range of mentally healthy to mentally ill Aborigine Indigenous police, their families, and the larger community of Queensland police, their family, and citizenry through his worthy and brilliant police colleague and student of his method and intervention, Sgt. Commander Matt Moloney. He's married with two kids.

Matthew J.A. Moloney, Active Queensland Police Sergeant

Matthew Moloney was born 1971 in Queensland, Australia. He spent some time in Papua New Guinea as a school boy and describes those years as formative. Sworn into the Queensland police Service in 1991 as a police officer, at present he actively holds the rank of Sergeant. He has performed duties as an officer in charge, supervisor, plain clothes investigator, training officer, Liaison officer, Watch officer and in the Water Police. He was nominated as a Peer Support Officer and Work Place Health and Safety Representative by his colleagues. Performing duties in Rockhampton, Winton, Thursday Island, Aurukun, Lockhart River, Cooktown, Coen, and Cairns, Matt has worked mainly in regional and remote areas of Queensland. Sgt Moloney has delivered police service in remote, isolated, indigenous communities where he was in the racial and cultural minority. He was seconded to the Australian Federal Police for two years in 2009, meaning he had worked in joint task forces. After returning to the Queensland police, he was mentioned in Parliament for his work obtaining recognition for indigenous people who have worked in law enforcement. He then won a prestigious Churchill Fellowship in 2014 where he travelled through the United States, Canada, and New Zealand to research 'culturally effective police responses to Indigenous persons in mental health crisis situations.' He has travelled extensively through Europe, Turkey, and the Middle East in a private capacity. On long service leave he lived in Asia with his then fiancé, where he taught English at high schools in China and Outer Mongolia producing students with broad Queensland accents and a tendency to use Australian slang. He is married with three kids.

www.ingramcontent.com/pod-product-compliance
Lightning Source LLC
Chambersburg PA
CBHW050212240426
43671CB00013B/2306